TRAVELS WITH MAGGIE

A Six-Month Journey with a Wondering Wanderer

By Pat Bean

Travels with Maggie
A Six-Month Journey with a Wondering Wanderer
Copyright © 2017 Pat Bean
patbean@msn.com
ISBN 978-1544628615

Cover and book design by Sherry Wachter
sherry@sherrrywachter.com

Printed by CreateSpace www.createspace.com

1 2 3 4 5 6 7 8 9 0

This book is dedicated to my
canine traveling companion, Maggie,
and to John Steinbeck.
His book, Travels with Charley, *was one of the*
inspirations for my vagabond lifestyle
and also for this book's title.
I would also like to thank the
hundreds of other great travel writers
who taunted me to discover
my own adventures.

CONTENTS

*"What is the feeling
when you're driving away from
people, and they recede on the plain
till you see their flecks dispersing?
It's the too huge world vaulting us,
and its good-bye.
But we lean forward to the
next crazy venture beneath the skies."*

— JACK KEROUAC

1

HOW IT ALL BEGAN

From the time I was a young girl, I could always see myself traveling across America and living on the road. Even before I read their books, I wanted to be William Least Heat Moon, John Steinbeck, Paul Theroux, Freya Stark, Tim Cahill, Charles Kuralt and all the other writers who visited exciting places and then wrote about their adventures.

Perhaps this thirst for adventure began after I read Osa Johnson's *I Married Adventure*, which is about photographing wild animals in Africa. It was named best non-fiction book of 1940, and it left me with a thirst for my own adventures. I couldn't have been more than ten years old when I read the book, which I found in the adult section of the library. I do believe I was born with wanderlust in my soul. My mother confirmed it by telling me I had inherited the trait from my grandfather, who could never pass an untraveled road without wanting to travel down it. That's exactly how I have always felt.

But for most of my life, travel was something that had to be squeezed in between life, which in my case included raising a family and constantly striving to keep the financial wolves away from the door. Travel, by necessity, was far down on my priority list. The closest I ever came to satisfying my wanderlust was a 30-day road trip to Alaska in 2001. This rambling trek up the Alaskan Highway was like giving one berry to a hungry bear. Nothing much is going to stop him from grabbing the whole basket, or in my case the whole road.

On returning from Alaska, and in anticipation of my retirement in just three years, I immediately began checking out motor homes. While I salivated like Pavlov's dogs over the 40-foot Class A's, which were loaded with everything but the backyard swimming pool, the thought of driving one while pulling a car behind me dried up the saliva glands. As a lone woman on the road, with only a small dog for a companion, I would need to keep things simple. I also didn't want to drive something so big I was constricted to major highways. My goal was to travel back roads and take the business routes through towns. I wanted to be surprised by the wonder of things, and meet new people whose lives were different from mine.

So, two weeks before I left a 37-year career as a journalist behind me, I bought a 22-foot Class C motor home powered by a gutsy six-cylinder Volkswagen engine. It had all the basics I needed, got reasonable gas mileage, and came with a sticker price I could afford. I saw the RV on an Ogden, Utah, sales lot one morning, and purchased it before the end of the day. It was the scariest day of my life. I was committing myself to a 180-degree change in lifestyle.

When I drove my new RV into my driveway for the first time, I heard my cocker spaniel, Maggie, barking wildly inside the house. It was a new sound for her, and she wanted to know what was going on. When I opened the door, and she saw it was me, her mouth gaped in surprise. Before I could stop her, she squeezed through my legs and ran outside to check out what had made that unfamiliar sound. I followed, and opened the RV door for her. She sniffed our new home on wheels – from the driver's seat to the rear toilet and tiny shower – then she jumped on the couch and gave me a look that I translated as meaning: When and where, are we going?

This was a good sign. I had rescued Maggie from a shelter five years earlier. She had been about a year old, and had been badly abused by her former owner's teenage boys, the shelter worker told me. Maggie's first instinct after I had taken her home had been to run for freedom anytime a door was opened; once I found myself chasing after her, barefoot in snow. It only took three weeks, however, for her to undergo a change in attitude. It happened the day a friend dropped by and found me in my backyard.

She left the gate open when she came in to chat, and Maggie immediately streaked toward the opening. But at the same instant I was moaning and getting ready for the chase, Maggie realized she had found a safe home with a kind mistress. She came to a screeching halt in front of the gate, and I swear she smiled as she did a U-turn and came back to check out my visitor.

But Maggie's decision that she had finally found a safe haven created a new problem. Now she didn't want to leave the premises. Riding in a car was particularly agonizing for her. Every time she was forced to do so, she would crouch down on the floorboard shivering. It took two road trips to Texas – a journey I made annually to visit family – before Maggie changed her attitude, and became as eager a traveler as her owner.

So, smiling now at what appeared to be an acceptance of our upcoming change in lifestyle, I sat down on the RV couch, which could also double as a bed, and answered her implied question out loud: "We'll be leaving soon – and we're going everywhere. Now what do you think we should call our new home?"

I've always talked to my pets, both dogs and cats, but Maggie was the first one that I truly believed understood.

Later that evening, friends came to check out my daring purchase, and to help me celebrate. With Maggie perched on the over-the-cab bed looking down at us, we christened my RV "Gypsy Lee," and drank a toast of Jack and Coke to my upcoming adventures. The name Gypsy was in honor of my wanderlust; Lee was for my grandfather, Charles Forrest Lee; my mother, whose maiden name was Lee; and for me, as Lee is my own middle name. I would explain this often as people mistakenly called my home on wheels Gypsy Rose Lee.

I took the next couple of months to get rid of stuff. I gave everything I valued, or they valued, to my kids; stashed a few bins of books and paintings I couldn't bear to part with in the basement of my best friend's home; and gave away or sold the rest of my belongings – including my home. I couldn't afford a life of travel plus a mortgage, utilities and house maintenance. It had to be one or the other. I chose my dream, and I've never looked back, nor had regrets.

Frank Tatchel, author of the 1923 book, *The Happy Traveler,* said: "The real fun of traveling can only be got by one who is content to go as a comparatively poor man. In fact, it is not money which travel demands so much as leisure and anyone with a small, fixed income can travel all the time." I now had both.

This book is the story of one of my adventures, a 7,000-mile, six-month road trip through 23 states and Canada. It began in early May of 2006, from my youngest daughter's home in Camden, Arkansas, and ended in time to spend Thanksgiving with my oldest daughter in Dallas, Texas. I traveled backroads, designated scenic routes when possible, and with few exceptions avoided interstates and freeways. Along with ogling and oohing at this country's awesome landscape, I learned a lot of history, met fascinating people, and felt more at home on the road than I had ever felt before in my life.

Except for a few notable occasions, I avoided large cities. I seldom ate out and bookstores, museums, guided tours and ice cream shoppes were my major luxuries. When my budget was stressed, I simply stayed longer in one place until I was back on the budget track.

I'd do the whole trip over again in a heartbeat if there still weren't new places to go and new things to see.

THE JOURNEY

CAMDEN TO MENA, ARKANSAS
146 MILES

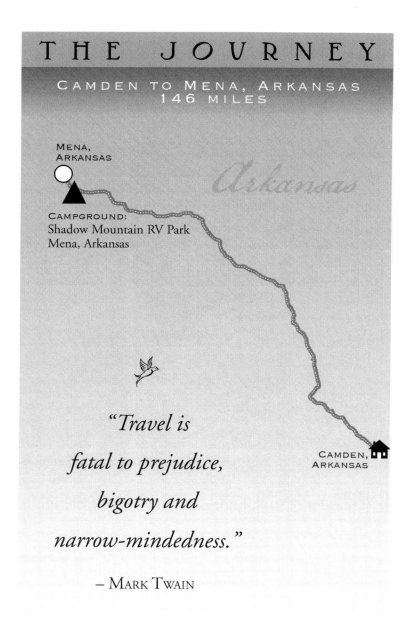

MENA,
ARKANSAS

CAMPGROUND:
Shadow Mountain RV Park
Mena, Arkansas

Arkansas

*"Travel is
fatal to prejudice,
bigotry and
narrow-mindedness."*

– MARK TWAIN

CAMDEN,
ARKANSAS

2

LETTING GO OF THE WORLD'S WORRIES

Every trip has a starting point. Our journey through life starts with a first gulp of air. The path to adulthood is opened to us the first time we put another person ahead of our own wants; and when we accept that life is not fair, we've begun traveling the pot-hole strewn road that will lead us to maturity. Hopefully along the way we've also discovered the byway to happiness, an internal road whose only map is blurry and ever-changing.

The starting point for my six-month meandering journey to New England began at the end of May in Camden, Arkansas, the home of Grapette soda and my youngest daughter. This small southern town sits on a bluff above the Ouachita River, and is populated with an abundance of churches and friendly people, including those who think nothing of revealing intimate details of their lives to strangers standing beside them in line at a bank or department store.

As an unashamed eavesdropper, I've heard such conversations as:

"My nephew's having a vasectomy today. 'bout time. They've had three kids in three years."

"Mom's divorcing Dad. She says he's having an affair."

And, "We had to have our dog put to sleep last week. I didn't know dogs could get cancer."

On a Sunday morning, the day before I began my travels, I found myself having one of these friendly chit-chats with a young

Black man while the two of us were waiting in the check-out line at the neighborhood grocery. The conversation ice-breaker was the dog food in both our carts.

The man's sharp-chiseled face was softened by a broad smile when he told me his dog was an old lab that his father had asked him to take care of when he moved in with his sister in Little Rock.

"Bo's 12 now, and beginning to slow down," he said. The pride for his hound was evident in the smile that lingered as he spoke. Mine, I said, was a spoiled cocker spaniel I had rescued from a Utah animal shelter and named Maggie. Our conversation then turned to the weather, the perennial hello-icebreaker that would be repeated everywhere I went. On this occasion, we both wished it was cooler and less humid.

Food was the next item for our waiting-in-line chat. The man, whose name I never did learn, said he had greens and pork chops for dinner the night before. I told him I had fried catfish and okra take-out from a small cook shack near my daughter's home. I couldn't help but notice that while our shared addiction to southern cooking betrayed itself on my older, pale hips, it was not the least bit evident on his dark, lean shape.

I found a pleasant kinship with this Black man, one my Southern grandparents would not have understood. The casual conversation became even more meaningful the next day as Maggie and I began our journey. After traveling only a few miles – 13 to be exact – we stopped to check out Poison Spring State Park, a designated Arkansas Civil War Historical Site located off Highway 24. The park proudly memorializes a Confederate victory over the Union Army.

Basking in the coolness of the morning, and the knowledge that I had no schedules or deadlines to meet, I took ample time to digest the site's historical exhibit. It told the story of a battle fought where tree-shaded picnic tables and rusty barbecue grills now reigned. While I read the signs, Maggie sniffed everything in sight, as if remnants from that fateful April 18, 1864, day still tainted the air.

This battle of brother Americans involved a Union supply caravan guarded by 1,170 Union soldiers. The plaques noted that 301 of them were killed along with 114 Confederate soldiers. The battle was glorified in its Confederacy-sided retelling that had the Union commander, Gen. Frederick Steele, and his surviving soldiers retreating in haste back to their stronghold in Little Rock, while recaptured supplies of corn and other items were returned to the southern owners from which they had been stolen.

What intrigued me about the story came in the plaque honoring the units that had fought in the battle. The inscription noted that the first Union men to attempt to repel the southern attack were from the 1st Kansas Colored Infantry, and that it was these Black men who suffered the most casualties. While I believed they had probably been proud to be fighting for freedom for their people, an irritating thought that perhaps they were first in battle because the Union Army valued them less got my brain tick-tocking a blues tune about the sacrifices America's soldiers are making out there on the battlefields today.

Since my oldest son, an Army Blackhawk helicopter pilot, was at the time deployed overseas, the thoughts were not pleasant; thousands of lives lost, and too many innocent among them – on both sides. While I'm certainly proud of my son and all of America's dedicated military sons and daughters, I fear the scars that war leave behind on countries and souls will never heal.

Time, I decided, to stop thinking about things I couldn't change and go back to simply being a wondering-wandering old broad in search of America's scenic delights – and North America's winged wildlife. It was only recently that I had become addicted to bird-watching, a passion that fit perfectly with my traveling plans. While some birds can be seen in all 50 states, other birds can only be found in just one state, and sometimes only in one small section of that state.

Escaping to explore the unknown had appealed to an unhappy youngster like me. I always felt I never fit in, and my schoolmates agreed. I also suspect that my continued dreams of locking the door and taking off down the road are fueled by a desire to leave behind the responsibilities and expectations of society, and a large family that turned me into a chameleon. I had given birth to five children and each is as different from the next – ideally, politically and occupationally – as a bald eagle is from a titmouse. My struggle to stay close and connected to each of them continually turned me into a chameleon who frequently changed colors to suit the mood and personality of whomever I was with at the time. This ability to fit in with each of my five children, and a wide variety of friends, is not all bad. It just makes it harder for me to stay true to myself. I need time alone, not always trying to fit in.

Meanwhile, knowing this day that my concerns for my son's safety would not change anything, I looked down at Maggie and said, as I would many times on this journey, "Let's go find Mother Nature."

She looked up at me with her velvet brown cocker eyes, wagged her short tail enthusiastically, and seemed to say: Let's go, let's go! It's pleasant to travel with a companion who is always up to adventure – and not a back-seat driver.

She and I found the earth goddess on a short trail that began beyond the picnic area. Its existence was noted by a colorful carved wooden sign, and a few wooden steps that put us on a path that followed a tiny stream bank dotted with lush green ferns. Dragonflies, their double wings glistening in the speckled sunlight that drifted through the tree canopy, darted here and there while chattering cardinals serenaded all. In such a setting one can easily forget that all is not right with the world.

I pulled out the small notebook I carried in my pocket, and added northern cardinal to a newly started bird list. It was the second bird of the morning, the first being an American crow whose cawing bid me a noisy good-bye as I pulled out of my daughter's driveway. I planned to keep track of all the bird species I saw on the trip. The list, after my short hike, also included house sparrow, mockingbird, common grackle and brown thrasher.

All but the thrasher would be seen frequently over the next 7,000 miles. Slightly larger than a mockingbird, the brown thrasher mostly skulks its life away in thick woods. I spied the one this day sitting on the path ahead as I rounded a curve. It offered only a quick glance of its it brown-speckled breast and yellow eye before scurrying out of sight among the vegetation that lined the trail.

I had seen my first brown thrasher, dozens of them actually, in the Camden backyard of my daughter's new home. One pair of the thrashers was in the process of raising chicks in thick wisteria vines growing on the latticed roof above the patio. There had been three hatchlings, the last of which I watched leave its nest for the first time. The almost weightless feather bundle dropped down from its high perch, and then half-flew, half-wobbled to the woody thicket that bordered my daughter's home on two sides. Its journey was guided by an anxious parent calling it to hurry. Given its vulnerability, and my daughter's two barn cats, I breathed a sigh of relief when it finally disappeared from view. Hopefully the other two had made it as well.

The next time I visited Camden, the wisteria was gone. My daughter's husband had cut it down because the fragrant lavender blooms of the plant attracted bees. I wanted to rant and rave at the loss, but for the sake of family peace, the chameleon in me squelched my tree-hugger voice. Today's brown thrasher was the first one I had seen since watching that fragile, first journey of the spirited fledgling. It seemed fitting to me that a park dedicated to honoring the dead was also a place where wild birds could live in peace. It was with an easier heart, and with a turkey vulture soaring overhead, that I left the park and drove on.

A short time later, I stopped at nearby White Oak Lake State Park to watch great egrets fishing. Continuing on in a stop-and-go sightseeing manner, I halted to take a few pictures, one of a huge blooming mimosa tree, and one of a sign on a small market that read: "Politics spoken here." The latter gave me a good chuckle. Around a bend in the road, a pair of blue jays watched me pass from their perch in a large white-blossomed magnolia tree. Human eyes occasionally followed my passage also. It was not unusual in this rural area of Arkansas for people to sit on their porches to watch passing traffic much as city folk watch television.

My meandering route to avoid freeways took me through the small towns of Bluff City, Whelen Springs and Gurdon. The latter's claim to fame is the Gurdon Light that haunts the railroad tracks a few miles out of town. The mysterious light, which many have claimed to have seen, was featured on the TV show "Unsolved Mysteries" in 1994, and is described in the *Encyclopedia of Arkansas*.

Believers claim the light is the lantern of a railroad worker who stumbled in front of a train and was killed; or that it is the lantern of William McClain, a railroad worker who was murdered in 1931 at about the same time the floating light was first claimed to have been seen. Skeptics look for a more natural phenomenon, such as quartz crystal in the area exuding electricity.

All I saw when I crossed the railroad track as it passed through Gurdon were rock pigeons perched on overhead utility wires. I suspected the small town's pigeon population was larger than its human one. I wondered if these city dwelling birds had ever seen the lights, and asked Maggie what she thought. I interpret her answers by the expressive looks she gives me. This time there was nothing to decipher. Maggie was curled up on her co-pilot seat comfortably snoozing.

Just outside the small town of Amity, several meadowlarks caught my attention as they hustled away from the side of the road and into patches of yarrow and wild roses. I recalled the first time I had ever seen a meadowlark through a pair of binoculars. Its throat had been so brilliantly yellow that my own throat gasped for breath. The color was duller this day, as seen through the passing window of my RV, but my eye's memory distorted it back to its original glow.

A few cows near a small farm house just before I entered the Ouachita (pronounced Wa-chi-ta) National Forest were accompanied by cattle egrets, a stocky bird whose white feathers are sprinkled with gold dust. An African migrant, these egrets feed mostly on insects found in grass and not in water as do their American cousins. The first record of cattle egrets breeding in the United States was in the 1950s in Florida. Forty years later, this prolific breeder had been seen in every state between Canada and Mexico. Just for the record, all these bird facts were recent trivia added to my little gray cells. Not only had I become fascinated watching birds, I was truly awed by the lives of these amazing winged creatures.

My slow meandering drive through Arkansas took me down oak and pine-lined stretches, and through the small settlements of Caddo Gap, Norman, Black Springs and Big Fork. If I had blinked I would have missed all but Norman, whose population numbers about 400.

As I drove, I identified brown-headed cowbirds, European starlings, scissor-tailed flycatchers, and mourning and white-winged doves. Each of these birds has a field mark that allows for easy identification from behind the wheel of a moving vehicle. A brown head on a sparrow-sized body for the cowbird; a distinctive profile with either black spots or white wing edges for the doves; a yellow beak on a black short-tailed body for the starling; and a dangling long, two-pronged tail for the flycatcher.

Smaller, less blatantly marked birds went unidentified. I knew from experience that if I stopped for a closer look (if there had been a place to pull over, but there wasn't), the birds would have most likely disappeared into the landscape.

I camped that night at Shadow Mountain RV Park on the outskirts of Mena, Arkansas. A red-headed woodpecker, whose knocking had alerted me to its presence at the campground when Maggie and I took our evening walk, brought the number of bird species seen on this day to 18. I'm sure if I had been a more experienced birder, the number would have been higher because of the many birds I saw that went unidentified.

Still, it had been a great day, I thought, as I went to sleep comfortable tucked up in my over-the-cab bed with Maggie at my feet and the words of Dr. Seuss drifting on the edge of a dream: "Oh the places we'll go ... and the things we'll see."

BIRDS ALONG THE WAY:
American crow, northern cardinal, house sparrow,
northern mockingbird, common grackle, brown thrasher,
turkey vulture, great egret, blue jay, rock pigeon,
eastern meadowlark, cattle egret, mourning dove,
brown-headed cowbird, European starling,
scissor-tailed flycatcher, white-winged dove
and red-headed woodpecker.

THE JOURNEY

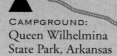

CAMPGROUND:
Queen Wilhelmina
State Park, Arkansas

*"It is good to have an end
to journey toward; but it is
the journey that matters."*

– URSULA K. LeGUIN

MENA,
ARKANSAS

CAMPGROUND:
Shadow Mountain RV Park
Mena, Arkansas

3

WHAT QUEEN WILHELMINA MISSED

Because I'm a writer traveling solo across America with my dog, my wordsmith colleague and friend, Charlie Trentelman, jokes that I'm the female version of John Steinbeck and his dog. I'm flattered. Steinbeck is one of my role models. I thought once about traveling the same route Steinbeck wrote about so artfully in *Travels with Charley*. Fortunately, I came to my senses. Instead of trying to repeat his journey, I realized I had to create my own. It's what each of us must do in order to give meaning to our lives as we stumble down life's rocky paths.

Tom Young had been doing just this when I met him at Queen Wilhelmina State Park in the Ouachita Mountains. Located on the Arkansas side of the Talimena Scenic Drive before it crosses into Oklahoma, the park was created in the late 1800s and named after Queen Wilhelmina, in hopes the young ruler of the Netherlands would visit.

While the park was only 20 miles from where I had spent my first night of this trip, it looked too inviting to pass by. That's the beauty of having no deadlines to meet. While I had carefully planned the route, I would take to Maine before retreating south to Texas in time to spend Thanksgiving with my oldest daughter, the timeline for my journey was left blank. At this point, six months seemed quite ample for my plans. My dawdling ways would have me thinking differently later on.

As would become my normal routine, I had begun this day leisurely, savoring two cups of cream-laced coffee while updating my journal. Maggie, as usual, slept in. It was well after 9 a.m. when she awoke and we took our morning walk. Once again, a cawing crow claimed the honor of being the first bird of the day. Chipping sparrows came in second. These small and cheery red-crowned birds were pecking away at the ground so intently that only the nearest ones moved off as Maggie and I passed by.

When I finally got back on the road, Maggie went back to sleep and I lollygagged through Mena, a town of about 6,000 residents with dozens of quaint boutique shops to attract the attention of tourists. I eventually followed Mena Drive north until it zigged onto Grand View Heights before re-entering the Ouachita National Forest, and then zagging onto the Talimena Scenic Byway.

Amazingly, I didn't take any wrong turns or end up on the highway that bypassed this less-traveled, scenic byway, which stretches for 55 miles atop a ridge and connects Talihini, Oklahoma, with Mena, Arkansas – hence the name Talimena.

Shortly after entering the forest, Maggie and I stopped to hike the Orchard Trail Loop maintained by the Forest Service. This short trail passes through an area where early settlers had built homesteads. Long abandoned, the homesteads had been reclaimed by nature. While there was scant evidence of the former human occupants, a red-bellied woodpecker made its present-day homesteading known by drumming a slurring beat.

I scanned the trees in the direction of the sound and found the bird about halfway up a pine tree. I identified it from its black and white barred back and bright red cap. Only a pale hue of red colored its mostly white belly. It's one of those birds whose names I question, like the ring-necked duck. That bird sports a quite visible ring around its bill, not its neck. I've been told that it does have a neck circle, but I've never seen it, and my National Geographic field guide doesn't show it either.

Trail walks with Maggie always seem to stimulate my brain into asking these inconsequential questions, and my wondering often goes unanswered – even if there's someone to ask.

For example, after the hike, I spent a few minutes chatting with the forest ranger who manned the small visitor center at the site. He noted that the trees, mostly pines and hardwoods that had escaped logging during the homesteading era, were twice as big today as they would have been in pioneer days.

I wondered what tales these trees would tell if they could talk, and voiced the thought. The ranger had no answer except a shrug of his shoulders. Oh well. Perhaps that was an unanswerable question.

There were several other pullouts with scenic views that demanded my attention as the road continued meandering upward toward the byway's summit. The vistas weren't the breath-gasping moment one gets when first time standing on a precipice overlooking the Grand Canyon, but they moved me just the same. Looking out at a sea of trees, whose green hues were as ripples on water, I felt at peace. I knew I was exactly where I should be at this moment in time.

When I came upon Queen Wilhelmina State Park, I also knew it was time to call a temporary halt to my travels. The rain storm that blanketed the area for the next few days, and which I wouldn't have wanted to drive through, confirmed my instincts. Because of the rain, I stayed indoors for the next two days. From my RV, I watched northern cardinals, eastern bluebirds and barn swallows flit among the trees; viewed several Season 7 Stargate episodes on DVDs that my daughter had loaned me for the trip; and caught up on my reading. I finished several issues of back birding magazines along with the book, *Plan B*, by Anne Lamott.

During one break in the storm, I walked up to the Queen Wilhelmina Lodge, where I devoured one of the tastiest cheeseburgers of my life while watching dark storm clouds build up for another burst. There's something in me that loves a storm, and the sound of rain drumming on my RV roof is as enjoyable as a well-played concert. I was glad, however, that I made it back to the coziness of my RV before the storm began anew. With me, was my last bite of cheeseburger wrapped in a napkin for Maggie. She always gets the last bite or two of my meals.

Continuing to luxuriate in my lazing, I watched in awe as my RV neighbors cheerfully kept four young grandchildren occupied during the rain. They were in and out of their RV frequently to play or eat at a picnic table they had moved under their awning.

When the sun finally came out, I was ready to stretch my legs There were several trails, and I chose to hike the one that went to Lover's Leap. It wouldn't be the first geological landmark with a Romeo and Juliet theme I would encounter during my trip. It seems high precipices – and the possibility of jumping off them to one's death – are not all that uncommon. Personally, such foolishness would never cross my mind.

The trail wandered through the woods to a high wooden deck that opened to a panoramic view of the Powell Valley below and the Rich Mountains beyond. Along the way, I spotted two more birds for my trip list, an eastern kingbird and an indigo bunting.

The kingbird belongs to the flycatcher family. It was behaving in a familiar fashion for its species: sitting up straight and flying out and back to the same perch after catching flying insects on which to feast. I watched it on the trail ahead through my binoculars for a while before moving on. Its crisp white breast against a dark back and head let me instinctively identify it, and the white on the end of its tail, like lace edging on a table cloth, confirmed my suspicion.

The bunting was in a branch overhanging the trail. I caught its movement in time to stop for a look before getting so close that it would fly away. Small, only about five inches in size, the bird was a young male. It didn't have the brilliant royal blue feathers of a breeding male, and its paler blue feathers were speckled with brown. I was just glad it was a male. The mostly brown females are much more difficult for me to identify.

Maggie didn't give the birds much attention, being more focused on the enticing scents of the wildlife and humans that had earlier walked the trail. She leaves the bird watching to me, except when squawking crows or ravens are around. These she likes to bark at and chase. Since these birds are large, easy to identify and common, I was glad they were her only feathered adversaries.

When we returned from the hike, I put Maggie back in the RV, and went to explore the wildlife center, which is where I met Tom. There was a $4 entry fee, which I was told upon paying supported wildlife rehabilitation activities.

For 30 minutes I walked around the small zoo, gawking at orphaned baby fawns and six-week-old bobcats being bottle fed. I also observed a pacing fat black bear that was actually a rich cinnamon color; a magnificent tawny cougar that I later learned was named Sheena; a colorful gobbling turkey; baby screech owls with eye problems; a sleek coyote; turtles sitting on a log in a small pond; and a pen with a timber wolf cub, a puppy and a young raccoon, all of which appeared innocent of their differences and were playfully wrestling together. It was delightful to watch the young before their prejudices would take over.

Most of the animals in the enclosures had been rescued after accidents or wrongful human activities, a fact emphasized on the side of a small unpainted wooden building where it was noted in large white lettering that 12 bears, 5,000 hawks, 2,000 owls, 22 bald eagles, 18 golden eagles and thousands of small mammals had been released back into the wild by Young. My instincts told me there was a story here if I could meet this person. But before looking for him, I took time to study a red-tailed hawk and a strange looking falcon that were holding center stage in this small wildlife zoo.

The birds were attached by a tether that allowed them to fly between their nesting boxes and stands a short distance away, where at the moment a large raw turkey neck had been placed on each. A rope encircled the area to keep humans back but the arrangement still allowed me to view these beautiful birds from less than three feet away without bars or screens. As a birder, the opportunity was savored.

While watching these birds, I also noted a young barred owl sitting out of reach atop a tall stand. This bird was not tethered. My curiosity was aroused and a talkative Paul Bailey, who was volunteering his help at the non-profit center, provided the answers.

The red-tail was his falconry bird. It was still young and, he said, he planned on releasing it when it was about four years old and breeding age. The odd falcon was a hybrid, a cross between a gyrfalcon and a peregrine falcon, and belonged to Tom, the falconer to whom Paul was apprenticed, and the driving force behind the center. As for the barred owl, it was young and being rehabilitated. When it was ready it would simply fly away and be on its own.

As we talked, a black vulture flew in and landed nearby. As soon as the vulture had landed, a slight, long-haired guy with romantic brown eyes and a thick mustache came running. He had a raw turkey neck in his hand, and he quickly squatted down and held it out to the vulture.

The bird had a wrinkled black face that lacked feathers, a trait that helps the species stay clean after poking its head into a meal of carrion. Turkey vultures have the same lack of feathers on their heads, but their skin is red, which makes the two easy to tell apart at close range. These birds are also easily identified when soaring overhead. The lower half and tips of a turkey vulture's wings are white, while only the tips of a black vulture's wings are white.

Turkey vultures are larger and more graceful fliers than the black vultures and have a greater sense of smell, but their talons are too weak to kill much of anything. Fifty percent of their diet is actually vegetarian. Black vultures, on the other hand, can actually kill small creatures, but their sense of smell is not as acute as that of their turkey cousin. Combining skills improves both birds chance of survival, which is why it is not uncommon to spot the two species in the same vicinity, and which is why I had spent a good bit of time learning to tell them apart.

The man holding out the turkey neck to this black vulture – bravely I thought considering the bird's size and fierce appearance –

was Thomas Young. The society-ugly bird slowly inched up to him, and in seconds had all the meat stripped away from the neck bone.

As I watched the scene from about 30 feet away, Paul told me the vulture was a bird Tom had rehabilitated. Later Tom told me it was actually the parent of the rescued bird. He said it was the first time this particular vulture had fed from his hand. I was amazed he could tell the difference between the two vultures.

"For some reason, it's come to trust me," Tom said of his vulture friend. "A while back it brought its young here for me to babysit while it flew off on some business for about three hours."

Paul had already told me this story in more detail, but I was still fascinated with Tom's less wordy rerun, along with a sparse sketch of his life. This man was a doer not a talker. His love for wildlife, he said, was inherited from his mother. He worked at one time for Fish and Game, and at times was the only licensed wildlife rehabilitator in this remote wilderness area of the Ouachita Mountains.

Tom said the center's lofty location made it ideal for releasing birds – like the beautiful red-shouldered hawk he set free before onlookers the next day from the overlook just beyond the park's lodge. The bird simply fell off the edge of the mountain and glided away, one of the most beautiful sights any birder could hope for. While I didn't add the red-tailed hawk to my trip list because it was a captive bird, I did add the red-shouldered hawk because I saw it flying free.

It was the first of many red-shouldered hawks I would see before my journey's end. Red-tailed hawks would be even more plentiful down the road. However, there would not be even a breath of a chance for me to see another hybrid peregrine falcon – it was quite rare. Even if two different bird species mate, their offspring, if any, are born sterile.

The public bird releases, Tom said, were usually done weekly to help attract paying visitors to the small wildlife center. The state's only contribution to Tom's efforts was to allow him to locate his center on park land for an annual lease of $5,000; for which he was grateful.

Tom posed for my camera with his bird, Snow, who at 37 years old was the same age as the falconer. He said the hawk had been left to him by a friend who had died. The falcon nuzzled Tom, as did the cougar, Sheena, a bit later.

This enthusiastic animal lover said he had worked with everything from big cats to possums, although admitting there might be too many of the latter. Tom said the time came when he had to admit he couldn't save the entire animal world, and so now focuses his efforts on saving and returning to the wild only animals native to Arkansas' Polk County.

Well, unless someone asks him to take in a timber wolf pup that's sick, or anonymously drops off an unwanted puppy.

For the rest of my stay at Queen Wilhelmina, the sun shone brightly, I hiked the remaining three trails located in the park and added two more birds to my trip list: an eastern wood-peewee, a small olive-gray flycatcher that gets its name from the pee-wee sounds it makes; and a barn swallow, the only swallow common to North America with a distinctive forked tail.

By the time I left the park, my total bird species for the trip was 28. As birding goes, it wasn't many. But each sighting of a new bird, or re-sighting of birds already on my list, gave me pleasure. There's something about seeing these feathered creatures living among us that touches a magic place in my heart.

It's too bad Queen Wilhelmina never knew what she missed.

BIRDS ALONG THE WAY:
Crow, northern cardinal, *chipping sparrow,
scissor-tailed flycatcher, mourning dove,
*red-bellied woodpecker, turkey vulture, *eastern kingbird,
*eastern bluebird, *barn swallow, *indigo bunting, *barred owl,
*black vulture, *red-shouldered hawk, brown-headed cowbird,
house sparrow, European starling, northern mockingbird,
rock pigeon, white-winged dove and *eastern wood peewee.

*First trip sighting of this species.

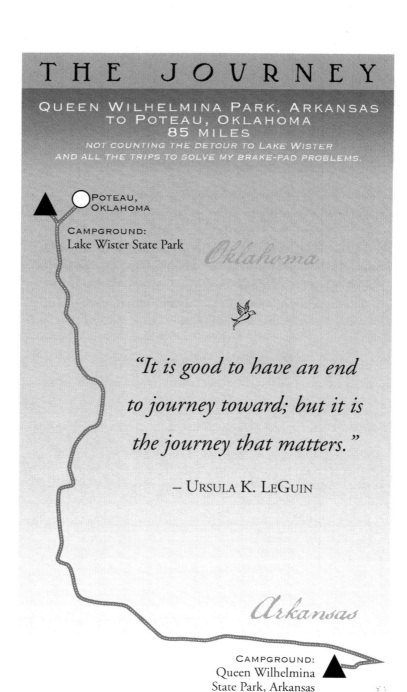

THE JOURNEY

POTEAU,
OKLAHOMA

CAMPGROUND:
Lake Wister State Park

Oklahoma

"It is good to have an end

to journey toward; but it is

the journey that matters."

— URSULA K. LEGUIN

Arkansas

CAMPGROUND:
Queen Wilhelmina
State Park, Arkansas

4

YES, VIRGINIA,
THERE IS A SILVER LINING

The morning sun flashed off the scarlet feathers of a cardinal just before I pulled back onto the Talimina Scenic Drive to continue my journey. What a fantastic day it was going to be, I thought, not yet aware that the trickster Murphy lay in wait a few miles up the road.

With traffic almost non-existent on the scenic byway, I dawdled, taking time to enjoy the multitude of scenic vistas from the high ridge the road followed. As part of the morning's sightseeing, I took a short walk to view the historic 1877 boundary marker near the Arkansas-Oklahoma border. Historians believe the marker, which once separated Arkansas from lands given to the Choctaw Indian Nation, was wrongly placed. The 136,000-acre error, as if you couldn't guess, was to the advantage of Arkansas's white settlers. I had bought a postcard depicting the marker at the Queen Wilhelmina Lodge. The slick picture on the card made the marker look larger than life, so I was surprised to discover it was simply a small, metal stake in the ground. For some reason, it brought to mind a long ago inscription in my high school yearbook: "Don't despair. Remember the mighty oak was once a nut like you."

I was still pondering this discrepancy in size and significance when the highway began a steep descent, causing me to apply my brakes. The RV slowed fine, but was accompanied by a gruff grinding noise. At the next pullout, the Kerr Nature Center where

I had planned to hike a nature trail, I stopped to look at my map. All thoughts of hiking had vanished, as had my plans to spend the night at the isolated Winding Stair Campground. My only thought now was to get to a populated place that might have a mechanic to solve my problem.

The map showed the closest place where help would likely be available as Poteau, Oklahoma, fortunately only 35 miles away. Even so, it seemed as if the downhill stretch of the road went on forever; each time I used my brakes the resulting screech left me white-knuckled. For the first time this trip, I forgot to look for birds.

Finally, off the scenic byway and onto a flatter, more populated stretch of highway, I stopped at the first service station I saw, and asked if anyone knew of an RV service center nearby. A couple of motorcyclists returning from a camping trip told me there was an RV center up the road just before Poteau. I found it a short time later, but since it was a Sunday the place was closed. I would have to spend the night elsewhere and return in the morning.

No problem. About a mile back up the road, I had passed a fishing resort with a large sign indicating it accommodated RVs. My brief relief, however, was dashed by Murphy when I learned the resort was brand new and had not yet put in its so proudly advertised RV sites.

The next closest possibility was Lake Wister State Park about 10 miles away. Since my brakes were still working well, although noisily, I decided to chance it. I arrived at the park without mishap about 20 minutes later, and hooked up in the campground that sat below the Wister Dam beside the Poteau River.

Since there was nothing else to do, I let myself enjoy the evening. Maggie and I took a walk through the campground, and then along the rocky edges of the river. A great blue heron stood silently on a ledge across the water, while several humans tossed their fishing lines into the water in the shadow of the dam.

My stomach then reminded me I had forgotten to eat lunch. The growling belly wanted comfort food, so I fixed a tuna casserole, ate two big helpings, and shared the last couple of bites with Maggie. Afterwards I watched fireflies dance through the night outside my window before falling deeply asleep. The day's stress had worn me out.

The next sounds I heard were those of a cheery robin with a backup chorus of Canada geese honking overhead. The sun was just peeking above the horizon, and since both birds were new for the trip I dutifully added their names to my list. I had fallen back into that oh so human trap of dismissing the present moment to worry about a future one.

The drive back to the RV center was uneventful, and soon I had a kindly young service manager addressing my problem. He said I simply needed new brake pads, but that it didn't look like I had done any damage to the more expensive brake cylinders yet.

"They should be replaced pretty quickly, however," he said, as he arose from a stooped position beside my driver's side tire. The words "Do it" were on the tip of my tongue when he added: "We don't do brake work." But before I had time to panic, he went on to note that there was a tire shop in downtown Poteau that could handle the job.

Fifteen minutes later, I arrived at the tire store, where another kindly young service manager confirmed the brake-pad problem. I okayed the work, and Maggie and I retired to the waiting room. She snoozed beneath my chair, but frequently woke to get petted by anyone who walked by. She's quite friendly, and gets her feelings hurt if strangers ignore her. One couldn't travel with a better conversation icebreaker.

About an hour later, the shop's manager walked over to me with my keys in his hand. I figured the work had been completed and I could be on my way. Wrong! He had come to tell me they had called all over town, but couldn't find any brake pads that would fit my RV. Murphy seemed to have hitched himself a ride with Maggie and me again.

The mechanic was apologetic and suggested that perhaps I could find help in Fort Smith, Arkansas, about 30 miles away. I remembered the list of recommended service centers given me when I bought the RV, and sure enough found a Volkswagen place in Fort Smith on the list. My Winnebago house sits atop a VW Eurovan chassis. As promised when I had bought it, the small RV was amazingly gutsy, but its downside, I was discovering, was finding parts and places to service it.

Forty-five minutes of nervous driving got me to Fort Smith. Murphy, however, had once again beaten me. The one and only asshole of my entire six-month trip – and in all of my on-the-road years following – worked at this Fort Smith Volkswagen Sales and Service Center. He told me my list was wrong and that they didn't work on VW Vistas, only Rialtas, the smaller VW Class B motor homes. This fat, ignorant, insensitive slob - perhaps that last description was a bit harsh as he was wearing a suit - was not only unhelpful but turned rude when I tried to elicit information from him about where other help might be available.

"Not my problem," he muttered, then turned his back and walked away.

I was near tears at this point, but not wanting to cry in front of this horrible man, I escaped to my RV and sat there pondering my options. I didn't care if I was blocking their parking lot. When I had finally composed myself, and put my brain back into gear, I got my list of service centers out again. The next closest place where I might find help was Little Rock, Arkansas, 157 miles from my present location.

Not willing to drive that distance without confirmation they could replace my brake pads, I called the VW service center there on my cell phone. The person I was finally transferred to sounded mentally challenged, or maybe it was Murphy himself. The man never could seem to understand my problem. He finally said he would call me back. I suspected he wouldn't – and he never did.

I got my list back out and saw that the next closest center that could most likely service my RV was in Dallas, Texas, over 300 miles away. If I had to drive back there, I would probably do serious damage to my brake cylinders. The up side was that my oldest daughter lived in Dallas, and I could stay with her while my RV was being repaired. With no other apparent options available, I called the Dallas center and was transferred to an angel named Jim. Murphy must have finally taken a wrong turn on the satellite beams.

Jim quickly comprehended my situation, and after I gave him my vehicle VIN number, he made a quick check and told me he had the brake pads I needed in stock. Together we decided a better option than my driving all the way back to Dallas was for him to ship the brake pads to the Poteau tire store. When all parties had confirmed the deal, I paid for the parts and shipping over the phone with my credit card, and then made my way back to Lake Wister to await their arrival.

This time I stayed in the park's upper campground that was located on tiny Quarry Island, and accessed by a short bridge. I awoke each morning to the sound of a chipper mockingbird greeting the day from the top of the picnic table outside my window. This bird's bright countenance and chipper personality is probably why five states, including my own home state of Texas, adopted the mockingbird as their own. The other four that have made it their state bird are Arkansas, Florida, Mississippi and Tennessee. A mockingbird, because of Texas history lessons taught in school, was one of the few birds I could identify before I took up birding. A gray bird with distinctive white wing bars, it gets its name from its propensity to ape the sounds of everything it hears – from insects and other birds to chugging tractors. It would continue being a familiar sight and sound during my travels the next six months.

Lake Wister, created when a dam on the Poteau River was completed in 1949, also greeted me every morning. It was visible out both my front and rear windows as Quarry Island was quite narrow. Maggie and I took frequent walks around it, usually accompanied by a couple of noisy blue jays. I added red-winged blackbirds, northern flickers and double-crested cormorants to my trip list, bringing the total bird species at this point up to 35.

On the third day of my stay at this Oklahoma park, the new brake pads arrived, which meant I could continue on my journey. I did so, with both regret for leaving such a peaceful setting and joy for getting back on the road. These oxymoronic emotions were oft repeated during my travels. It was also oxymoronic that after all the worry and tension of my mechanical problems, I found its silver lining. Ever since purchasing Gypsy Lee, I had feared breaking down on the road. That fear was now gone, replaced with confidence that I would always be able to solve whatever else Murphy might throw at me.

BIRDS ALONG THE WAY:
Northern cardinal, eastern bluebird, turkey vulture,
blue jay, mourning dove, black vulture, scissor-tailed flycatcher,
brown-headed cowbird, great egret, *great blue heron,
*American robin, northern mockingbird, barn swallow,
American crow, *Canada goose, eastern kingbird,
*double-crested cormorant, common grackle, indigo bunting,
eastern meadowlark, *red-tailed hawk, *northern flicker
and eastern wood peewee.

*First trip sighting of this species.

THE JOURNEY

LAKE WISTER STATE PARK
TO NATURAL FALLS, OKLAHOMA
140 MILES

NATURAL FALLS TO
BERNICE STATE PARK, OKLAHOMA
37 MILES

CAMPGROUND:
Bernice State Park
Bernice, Oklahoma

Oklahoma

CAMPGROUND:
Natural Falls State Park
West Siloam, Oklahoma

*"To my mind,
the greatest reward
and luxury of travel is
to be able to experience
everyday things as if for
the first time, to be
in a position in which
almost nothing is so familiar
it is taken for granted."*

– BILL BRYSON

CAMPGROUND:
Lake Wister State Park

5
TWO MORE OKLAHOMA PARKS —
AND A LIFER

It felt good to be back on the road and driving a vehicle that didn't cry ouch every time the brakes were applied.

From Lake Wister, I backtracked once again to Poteau, a pleasant little town of about 10,000, whose personality I failed to appreciate while Gypsy Lee was ailing. Poteau, which absorbed the old mining town of Witteville around the time of the Great Depression in the 1930s, was founded in 1885 by a group of French explorers. They named it Poteau, which in French simply means outpost.

The city's chamber of commerce promotes the city today as home of the world's tallest hill, that being 1,999-foot tall Cavanal Hill. The claim, despite the fact that the hill is officially called Cavanal Mountain, is based on the geological understanding that a landscape feature is a mountain if it's 2,000 feet or taller, and a hill if it is less than 2,000 feet tall. Whether a hill or a mountain, its summit provides excellent views of nearby Sugar Loaf Mountain, which at 2,833 feet high is most certainly a mountain – and the tallest landmark in the county.

Leaving Poteau behind, I took Highway 59/271 north. This route took me through the small towns of Panama and Ward, then across the Arkansas River near its junction with the Robert S. Kerr Reservoir. The lake's namesake, who was born in 1896 and died in 1963, was one of those good old southern boys who got a lot done for his home state. He founded a petroleum company, was Oklahoma's 12th governor, and then served three terms in the U.S. Senate, where he left a legacy of water projects in his wake. I checked Kerr out because when something as large as a 43,000-acre lake is named after a person, it makes this wondering-wanderer curious.

My drive continued on Highway 59 and took me to the outskirts of Sallisaw, a French word for salt. The name was most likely given the city because early traders salted their bison kills at a creek here. I bypassed the town to zig over and catch Highway 82, one of those routes on my map marked by green dots indicating a scenic drive. While William Least Heat Moon's choice of back roads taken on his travels over 30 years ago, and described in his still popular book *Blue Highways*, were marked in blue, my choice of routes were the green-dotted ones.

Moon, like Steinbeck, was a role model for my vagabond life, but just as I decided not to retrace Steinbeck's steps, I would not follow in Moon's path, nor would I bemoan how different America is today from what it was yesterday. There are enough travel books out there that already do this. Sometimes I agree with them, but mostly I don't; perhaps because I'm always looking for the good in things.

Change is life, sometimes good and sometimes not. Often it just is. For example, the blue lines on the maps I was using represented major freeways, not the small back roads of Moon's maps. My whole journey would have been different if I had followed my map's thick blue lines instead of avoiding them. While doing so often added miles and days to the journey, I had the time. It was a treasured freedom because it wasn't always so.

Continuing on, I passed through Vian, whose best feature was its nearby location to Sequoyah National Wildlife Refuge, the meeting place for the Arkansas and Canadian rivers, and habitat for the alligator snapping turtle and over 250 bird species, including around 20,000 snow geese during winter migration. My route then took me across Lake Tenkiller, a 12,500-acre reservoir formed by damming the Illinois River. According to a visitor's guide, the lake was named after a Cherokee family, the Tenkillers, who owned land and operated a ferry on the lake. The name Tenkiller supposedly was given to a Cherokee warrior by Fort Gibson soldiers after they noticed the ten notches that had been carved into his bow.

After Tenkiller, I passed through the towns of Cookson, Pettit and Quails, and finally Tahlequah, one of many Oklahoma sites bearing Native American names, a remnant of the state's role in history as a designated Indian territory. The long list begins with the state's name itself, which comes from the joining of two Choctaw words: *Okla*, meaning people, and *humma*, meaning red. Tahlequah is a Cherokee word that loosely translated means "two is enough." Legend has it that the site, now the capital of the Cherokee Nation, is where two elders met shortly after the Trail of Tears. An expected third elder never showed up, and the pair then decided "two is enough."

After Tahlequa, I zagged to get onto Highway 10, yet another green-dotted route and one that would take me to Natural Falls State Park. After my pleasant stay at Lake Wister, I was eager to check out other Oklahoma parks. With what had already become a regular routine, I hadn't begun my drive until around 10 a.m., after my writing goals and a short hike with Maggie were accomplished. Because I never traveled much over 100 miles on any leg of my journey, this still left plenty of time to dawdle and investigate whatever caught my eye. And plenty of things always did.

I arrived at Natural Falls early in the afternoon. The campground had large, tree-shaded campsites with paved parking spaces, and hookups especially designed to accommodate RV-ers. No need to use my orange Lego levelers here. The park brochure indicated several hiking trails and the location of a formal garden area. It also noted that the park had been the scenic setting for the movie, "Where the Red Fern Grows," one of my favorite books, both as a child and as an adult.

I was eager to explore the park but made it only to the falls overlook before heat and humidity turned me into a wimp, and forced me back to my air-conditioned RV. I spent the rest of the evening reading Janet Evanovich's latest Stephanie Plum mystery. I love that Jersey girl, and couldn't put the book down until I finished it at 2 a.m. in the morning.

Even so, I was up early to explore the park's hiking paths while it was still at least somewhat cool outside. The trail I took meandered around a small lake and through the woods. Natural Falls, the park's 77-foot namesake, was visible from several vantage points along the route. Sometimes Maggie and I were above the narrow stream that poured into a dark pond beneath, and sometimes beside it, where the stream of water widened and turned white with froth.

At one point along the trail a wooden footbridge took us up to tree branch level. I paused here to watch a pair of cardinals, the male bright red and the female golden with red trimmings. I couldn't decide which was more splendid. The male, with its fanciful scarlet crest and distinctive black mask is usually the one you see sitting on a limb in winter on Christmas card greetings. The bird was named after the Catholic Church's cardinals, whose robes are as scarlet as the male bird's feathers.

By tracking its melodious tune, I also located a song sparrow that sang from a low branch beneath me. Its buzzy trill was quite different from the cardinal's cheer-cheer-cheer. While I can sometimes identify a cardinal by its voice, it took me a good look at this sparrow's striped chest, interrupted by a single dark spot in the center, before I knew I was listening to a song sparrow. I have a very poor birding ear.

Nearby, a yellow-rumped warbler, or butter-butt as birders call it, added its drum-beat chirp to the chorus. I identified it when it flashed its yellow rump at me. There are two subspecies of yellow rumps: The Myrtle, which has a white throat and is more dominant in the east, and the Audubon, which has a yellow throat and favors the western territory, where I was living when I first started watching birds in 1999.

While North America has nearly 1,000 bird species – of the approximately 10,000 that exist worldwide – many can only be found in small scattered pockets around the continent. Visiting one of these pockets – like southeastern Arizona where I made my first trip in Gypsy Lee with the goal of seeing an elegant trogon – made my travels meaningful as well as just plain fun.

Butter-butts, however, can be seen everywhere in North America. The one that joined the chorus I was listening to this day was a Myrtle, and it brought back memories of the first time I had seen this subspecies. It was in Utah's Ogden Valley, and when the only yellow-rump I had seen previously was the Audubon subspecies – and didn't even know about subspecies. When my birding comrades pointed out the bird, and called it a Myrtle, I thought it was a new bird for my life list, and was inappropriately excited.

I later learned that the two yellow-rump subspecies had actually been two separate species until the American Ornithology Union, which has the final word on bird biology, decided the two birds were the same species and renamed them the Audubon and the Myrtle yellow-rump subspecies. As if to acknowledge the reason for their name, the one I was currently watching flashed me. I smiled. This was one mooning I didn't mind.

By the time I finished my bird watching and arrived back at my RV, I was dripping wet with sweat. Maggie hopped up on the overhead bed and planted herself at the spot where the air conditioning vents blew the coolest. I, meanwhile, used the park's shower to cool off. While my RV had its own shower, I only used it when there was no alternative. Not only was mine small, it was also a place I stored everyday items. It was cleared out more during the trip to bathe Maggie than myself. Keeping her groomed and smelling sweet enough to share that overhead bed she loved was a weekly chore while we were on the road.

After spending two nights at Natural Falls, I continued north on Highway10/59 to Bernice State Park, which would be my final stop in Oklahoma. It was a pleasant drive with few distractions along the way, allowing me to arrive at the park about noon. I chose a camp site near the shore of Grand Lake o' the Cherokees, which got its name because this northeastern area of Oklahoma belonged to the Cherokee Nation, at least until 1893, when the Indians were forced to replace tribal ownership with individual acreage allotment.

After I hooked up, I surveyed my fellow campers, noting they were mostly boaters and fishermen. Bernice is designated the "Crappie Fishing Capital of Oklahoma" and Grand Lake's 46,500-acre surface and 1,300 miles of shoreline offer plenty of opportunities to indulge both fishermen and boaters. There was a family atmosphere in the park, and I watched as several youngsters played in the water under the watchful eyes of adults. After covering too many incidents of child neglect and abuse during my journalistic career, the scene was aloe to my spirit.

I ate a late lunch, took a short walk by the lake with Maggie, and then meandered over to a small nature center located at the far end of the park. It was nice to learn about the area's flora and fauna in an air-conditioned setting as, again, it was quite hot and humid outside. I spent a pleasant hour looking at the exhibits and chatting with a volunteer who worked there. She suggested I take the nearby nature trail.

I set out to do so, but because of the heat decided it could wait until early morning. Instead I stopped to bird watch for a little bit in a tree-shaded spot near the lake shore, and was rewarded with my first catbird of the year. This dark gray fellow with a black cap is just slightly smaller than a robin. Its dark form and preference for perching in thick foliage make it difficult to identify unless it exposes the underside of its tail, which is rusty red. I caught the color. The bird, as I'm sure you suspected, gets its name because its call can sound exactly like a meowing cat.

Pleased with the find, I cheerfully returned to the RV, where I caught up on my e-mail, fixed myself a bowl of soup, walked Maggie one last time, and then checked to see if I was picking up anything good on TV. I went a year without one after I bought my RV, but finally relented and bought a small set, mostly to play DVDs. I found this night's television programing an excellent sleeping pill. I fell quickly into dreamland, and the sleep button I had set automatically turned the television off.

I was up by 6 a.m. and after a quick cup of cream-laced coffee and a short walk with Maggie, I took off alone to explore the park's nature trail. Maggie had seemed quite agreeable to be left behind to sit in her favorite perch in front of the air conditioner. She did like her comforts, and already the day was thick with humidity.

It had rained heavily during the night, but I didn't have to walk in mud as the nature path was paved and well maintained. Several bird feeders set out near the trailhead had attracted Carolina chickadees and American goldfinches. As I watched, I heard a woodpecker drumming a tune from a nearby tree. It was a downy, North America's most common and smallest woodpecker.

As I continued on down the path, I took plenty of time to breathe in the simple beauty around me: a yellow patch of wall flowers, the artistic composition of a small dead tree reclaimed by vines, and an occasional peek of a glistening, sun-speckled lake through thick foliage. How do people who don't take nature breaks stay sane in today's fast-paced world? I suspected the angry psychopaths who do evil and harm are among the deprived.

My thoughts were interrupted when a doe and her freckled fawn came into sight around a curve in the path. I froze, as did the two deer. We all stared intently. When I finally took a step forward, mom stepped into the woods. Her baby gave me one last look of interest then quickly followed. It amazes me how fast wildlife can disappear from sight.

My thoughts were still on the deer when a flash of orange drew my attention. With eyes glued to my binoculars, I followed the color through the tree branches, and realized I was most likely looking at a Baltimore oriole. While common in the East, these orioles don't visit the West, where I had lived when I took up bird-watching. Out West, the Baltimore's look-alike cousin is the Bullock oriole. I had seen hundreds of Bullocks, but this was my first Baltimore. It was what we birders call a lifer. While I rejoiced, I lamented the too brief view I had before the bird disappeared amongst the trees. I had identified the bird more because of its color and location than because of specific field marks.

Later in the day, as I was sitting at my table writing, the omission was rectified. A Baltimore oriole flew right outside my RV window, and then lingered in the area. It was a breeding male with a black head atop a bright orange body that had thin white streaks on black wings. A Bullock wears only a black cap atop its head and its black wings have prominent white patches on them.

After the oriole flew away, I got out my world bird list and added the Baltimore oriole to it. It was bird 477. I had been hesitant to put it on the list earlier because of the poor sighting. Life is good, I thought, as I added the date and place of its sighting beside the bird's name.

When I left Bernice Park, my trip list of birds had grown to 50. I'm sure the number would have been much higher if I had been birding with some of my more experienced bird-watching friends, but I was also enjoying the challenge of identifying birds on my own, which seemed more important than a triple digit list.

BIRDS ALONG THE WAY:
American robin, northern cardinal, Canada goose,
*bank swallow, American crow, turkey vulture,
northern mockingbird, mourning dove, rock pigeon,
house sparrow, *Brewer's blackbird, great egret,
eastern meadowlark, *laughing gull, *mallard, black vulture,
*snowy egret, indigo bunting, *house finch, eastern bluebird,
*gray catbird, great blue heron, scissor-tailed flycatcher, *killdeer,
common grackle, brown-headed cowbird, red-winged blackbird,
*Carolina chickadee, *American goldfinch, *white-eyed vireo,
*downy woodpecker, **Baltimore oriole,
*yellow-rumped warbler
and *song sparrow.

*First sighting of this species on the journey
**A lifer.

THE JOURNEY

CAMPGROUND:
Big Red Barn RV Park
Carthage, Missouri

Missouri

"Without new experiences,

something inside of us sleeps.

The sleeper must awaken."

— FRANK HERBERT

CAMPGROUND:
Bernice State Park
Oklahoma

Oklahoma

6

CHILDHOOD MEMORIES, A KINDRED SOUL AND MARLIN PERKINS

Never mind that I hadn't traveled far, it was time to let my mail catch up with me. After checking out my "Trailer Life" directory, a lengthy list of RV campgrounds with ratings and costs, I decided the Big Red Barn RV Park in Carthage, Missouri, less than 100 miles away, and with a greatly reduced weekly rate, would be the perfect place to hold up for a while.

To get there, I backtracked to Highway 59 and headed north to Grove, a small town with an eye-popping botanical park, Lendonwood Gardens. While I'm not much of a gardener – the truth is I don't enjoy digging in the dirt like most of my friends – I quite enjoy the hard work others have put into creating manicured and flowery landscapes.

The specialty of Lendonwood, which is a part of the Oklahoma Botanical Garden System, is the rhododendron. The garden's brochure claimed there were about 250 or so varieties of this woody plant located in the garden, along with about 25 varieties of dogwood trees. In addition, daylilies were everywhere, some 500 varieties of these colorful flowers. I was tempted to count, but didn't. Lendonwood is a display garden for the American Hermocallis Society. Hermocallis, in case you didn't know - and I didn't until I looked it up – is the scientific name for daylilies.

After the colorful stop in Grove, I took Highway 25 east into Missouri, zigging at Anderson to catch Highway 71. The Big Red

Barn sat just off the highway, beside one of the few remaining sections of Route 66, which once stretched from Chicago to Los Angeles. Since its heydays in the mid-1900s, this Old Mother Road has been chomped up and eaten by multi-laned interstates and highways. When I come across Route 66 remnants these days, memory takes me back in time to the 1950s, when my Uncle Adrian, with my Aunt Marie by his side, and me in the back seat with my 18-month-old cousin, traveled the uncrowded highway between Texas and California. It was my first road trip. I also recall, with fondness, sitting in front of a television set watching George Maharis as Buz and Martin Milner as Tod get their kicks on Route 66, a weekly event that also added to my innate wanderlust.

The Red Barn turned out to be an excellence choice for a week's stay. It was well-maintained with friendly owners; and I snagged a prime end row site next to a small tree, where each day I watched a white-breasted nuthatch scamper among its branches.

Nuthatches have a habit of walking up and down tree trunks, defying gravity like astronauts in space. This one's antics brought to mind an old Chinaberry tree in a field behind my grandmother's house on the outskirts of Dallas. I spent many hours up in that tree. It was a favorite activity until the hot summer day I discovered a large rattlesnake coiled beneath it on the very same rock I used to boost myself up into the branches.

While that snake was probably just as afraid of me as I was of it, and quickly slithered away, I never climbed that tree again. Looking back, I now realize it was my first lesson about how fear can paralyze people from enjoying life. Time taught me to fear the snake when it was where I would place my foot, but not to fear it when it wasn't there. It was a well-learned lesson that gave me many years of freedom in the outdoors, and the courage to face the unknown unafraid.

As a lone female on the road, I traveled during daylight hours, camped in secure places and locked myself in my RV at night. With these precautions, and Maggie as my alarm system, I felt as safe as if I was simply going to the grocery store a mile down the road in a residential neighborhood. While men I knew, or met along the way, told me I was brave, or stupid, or suggested that I should travel with a gun, which is too often how they deal with fear, women usually expressed envy at my lifestyle. Perhaps this is why I was always meeting other lone female travelers. I discovered there were quite a few of us on the road. Like me, they had learned to read maps, dump the sewage, back up their rigs and take care of all their own needs themselves.

One of these was Sue House, who was staying for a couple of months at the Red Barn. I thought her especially brave. Her RV was four feet longer than mine, and she was pulling a car behind it as well. We recognized we were kindred spirits almost the minute we met, and spent the next week exploring the area together. Sue, like me, preferred roaming around in nature more than wandering around in shopping malls.

We visited the nearby George Washington Carver National Monument, where I hiked a pleasant trail that passed through woods and around a small pond to the place where Carver was born into slavery in 1864 or 1865. He never knew his exact birth date. Sue didn't hike because of a knee disability. She encouraged me to do so, however, saying it gave her extra time to explore the visitor center and its surrounding landscape. I took digital pictures along the trail, and showed them to Sue when I returned so she could at least share in the hike. In this same way, we explored several other areas around Carthage, including Kellogg Lake and Wildcat Glades Conservation Sanctuary.

The glades added three more bird species to my trip list. The first was a tufted titmouse, an energetic tiny bird whose *peet-r, peet-r, peet-r* call alerted me to its presence.

The next was a Cooper's hawk, one of North America's three accipiters. This family of birds has short, rounded wings that allow them to maneuver through forests better than most other birds of prey. Fortunately, the one I saw at Wildcat Glades gave us a spectacular flyover because usually I'm hard-pressed to tell it apart from its smaller accipiter cousin, the sharp-shinned hawk.

Finally, there were several white-fronted geese hanging out at Kellogg Lake. These geese are a familiar sight around ponds all across the country. I also enjoyed repeat sightings of most of the other birds seen earlier on this trip.

Sue, while not a birder, seemed to enjoy our bird-watching as much as I did. But for a change one day, we drove into downtown Carthage for lunch and a bit of sight-seeing in America's Maple Tree City, home to about 12,000 residents. After a tasty meal, at a simple restaurant that was easy on the pocketbooks, we headed back to the campground. On the way, we passed by a small park with a statue in the center that caught my attention. I asked Sue if she knew whom the statue represented. She said no, then pulled a U-turn, parked the car, and told me to go find out and come back and tell her its identity. Nothing could have delighted me more than to discover the statue honored Marlin Perkins. This gentle man's exotic animal adventures on TV's Mutual of Omaha's Wild Kingdom, in the 1960s and early '70s, had fed both my love of nature and my wanderlust. A native of Carthage, Perkins was among the first to bring exotic wildlife into America's living rooms.

The bronze statue of Perkins, created by Carthage artists Bob Tommey and Bill Snow, has him kneeling with a giant pair of binoculars in one hand. Since my own binoculars are never far from hand, I felt a renewed kinship with Mr. Perkins, who loved and worked to protect nature and all that exists in it.

The discovery of Perkins' statue is really what travel is all about. Although I do a lot of advance study and reading about places I plan to see on my journeys, it's the little things, the unexpected things, that give me the most pleasure. It is especially meaningful when I make connections to what I'm seeing, and when such sights help me better understand the influences that shaped me. My journey was proving the oft quoted phrase that travel is as much about learning about ourselves as it is about seeing new things.

BIRDS ALONG THE WAY:
American robin, northern cardinal, mallard, snowy egret,
European starling, *tufted titmouse, killdeer, house sparrow,
northern mockingbird, common grackle, Canada goose,
mourning dove, indigo bunting, red-headed woodpecker,
cattle egret, turkey vulture, scissor-tailed flycatcher,
bank swallow, great egret, eastern meadowlark, eastern kingbird,
barn swallow, red-winged blackbird, *white-breasted nuthatch,
house finch, brown thrasher, *Cooper's hawk, Baltimore oriole,
downy woodpecker, American goldfinch, rock pigeon,
blue jay, great blue heron, *white-fronted goose,
eastern wood-peewee, Carolina chickadee.

*First sighting of this species on the journey

THE JOURNEY

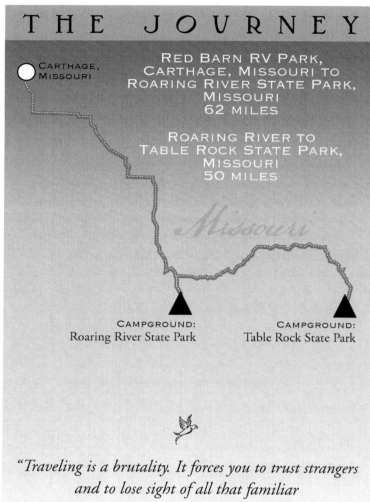

CARTHAGE,
MISSOURI

RED BARN RV PARK,
CARTHAGE, MISSOURI TO
ROARING RIVER STATE PARK,
MISSOURI
62 MILES

ROARING RIVER TO
TABLE ROCK STATE PARK,
MISSOURI
50 MILES

Missouri

CAMPGROUND:
Roaring River State Park

CAMPGROUND:
Table Rock State Park

*"Traveling is a brutality. It forces you to trust strangers
and to lose sight of all that familiar
comfort of home and friends. You are constantly
off balance. Nothing is yours except the essential things
— air, sleep, dreams, the sea, the sky —
all things tending towards the eternal or
what we imagine of it."*

— CESARE PAVESE

7
HEART OF THE OZARKS

While in Carthage, I read a book that was loaned to me after I had expressed disappointment about a trip to Texas' Big Bend National Park. I said it compared poorly with the more colorful national parks in Utah, which is a traitorous thing for a native Texan to say – even if it is true. I said the trip had been a lot of driving to the end of nowhere for over-rated scenery except, my Texas conscience added, for the magnificent fields of bluebonnets that were at their peak during my journey.

"That's too bad," my Utah friend, Pat Williams, commented about my disappointment in Texas' southernmost national park. "Bill and I visited Big Bend, and we loved it, especially after reading about the early settlers in the area." She then gave me Hallie Crawford Stillwell's *Gathering My Geese*, a woman's tale of Big Bend ranching in the early 1900s, which I finally got around to reading during my week's stay at the Big Red Barn.

The book did give me more appreciation for the vast, wide open spaces of Big Bend, but mostly I simply enjoyed the tale of a woman who wasn't afraid to tackle the unknown. While she was growing up, Hallie's father often complained about his daughter constantly going off on one wild goose chase after another.

"Then I'll just gather my geese," she told him, hence the book's title.

I was still thinking about Hallie when I bade farewell to Carthage. Perhaps it was because, as usual, I was a bit apprehensive about what was ahead of me. Would I find a safe place to stay each night? Would the people I meet be trustworthy? Would I take a wrong turn? Would I get a flat tire? Would the restrooms be clean? Or worse? Would I forget to make sure there was toilet paper before I sat down?

All these woulds are what made one couple I met decide, after just one day on the road in a brand new 40-foot RV, that the traveling lifestyle wasn't for them. Instead, they chose a wooded RV park an hour away from their home, bought one of its spaces, parked their RV there, and used it as a getaway cottage. A creative way to go, I thought, when the female half of the couple told me about their decision as we shared the park's Laundromat.

But not my way.

Even if I'm hesitant to face those first few miles of travel into unknown territory, I still want the thrill of driving down a road I've never been on before, particularly if it's a quiet back road with little traffic. This last criterion was why I chose the long way around to get to St. Louis, where I planned to spend a week and do some major sightseeing. Via Interstate 44, Missouri's second largest city was only 280 miles from Carthage. The less-traveled route I chose doubled those miles, but took me through Mark Twain National Forest, and allowed me to camp in the heart of the Ozarks at two Missouri state parks.

My first destination after leaving Carthage was Roaring River State Park. To get there, I headed south on Highway 37. The drive took me through Sarcoxie, Pierce City, Monett, Purdy, Butterfield and Cassville, all small rural towns past their prime if one judged them by the abundance of boarded up buildings, and tacky stores selling stuff they called antiques and collectibles. There was little traffic, and I stopped often to identify a bird, search out historical markers, and to explore a couple of the towns.

Sarcoxie was the most interesting. It was named for Chief Sarcoxie, head of the Turtle Band of the Delaware Tribe. The name

Sarcoxie means "Tall As He Is," which pondering historians say could either mean "he was high up in tribal government" or that he was simply tall.

According to the town's Chamber of Commerce, the first Confederate "Stars and Bars" flag was flown on Sarcoxie Square. During the town's heydays in the lake 1800's, it served as a major stopping point for Texas cowboys driving cattle to the railhead at Sedalia. Sarcoxie was also one of the first Missouri towns to get Thomas Edison's newly discovered electric lights, thanks to the local mill owner, J. J. Sprague, who ordered 10 incandescent bulbs from the ingenious inventor.

In Cassville, I jogged onto Highway 112, which took me straight into Roaring River State Park. Even though it was a weekday, I discovered the main campground nearly full when I arrived. I was told when I checked in that I was lucky there was a vacancy. I felt even luckier when I pulled into my assigned site, a tree-shaded spot that backed up to a creek bed. Looking around I noted that all the sites looked just as inviting – but where was the river that gave the park its name?

I didn't find it this day, but when it cooled off a bit, Maggie and I did find the Pibern Trail, a winding path off the campground that meandered in a loop through trees and thick vegetation for about a mile and a half. About halfway along the trail, I spotted my second lifer of the trip. It was a Louisiana waterthrush, a small bird with a streaky breast and a prominent white eyebrow. It was poking about beneath a bush and I was able to watch it through my binoculars for several minutes before it disappeared back into the brush.

Back at the RV, I cheerfully added the new bird to my life list, and then Maggie and I shared a dinner of chicken and rice, which I made with a small package of saffron rice, a 4-ounce can of chicken, and a bit of butter, poultry seasoning and black pepper. Some cherry Jell-O I had made with fruit cocktail was dessert.

Early next morning I went looking for that "roaring river." What I found was a softly purring stream whose banks were dotted with fly fishermen hoping to snag a trout. Maggie and I walked along the river, and I tried to imagine it roaring after a heavy downpour. I was sure it did just that; else why the name?

Several eastern phoebes, my first for the trip, were sitting on tree branches overlooking the water. They were common in the areas I had traveled, and I was surprised I hadn't seen one before now. The eastern phoebe belongs to the flycatcher family, and the brownish-gray and white birds are easily recognizable from look-alikes by their habit of bobbing their tails up and down. I've never watched this phoebe for more than a minute or two that I haven't seen this bobbing motion. Today was no exception. These birds get their name from their call of *fee-be, fee-be.*

After my river and bird-watching walk, I wandered over to the park's rustic nature center. It offered a closer example of some of the area's creepy-crawlies than I would have liked, and I rather quickly left the center to a family whose two young boys were thrilled by all the snakes and bugs. By now the sun had turned the day steamy. I returned to my camp site, where I watched nature outside my RV window in the air-conditioned comfort of my tiny home, and planned the next leg of the journey.

I decided it would be a stop at Table Rock State Park near Branson, Missouri. State parks were fast becoming my favorite places to camp. They were not only less expensive than commercial parks, but came with roomier, more scenic camp sites, and the bonus of hiking trails. But before getting on the road to Table Rock the next morning, Maggie and I took another hike – this time just around the large landscaped campground as I had discovered a tick on Maggie and one on myself after the Pibern Trail adventure. Maggie's was dead, thanks to her monthly application of flea and tick prevention, but mine, which was on the back of my calf, was still alive and sucking when I pulled it off. It was the last time I went hiking in the Ozarks without a liberal dose of insect repellent, particularly on my lower legs. Nature, like life, has its share of unpleasant situations to muddle through. But if you don't muddle, you don't get nature's surprising rewards, like watching an ant carry a leaf four times its size, or a robin feed a juicy worm to its clamoring young.

After the hike, Maggie and I quickly got on the road. While I only had 50 miles to go, I wanted to get to Table Rock in time to ensure a site for the upcoming weekend.

Continuing south, I followed Highway 86, also known as the Sugar Camp Scenic Byway, a 28-mile stretch of road that meanders through a forest, up and down hills and across valleys. It was my kind of travel. The drive took us through the tiny communities of Eagle Rock, Golden and Nauvoo. Blink and you missed them. The road also crossed several of Table Rock Lake's many fingers. The snake-twisting outline of the reservoir, created by a dam on the White River, defines 750 miles of shoreline.

As I had suspected, my early arrival at Table Rock had been a good idea. I snagged one of the last open camp sites. I paid for three nights so as not to find myself searching for a campground on a Friday or Saturday night. It was a pattern I repeated often during my travels, staying in one place anywhere from two days to a week, depending on the scenery, possible activities, and the ability of my budget to keep up with the cost of gas.

My camp site here backed up to a three-mile long paved walking trail that went across a couple of wooden bridges to a marina in one direction and to the Branson Belle Showboat in the opposite direction. Table Lake was just beyond the path, which I walked early every morning with Maggie. I pretty much kept to myself after that – reading, writing and watching an occasional DVD or TV in the RV. It was hot and humid, and I was content to simply view the lake and campground goings on through my window. I thought about taking in the show on the Belle, but decided I didn't want to spoil my lazy solitude. That's one of the joys of traveling alone, not having to meet another person's travel expectations.

My walks, meanwhile, turned up three more new birds for the trip: northern rough-winged swallow, a plain brown and white bird that can easily be mistaken for a bank swallow — if the bank swallow didn't wear a bow tie, like a banker, low around its neck; a Carolina wren, a cheerful little bird with a pale cinnamon belly and a prominent and dashing white eyebrow; and a northern bob-white, a very distinctive member of the quail family. Like so many other birds, it gets its name from its call, *bob-white, bob-white.* It also softly clucks. These additions brought my number of trip species up to 59.

BIRDS ALONG THE WAY:
Brown thrasher, American robin, Carolina chickadee,
Baltimore oriole, northern cardinal, northern mockingbird,
red-winged blackbird, mourning dove, scissor-tailed flycatcher,
eastern meadowlark, common grackle, European starling,
black vulture, blue jay, house sparrow, turkey vulture,
American crow, Brewer's blackbird, *eastern phoebe,
chipping sparrow, **Louisiana waterthrush, gray catbird,
*rough-winged swallow, eastern kingbird, house finch,
indigo bunting, *Carolina wren, *northern bobwhite,
barn swallow, eastern bluebird.

*First sighting of this species on the journey
**Lifer

THE JOURNEY

CAMPGROUND:
Henry's RV Park
West Plains, Missouri

CAMPGROUND:
Table Rock
State Park

"What you've done becomes the judge of what
you're going to do —
especially in other people's minds.
When you're traveling, you are what
you are right there and then.
People don't have your past to
hold against you.
No yesterdays on the road."

— WILLIAM LEAST HEAT MOON

8

ROY ROGERS, A TRAGIC PAST
AND AN OUCH

Sunday morning found me back on the road, experiencing the exact opposite of my past few days of peacefulness. Instead of taking the loop around Branson, I had chosen to drive down its Main Street. I wanted to see why tourists flocked in huge numbers to visit this town. Branson, I saw, was where the Titanic and Elvis still lived, and where legendary singers past their prime performed to appreciative audiences past their prime. It was also home to the Roy Rogers Museum.

As a bratty child, he was my hero, idolized to the point I wouldn't play cowboys and Indians with the neighborhood kids unless I could be Roy. I had an advantage to keeping the role because every Saturday my mom would drive me and a couple kids of my choice to the Lisbon Theater in Dallas, where there was almost always a Roy Rogers movie playing in glorious black and white. Occasionally it was a Gene Autry or Hopalong Cassidy movie, along with the latest Flash Gordon cliff-hanger serial, but I lived for the Saturdays Roy and Trigger dominated the screen. I could have done without that cheeky Dale Evans, however.

I had plenty of time to let my mind wander back to those days as it took me over an hour to drive just five miles. It was bumper-to-bumper traffic, moving as slowly as it took my meat-and-potato-loving oldest son to eat his veggies when he was a youngster. Branson's main thoroughfare does a middling impersonation of the Las Vegas Strip.

I was tempted to stop and visit the Roy Rogers Museum in the middle of the chaos, but the mass of humanity convinced me otherwise. Besides I had visited the museum when it sat alongside Highway 15 in Victorville, California. I had stopped at it a few years ago when I was on my way to San Diego to visit one of my children. I was one of only about six other paying customers that day, which is why, I suspect, the coin-counters decided to move Roy and Trigger to Branson. From the mass of people in the city, it looked like the scheme was working well.

I took Highway 76 after getting out of town, and then veered onto Highway 160. My route crossed the long, winding Bull Shoals Lake twice, once just outside of Branson and again near Theodosia about 50 miles away. The lake, which on the map looks more like a large river, winds through both Arkansas and Missouri. It was created in 1952 when one of America's largest concrete dams was completed on the White River near Flippin, Arkansas. Its shorelines stretch and wind in back and forth circles for a thousand miles through the Ozarks.

Today's drive took me through the tiny communities of Kirbyville, Kissee Mills, Rueter, Theodosia, Isabella, and one corner of the Mark Twain Forest on its way to Gainesville. Along the way, I passed signs that read Booger Hollow, Slouch Slough and Coon Creek Road, names to fuel the Ozarks' hillbilly image – and names that made me smile.

The word Ozarks might either have been taken from an early French trading post, Aux Arks, which was located on the Mississippi River, or a natural bridge, Aux Arc, that was located in the Ozark-St. Francis National Forest. Today, the word Ozarks is a generic term for 50,000 square miles of varied territory that covers much of southern Missouri and northern Arkansas, a northeast chunk of Oklahoma, and a tiny piece of southeast Kansas.

After Gainesville, which had a population of about 650, it was back to tiny villages again, Tecumseh, named after a Shawnee chief who lived in the area; Caulfield, named after a former Missouri governor; and South Fork, so named because it's the south fork of the Spring River. It was an enjoyable drive, with almost no traffic – once I had left Branson behind. Maggie slept the whole way, only raising her head when I ended the day's journey in West Plains, Missouri, at Henry's RV Park.

I had left Table Rock with no reservations, deciding that I would simply stop at the first RV park I came upon after I had traveled 100 miles. Henry's was it.

West Plains, with a population of about 12,000 was pretty much nondescript. I learned that its primary claim to fame wasn't a happy one. In 1928, an explosion, possibly from a gas leak or possibly from a truck full of dynamite that had been parked nearby, destroyed the town's dance hall, killing 37 people and injuring 22. The explosion demolished cars parked on the street and damaged the nearby town courthouse to the point that it had to be demolished. The dynamite theory is suggested in the book, *West Plains As I Knew It*, written by lifelong town resident, Robert Neathery, who died at the age of 93 in 2003.

History of a place always fascinates me, but this tale from the past left me a bit sad. I prefer humorous trivia, or stories of bravery or skullduggery, to mass death. But things are what they are, as my own tale at the end of this driving day would prove.

Since I had been dawdling so much, I was only going to spend one night in West Plains. My plans were changed when I accidentally backed into a fence at the small campground.

I had already parked Gypsy Lee, but needed to put one of my Lego blocks beneath my back wheel to level her – Henry's wasn't exactly a KOA kind of place. After situating the leveler, I only got half-way back into the driver's seat to back the vehicle up the necessary six inches. Instead, I went back three feet before my foot could find the brake pedal. Since a fence was just two feet behind me, I did a bit of damage, mostly to the fence. Taking care of the details of getting that fixed kept me in town a couple of extra days.

My insurance took care of the fence and thankfully, since the insurance I carried came with a $250 deductible clause, the RV place I found to fix the minor ouch to my rear bumper charged me only $40 to straighten it. While it was a delay I would have preferred to do without, the people at the RV park were friendly, and the time passed quickly.

BIRDS ALONG THE WAY:
American robin, eastern bluebird, rough-winged swallow,
mourning dove, European starling, northern mockingbird,
northern cardinal, black vulture, eastern meadowlark,
turkey vulture, common grackle, Canada geese,
eastern kingbird, red-winged blackbird,
house sparrow and blue jay.

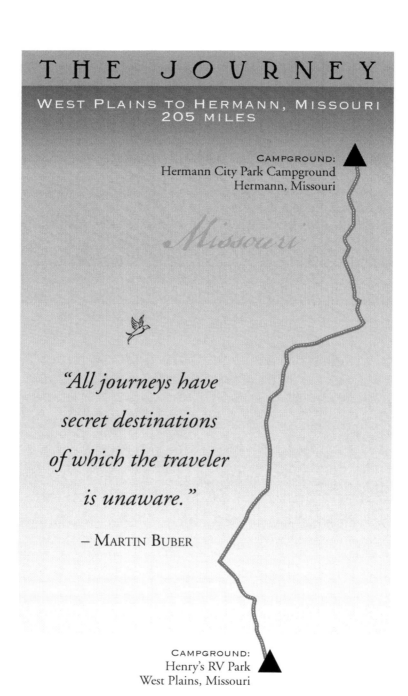

THE JOURNEY

CAMPGROUND:
Hermann City Park Campground
Hermann, Missouri

Missouri

"All journeys have

secret destinations

of which the traveler

is unaware."

– MARTIN BUBER

CAMPGROUND:
Henry's RV Park
West Plains, Missouri

9

A SCENIC RIVERWAY, A GERMAN TOWN AND A MARGARITA NIGHT

When West Plains was finally in my rear-view mirror, and the bumper incident behind me, I breathed a sigh of relief. Today's destination was Hermann's City Park Campground, where I had reservations for the night. Today would be my longest drive of the trip, and knowing I had a place to stay would keep me from hurrying my travels.

Maggie, a bird list for the area (compliments of Henry's cheerful owners after they discovered I was a birder) and a cheat-sheet of right and left turns for my day's drive were by my side. The latter was compensation for the fact that I have no sense of direction. The only time I knew which direction I was always headed was when I lived in Northern Utah, in sight of the awesome Wasatch Mountains. They stood tall, quite visible, and always on the east. They never moved.

As usual, my chosen route had more to do with scenic landscape than distance. I chose to travel Highway 19 because it was a designated scenic byway. The green dots running beside the road on my map went all the way from where I would join it at Alton, a town of about 600 residents 30 miles up the road on Highway 160 from West Plains, to Hermann.

The byway ran through a good-sized chunk of the Mark Twain National Forest and through Ozark Scenic Riverways National Park, which was created in 1964 to protect the Jacks Fork and Current rivers. It was a peaceful drive on a narrow two-lane, tree-lined road with little traffic. My eclectic thoughts were only occasionally interrupted by the passage of a swaying logging truck, which the highway had originally been built to serve. The rural road passed through the communities of Woodside, Greer and New Liberty on its way to Winona, the first town with more than 1,000 people since West Plains.

My one disappointment with the journey was that there was never anywhere to pull off to the side of the narrow road, giving me no opportunity to stop when I saw birds I couldn't identify while driving. All my earlier and eager study of the area's bird list I had beside me was for naught. While I was sure there would have been a lifer or two among the birds flitting among tree branches, I had to reconcile myself with the fact they would not be added to my bird list this day. It was becoming the mantra of my journey.

There were also many side roads off Highway 19 that I longed to explore, but today's drive was longer than usual; and since I didn't want to be driving in the dark, I reluctantly had to resist. Dallying had already put me a couple of weeks behind schedule so as to arrive in New England in time to see its landscape change into a coat-of-many-colors. I satisfied myself with a stop for a peanut butter and orange marmalade sandwich at a pull-off for the Riverways Park near Eminence.

With a population of only about 650, Eminence was proclaimed one of the top 50 outdoor towns in America by Sports Afield magazine, and the town self-proclaims itself the Canoe Capital of the World because of its access to the Jacks Fork and Current rivers. It was a quaint town with an old-fashioned feel to it that the Chamber of Commerce played on to attract tourists. I drove through slowly but didn't stop.

My map showed other populated sites along the way – Venice, Round Spring, Timber, Shannondale, Gladden, Custer and Salem, but some were so small I passed them by without realizing it. Salem was the largest, and like Eminence, catered to outdoor tourists.

Occasional logging trucks continued to be almost the only traffic I passed as I continued north through the small, sometimes seemingly non-existent, communities of Howes, Short Bend, Sligo, Limberlost, Cherryville, Steelville and Cuba, the latter being the only one that captured my interest. Located on old Route 66 near its current-day junction with Interstate 44, Cuba was designated as the Mother Road's Mural City.

I stopped here briefly to look at the outdoor art work, and would have visited the local historical museum except it was closed. Among the many murals were ones that paid tribute to Harry Truman's visit to Cuba, the Civil War and the Model T. Bette Davis and Amelia Earhart had also visited the city, and had murals representing them, too. Cuba, Missouri, turned out to be one of those unexpected travel surprises that made my travels so delightful. I would never have known such a place existed if I hadn't unexpectedly come upon it.

Back on the road, continuing north on Highway 19, I passed Berm, Tea, Drake and Swiss before arriving in Hermann. Because I had left West Plains early, and hadn't dallied too much along the way, it was only late afternoon when I found the city park and hooked up. My plan was to spend a quiet weekend, writing and reading before tackling St. Louis. While large cities weren't my thing, St. Louis, the Gateway to the West, was not a city to miss.

My time in Hermann, meanwhile, would give me a chance to absorb with my mind, the things my eyes had been seeing – and to record all the impressions in my journal. If I didn't take these breaks, my travel experiences would vanish into a misty wasteland of forgotten memories. Travel, I learned long before becoming a full-time RV-er, is best done with both the feet and the mind. The feet require stamina and the mind needs to be open and thoughtful.

There were few campers in the park when I arrived in Hermann, but a lot of the spaces – mostly the best ones – had reserved signs on them. I finally chose a shady end site near a huge four-trunked tree and a creek, its only disadvantage being that traffic zoomed over a nearby bridge that crossed the stream. Not to worry. It was so hot I figured the sound of my air conditioner running 24 hours a day would blank out the noise of passing vehicles.

Once hooked up, Maggie and I went exploring. Both our legs needed limbering up after the long drive. I found a path that led up a hill to the center of the town and followed it. Hermann was built on what the locals call "vertical acreage," a situation that did not please its first German settlers who had purchased the lots sight unseen.

The town was founded in 1836 by the German Settlement Society of Philadelphia, whose members had concerns that the English influence was destroying German traditions. Land for the new town, originally about 12,000 acres, was purchased by the society's representative, George Bayer, for about $15,000. Bayer, unlike those who followed him west in 1837, was undeterred by the hilliness of the property. But the rough landscape made survival difficult for the new settlers, and while the town did eventually prosper, it never achieved the status of a city to rival Philadelphia, as the society had dreamed of it becoming.

Today, Hermann's population is less than 3,000 – but the city's Market Street is 10 feet wider than the one in Philadelphia, according to the local vineyard brochure I came across. Vineyards are the area's largest industry, and before prohibition, it produced 100 million gallons of wine annually. What I observed personally, as I briefly wandered a few of the town streets, were a lot of historic buildings, large old stately homes, and a scenic river-front downtown. Hermann sits on the banks of the mighty Missouri.

Sweating profusely in the humid air, I meandered back down hill to my RV, where my first priority was a cool shower. Refreshed, I fixed Maggie and myself a bite to eat, and then began reading Peter Cashwell's book, *The Verb To Bird*. I felt an immediate kinship with Cashwell, who wrote in his first chapter that birding was not something one chose to do as much as it was something one could not help doing. These are exactly my feelings about both travel and birding.

I spent most of the next morning writing and gazing out the window, watching as the camp sites filled up. The reserved spots next to my RV were occupied by what appeared to be one large, noisy family group with lots of younger children. Later in the day, when I took Maggie for a walk, one of the men greeted me and apologized for any disturbance. He even offered to exchange camp sites with me as his RV unit was located farthest from the center of the gathering. I told him I was fine, and that the sound of people having fun never bothered me.

It was the truth, but the comment earned me an invitation for margaritas that evening after the young ones were all in bed; I eagerly accepted. Not only do I try and take every opportunity while on the road to meet people, sitting around a campfire is one of my favorite things to do any evening of the year. There's something magical about being under a star-filled sky and staring at crackling flames that connect people.

The group, I learned, was not one large family as I had suspected, merely a hodgepodge of boating friends from nearby St. Louis who took breaks from their busy lives to gather at the Hermann campground several times a year. They were curious about my solo life on the road, and I was interested in learning about sightseeing in St. Louis. The exchange of this information, along with a few tall-tale boating stories and weighty discussions about solving the world's problems, chased the hands around the clock. It was midnight when I gingerly did a tequila walk back to my RV and scooted Maggie off my side of the bed.

Before I left Hermann, I did a bit more exploring of the city, this time driving my RV up the hill into town. I parked at the city's Riverfront Park and took a stroll along the Missouri River. With my always handy binoculars, I spotted a belted kingfisher sitting on a bank stump across the river. It was on the lookout for a fish dinner, but a passing boat scared it away – just like the first 17

German settlers who arrived at this site in a steamboat might have scared away one of her ancestors.

I said "her" in reference to the kingfisher, because it was wearing a rusty red cummerbund that the male lacks. This kingfisher species is one of the few birds in which the female is the more colorful gender. Despite my high birding hopes, the kingfisher was only the third species to be added to my trip list since leaving West Plains. I had caught separate glimpses of three great blue herons along streams I passed while driving Highway 19, and had observed several American pipits wandering around the city campground.

Now, as I walked along, something other than a bird captured my attention: the tall bridge across the Missouri River. Information that I had picked up about the city told me it had been built in 1929. Before its construction, people had to be ferried from one side of the river to the other, well except in the occasional winters when the water froze solid and they could walk across.

As just one of my many whims on the journey, I decided I needed to drive across the imposing structure that loomed overhead, even though it would take me in the opposite direction from my route. And so I did. The detour, which took me high on the narrow bridge across the mighty river, gave me goose bumps, the same kind of feeling I used to get as a youngster riding the old wooden roller coaster at the Texas State Fair. Remembering this made me smile, and the return trip across the bridge was made without the goose bumps.

I read once that riding roller coasters, which I still do with my grandkids at every opportunity, stimulates the brain. I figured driving across this nearly 80-year-old bridge might be stimulating, too. And for no good reason I was pleased with myself.

BIRDS ALONG THE WAY:
American robin, *great blue heron, eastern bluebird,
rough-winged swallow, mourning dove, European
starling, northern cardinal, black vulture, eastern meadowlark,
turkey vulture, common grackle, northern mockingbird,
Canada goose, American crow, rock pigeon, eastern kingbird,
red-winged blackbird, northern bobwhite, blue jay,
house sparrow, barn swallow, *American pipit, bank swallow,
*belted kingfisher, American goldfinch and
red-headed woodpecker.

*First sighting of this species on the journey

THE JOURNEY

CAMPGROUND:
Hermann City Park Campground
Hermann, Missouri

CAMPGROUND:
St. Louis RV Park
St. Louis, Missouri

Missouri

*"Certainly, travel is more than
the seeing of sights; it is a change
that goes on, deep and permanent,
in the ideas of living."*

— MIRIAM BEARD

10

SAINT LOUIS: CHIHULY, A BIRDCAGE, AN ARCH AND BEER

When I was working as a writer/editor at Utah State University, the school's geology department hooked up to the state's earthquake monitoring program with a seismograph machine installed in a hallway. Passers-by could glimpse what was going on deep beneath their feet by noting the squiggly lines of peaks and valleys printed out on the continuous roll of paper flowing through the machine. I was fascinated, and often found myself going out of my way to take a look.

The apparatus mostly scratched out short vertical strokes weaving across the page, representing movements below that were too small for humans above to feel. Every once in a while, however, the lines grew tall and bold, representing a significant shaking of the earth somewhere. If my journey to New England had been plotted out in such a visible way, my week's stay in St. Louis would have been recorded in those long bold strokes.

While I had happily been avoiding the messy industriousness and cacophony of big cities, I was ready for a change of pace that this western gateway, where Lewis and Clark began their historic trek, had to offer. But not as eager, however, to face freeway traffic any sooner than necessary, which is why I bypassed interstates 64 and 44 and took Highway 100 into the city from Hermann.

My drive took me through the city of New Haven, which began life in 1836 as a river boat stop called Miller's Landing. The name was changed 20 years later to signify that the town, now boasting a Union Pacific railway station, was more than just a boat landing.

My chosen route continued through Washington, which was the Corn Cob Pipe Capital of the World, a title owed to the fact that the town is the home of corn cob pipe manufacturer Missouri Meerschaum. Corn cob pipe fans include General Douglas MacArthur, Mark Twain, Norman Rockwell, Popeye and Frosty the Snowman, Highway 100 also took me through Ellisville, a town of about 10,000 that Money Magazine, in 2009, ranked 25th as being one of the best places in America to live.

Then there were the St. Louis' suburb towns of Ballwin, Manchester, Des Peres, Maplewood, etc., etc., that all seemed part of St. Louis itself. People move to the suburbs to get away from the city, and then the city comes to them. I watched it happen in Dallas, where I was born, and which I still visit annually.

Fruitdale, the Dallas suburb where my grandmother lived when I was growing up, was a quiet place where everyone had gardens and chickens. My grandmother raised pigs and rabbits for the dinner table as well, and the nearest home was at least a half block away. I recently took a trip down memory lane there, and saw three houses occupying what was once my grandmother's garden. I could also hear the roar of traffic from a nearby major traffic-mover road as I stood in front of her former small home.

I had plenty of time to let this memory rattle around in my brain as the nearer to St. Louis I got, the more stop and go traffic I encountered. Eventually, however, I arrived at the St. Louis RV Park, where I had reservations for a week. Although expected, because of the description in my Trailer Life Directory, its lack of nature amenities and scenic setting still disappointed me. Located in the heart of downtown, it was an asphalt parking lot with not much more than six feet separating the parked RVs. The paved interior intensified the summer heat, and the only place to walk Maggie was a thin strip of grass outside the fenced park. As

Realtors love to say, the three best things going for this place was location, location, location.

Once I registered, and accumulated brochures of things to do in the city that the friendly clerk heaped on me, I hooked up, turned on the air conditioner, and then used my cell phone to make arrangements for a rental car to be delivered the next morning. Maggie couldn't go with me to the places I wanted to visit, and my affection for her demanded I leave her behind in air-conditioned comfort. I then spent the next several hours plotting out which sights to see during the coming week before attempting to take advantage of the park's cable television service.

As usual, there was nothing on I cared to watch. After about 15 minutes of surfing with the remote, I gave up and settled down to spend some time with Anna Pigeon, Nevada Barr's fictional National Park Service ranger. In this murder-mystery adventure, *Liberty Falling*, Anna was in New York, temporarily assigned to the Statue of Liberty and Ellis Island National monuments. Barr's novel was full of facts about the book's park setting, which fascinated me. Anna kept my attention until well after midnight before I finally forced myself to put the book down and get some sleep for the day ahead.

I should have read longer. It was 10 a.m. before the economy blue Neon I had rented for the week showed up at the RV park. The driver pleaded that his helper was off sick for the day. He also said I needed to take him back to the office to complete the rental agreement. On the way back to the office, the driver pointed out Union Station, where I would later encounter a huge mural depicting J. K. Rowling's imaginary "Platform 9 and 3/4th." Our route to the rental office took us down Market Street, which offered a frontal view of the city's towering Gateway Arch. We were only a few blocks from the 630-foot tall landmark when the driver turned into what appeared to be a back alleyway, and parked in front of an annex to a large hotel.

"That's Busch Stadium, home of our Cardinals," he said pointing to the large structure adjacent to the car rental office. I didn't figure I would have much problem finding this place again.

When all the paperwork was finally settled, I set off for the Missouri Botanical Gardens. Its nature essence had been the thing I had chosen to help ease my way into the big city, besides, I was eager to see the Dale Chihuly exhibit currently on display in the gardens' Climatron. This geodesic dome greenhouse, according to my brochures, enclosed an international forest of tropical plants for which the 150-year-old gardens is acclaimed. Chihuly, I already knew, was world renown for his stunning glass art, much of which is on display in museums across the world.

As I walked through the dome's earthy rain forest, I couldn't stop taking pictures. Usually I find too much time with a camera in front of my eyes dulls the senses, so I snap a picture or two then put my camera away, and bring out my notebook. While it's said "one picture is worth a thousand words," as a writer I appreciate that it takes words to express that very idea.

But this day, staring at Chihuly's colorful glass creations, representing everything from reeds and Mexican hats to herons and meteorite-looking balls plopped down among a bounty of brilliantly hued flowers, left me wordless. When I later looked at the photos, I found I had mingled Chihuly's art with the creations of nature so well that I sometimes had to stop and ask myself which was which. If ever there were to be the perfect marriage, Mother Nature and Chihuly would wear the wedding rings.

The rest of my tour of the gardens' botanical wonders, which lasted until the place closed at 5 p.m., included a rather dry sandwich at the Garden Cafe and sweaty walks covering 79 acres of landscaped gardens. There was a tram tour one could take, but which I always seemed to miss.

It felt good to get back to my RV and Maggie. After walking her, and a cool shower, I heated up a frozen lasagna dinner and topped the meal off with a big bowl of vanilla ice cream drenched in chocolate syrup. Life is good, I thought, as I brought my journal up to date. Maggie and I then took another walk, circling the block around the RV park twice before I picked up where I had left off with Anna Pigeon. My eyes were tired, however, and I soon turned out the light to lay in the dark with my thoughts.

How does a genius like Chihuly come to be? I already knew the answer: Single-minded focus and dedication. For almost as long as I could remember, I had wanted to be a "great" writer, yet I was always finding excuses for not writing. I knew I lacked the focus of a Chihuly, or a Van Gogh, or even an old boyfriend who religiously practiced his guitar four hours a day, seven days a week. I was always getting distracted, and when the writing went undone, I flagellated myself.

Such abuse went on for years, until I finally realized that giving up riding roller coasters with my grandkids, arguing politics with my friends, discovering who my grownup children had become, exploring new hiking trails, white-water rafting with my river-rat buddies, mindlessly watching the sun rise and set, piddling with my watercolors, reading Harry Potter the day it came out, and sniffing every flower in life I came across, were more important to me than being a great writer. Writing is a part of my life, and will always be, but it will never be my whole life. Knowing this, accepting this, and now content with this, I lay silently in bed listening to Maggie gently snoring at my feet, and then finally let the waves of sleep take me.

The rest of my time in St. Louis was spent in a frenzy of sight-seeing. I knew I might never pass this way again, and I didn't want to miss a thing.

I spent two of my days in Forest Park – St. Louis' version of New York City's Grand Central Park. It was here that the 1904 World's Fair was held, an international event that attracted 19 million visitors. The park is home to the St. Louis Zoo and the St. Louis Art Museum, both permanent reminders of the world event.

The museum was created specifically for the fair at the astronomical cost, considering the year, of about $1 million. It was called the Palace of Fine Arts, and its great Sculpture Hall was modeled after the Roman Baths of Caracalla, whose ruins are now an Italian tourist attraction. While I enjoyed the four hours spent roaming through the museum, I have to admit I found it a bit on the "stuffy" side. Although not belittling its excellent credentials for being one of the nation's best museums, I found too many ancient relics and Old World art and too little of the excitement that artists like Gauguin, Monet, Mattisse, Renoir, Nolde and Degas generated. It is these rule-breaking artists of the Impressionist years, and their colorful palettes, that speak most joyfully to me.

The World's Fair remnant at the zoo is the Birdcage, an enclosed walk-through aviary that was once the largest of its kind in the world. It was built by the Smithsonian Institution at a cost of $17,500, and was supposed to be moved to the organization's National Zoo in Washington D.C. after the fair ended. St. Louis residents protested its removal, however, and the Smithsonian allowed the city to buy the flight cage for $3,500. Cost of the birds was extra. Records show that these charges included $7.50 for a pair of Mandarin ducks and $20 for four Canada geese.

My sense of direction and interpretation of the zoo map failed me several times before I finally found the back path that led me to the aviary. Today it's been turned into a cypress swamp for aquatic birds commonly found along the Mississippi River. A boardwalk takes visitors through the created landscape, and until one looks up at the aviary's skylight frame, it's easy to imagine oneself actually outside in nature.

I shot photos of a roseate spoonbill with its pink feathers reflecting a double image in a shallow pond, and one of a snowy egret whose reflection was artistically broken up by the aviary's framework. While captive birds don't count on an official American Ornithological Union bird list, I was still a happy birder.

Along with spending time in the aviary, I spent time enjoying the zoo animals, although I sometimes found myself watching people more than the animals. I found them just as interesting. As I've already admitted, I'm an unashamed eavesdropper, and the conversation I overheard at the spider monkey exhibit made me smile.

"I wonder how we would use our tails if we had one," a young boy asked the woman holding his hand."

I wondered, too. But the only answer the boy and I received from the woman was: "Don't ask so many questions." I get that response a lot.

* * *

The next day found me strolling through the manicured flower gardens at St. Louis' Anheuser-Busch Brewery. Of particular delight for me this day were the crystal-chandelier lighted stables for the Budweiser Clydesdales. The keepers of these giants, which once pulled the company's beer wagons for real and not just show, kept their stalls smelling as sweet as any outdoor garden. As one who has mucked out a few stalls herself, I know firsthand what an endless task that would be.

At the end of the 45-minute free guided tour, it being yet another hot day, I eagerly took advantage of the free beer offered the visitors. I even got a second free beer the next day when I visited Grant's Farm. The former home of our 18th president, Ulysses S. Grant, the property is now a 281-acre wildlife reserve that is owned and operated by the Anheuser-Busch family. The tour of the farm begins with an open-air train ride that transports visitors to a small zoo area, where I was entranced watching a dozen or so real macaws while listening to a fake mariachi band's lively music. This visit also offered a chance to get a better look at the famous Clydesdales – and the opportunity to get your picture taken with one of the horses. I declined the offer.

I did, however, fork over money for a picture to be taken the next day when I did what all St. Louis tourists should do; I went up to the top of the Gateway Arch. I figured I had earned picture rights after enduring a four-minute jolting ride to the top in a windowless ball. It's actually called a capsule and eight of them form a tram inside the arch that gimbals to the top in Ferris-wheel fashion. There are seats in each for five people, but unless you're petite you can't sit up straight. I'm sure I had to breathe on the way up but the large intake of air I drew in when we finally reached the top, and could see the outside world again, felt as if it was the first I had taken since the door had closed on that cramped conveyance. Have I mentioned that I'm claustrophobic?

The arch was completed in 1965 to commemorate the Louisiana Purchase and the nation's 19th century westward expansion. A contest for its design was sponsored by the Jefferson National Expansion Memorial Association in 1947. It was won by Eero Saarinen, an American architect who immigrated to this country with his parents from Finland when he was 13 years old. While his impressive stainless steel arch design appears deceptively simply to someone like me, I learned that its catenary curve is considered an engineering marvel. The arch is twice as tall as the Statue of Liberty and 75 feet higher than the George Washington Monument.

Heights don't bother me so I lingered at the top as long as possible, enjoying the aerial view through the arch windows. St. Louis was spread out before me on one side and the Mississippi River on the other. But finally, I had to step back into that dreadful ball. The ride down seemed to take less time than going up, thankfully, and I celebrated my courage by having my picture taken and inserted in the forefront of a photograph of the arch. It was a great souvenir for my travel journal.

After the photo session, I meandered through the Museum of Westward Expansion that sits below ground and beneath the arch. The museum's exhibits trace the journey of Lewis and Clark, whose amazing journey across this country's former wilderness always leaves me in awe. While I can't say I reserved the best of St. Louis for the last, I can say my arch adventure was one of the more memorable of my St. Louis visit. It was the one thing I did in which I felt part of the action instead of just an onlooker.

That night, after my twice around the block walk with Maggie, cool shower, and then two bowls of cereal for dinner, I crawled into bed once again with Anna Pigeon, this time staying awake until I finished the book. Tomorrow I would leave big city life behind, and once again search out Mother Nature. I was eager to do so, and I suspected Maggie was just as eager.

BIRDS ALONG THE WAY:
American robin, eastern bluebird, northern cardinal, common grackle, northern mockingbird, house sparrow, turkey vulture, mourning dove, bank swallow, blue jay, European starling, rock pigeon, American pipit, American goldfinch, red-headed woodpecker, American crow, bank swallow, belted kingfisher, eastern phoebe, great blue heron and chipping sparrow, not counting the many exotic birds at the zoo and farm.
As slow as my trip bird list was going, it would have been nice to add them.

THE JOURNEY

ST. LOUIS TO HANNIBAL, MISSOURI
126 MILES

○ HANNIBAL, MISSOURI

▲ CAMPGROUND:
Injun Joe Campground
New London, Missouri

Missouri

CAMPGROUND:
St. Louis RV Park
St. Louis, Missouri

"Nothing so liberalizes a man and expands the kindly instincts that nature put in him as travel and contact with many kinds of people."

– MARK TWAIN

11

IN THE FOOTSTEPS OF MARK TWAIN

U nlike my back-road travel to St Louis, I couldn't find a satisfactory way to avoid taking the freeway out of town. Instead, I found myself on Interstate 70, mucking through heavy traffic and passing through the suburb towns of St. Charles and St. Peter. What's with all the saint names, I mused, as my RV turned into a ponderous, motorized snail.

A bit of research partially answered the question. Saint Louis was named for King Louis XIV, after La Salle claimed the area for France in the late 1600s. He actually named the entire area Louisiana, hence what we know today as the Louisiana Purchase. I didn't have a satisfactory answer for why it became "Saint" Louis. My suspicion is that it was simply the influence of the early Catholic missions in the area.

That was certainly the case for St. Charles, which was originally named Les Petites Cotes, or The Little Hills, when it was founded in 1769 by Canadian fur trader Louis Blanchette. The city was renamed in 1791 after the area's first church, which was dedicated to Saint Carlos Borromeo, a 16th Century archbishop of Milan who played a major role in the reformation of the Catholic Church.

The city of St. Peter took its name from the area's first log church, St. Peters on Dardenne Creek. The church was established in 1815, but the area didn't incorporate as a village until 1910. It only became a city in 1959. At which time it had a grand population of 404. Today, St. Peters boasts a population of over

60,000, and is home to the largest recycling plant in the world. Anheuser-Busch uses its recycled aluminum to make beer cans.

I was glad when I finally left the "saints" and their snake of traffic behind me when I turned onto Highway 79, a two-lane scenic byway that would take me to my day's destination just outside Hannibal. The byway was little traveled, most likely because paralleling it to the west was Highway 61, a major freeway between St. Louis and Hannibal on which drivers could put the pedal to the metal. To the east of 79 was the Mississippi River, hence the road's nickname as the Little Dixie Highway of the Great River Road.

With traffic practically nil, I was able to once again enjoy the quiet rural landscape, which this day offered frequent glimpses of "Old Man River." The first town I passed was Old Monroe. In order after that came: Winfield, Foley, Elsberry, Clarksville, Louisiana and Ilasco, with populations ranging from less than 200 to about 4,000. The only one I lingered in for a bit was Clarksville, which sits right on the Mississippi River. Founded in 1817, Clarksville is on the National Register of Historic Places. I suspected from the looks of its downtown that the majority of the town's 500 or so residents were either artists or antique dealers.

About 10 miles up the road from Clarksville, I crossed Interstate 54, which began its journey eastward in El Paso, Texas. The highway looked to be the only route with a bridge that crossed the Mississippi into Illinois between St. Louis and Hannibal. The river, I fancied, was one of those "good fences" Robert Frost wrote about that makes Missouri and Illinois "good neighbors."

At Hannibal, about 30 miles farther up the road, I backtracked a short distance on Interstate 61 to reach the Injun Joe Campground. It seemed like a good spot from which to explore the town where Samuel Clemens, better known to all as Mark Twain, grew up, and which he fictionalized in his writings. The town now plagiarizes its native son to attract tourists. For example, the large Injun Joe RV Park I chose for my home for the next four days got its name from the murderous villain in Twain's "Tom Sawyer."

Some say the character of Injun Joe was based on Joe Douglas, a half-Indian/half Black resident of Hannibal in Twain's day.

Douglas, however, was a respectable property owner and not a murderer. And while Injun Joe died before his time, Douglas lived to be 102. Injun Joe Campground also contrasted to its namesake in that it was a cheerful place with a trading post, a pool where children splashed about and an ice cream shoppe near its entrance.

After hooking up, I turned on the TV and discovered that June Allyson had died. She had been one of my favorite Hollywood icons growing up. Perhaps it was the upbeat quality of her early movies. My favorite was "As the Clouds Roll By," in which she sang "Look for the Silver Lining." I was only 10 when I heard it for the first time, and I suspect it helped format my cheery – if sometimes annoying-to-others – attitude toward life. I try, even though I finally accepted the sad truth that life is neither logical nor fair, to look for that glimmer of sunshine behind the tragic storms that at times touch us all.

June's death, meanwhile, left me in need of a bit of that sunshine. I figured I'd probably find it if I took a walk through the park with Maggie. As usual, this spoon-full of medicine worked its magic. Maggie's stubby wagging tail, which vibrates her entire body when in motion, inspired smiles from several campers. Their smiles required an echoing face, and perhaps a few words from me in return. The rusty red crowns and joyful trilling of a dozen or so chipping sparrows broadened the smile. After I had devoured a double-scoop, chocolate ice cream cone, I was smiling for real again, and ready to shuffle through the stack of tourist brochures I had picked up when checking into the campground.

There was, I saw, plenty to do. Hannibal's entrepreneurs had organized tours through the homes of Twain and Becky Thatcher and the Mark Twain Cave. There was also a Mark Twain museum to explore and a cruise aboard a riverboat down the Mississippi. The next day I signed up for them all, forking over $38 for the Adventure Passport package. In addition, I decided to take a two-hour trolley tour for $8 to get my bearings of the area. I thought the ticket prices quite reasonable, but like everything else, I'm sure the tours will cost more today. I know that the nice, $20 RV parks that I found during my first few years on the road had become $30-35 per night toward the end of my nine years on the road.

It was cooler in Hannibal than it had been in St. Louis, and with the smaller, less crowded, atmosphere of the town, I was always able to find shade in which to park my RV while I went off on my ramblings. I knew that with the windows and vents left open that the motor home would remain reasonably cool for Maggie's benefit. I knew, because on such days as these, I usually didn't turn the air conditioner on when both she and I were occupying it.

The trolley ride was my first order of business. The driver's name was Maudine. She was a cheerful, spunky lady, clearly over retirement age who had the Mark Twain and Hannibal stories down pat. I enjoyed them all, but the unexpected bonus for me on the tour was the home of "Unsinkable Molly Brown" of Titanic fame. The cottage where Molly started out life sat just a block west of the Mississippi River, and a few blocks from Hannibal's historic downtown. It has been restored to the degree that it looked a lot nicer than its depiction in the movie in which Molly, played by Debbie Reynolds, started out in life.

It was noon when Maudine finished her spiel. After a quick check of Maggie, whom I found comfortably snoozing in the over-the-cab bed with a cross breeze blowing across her, I sought out a place to feed my stomach's grumble. This turned out to be Sid's National Bar and Grill. I sat at the bar, ordered a Philly sandwich and a cold beer, and struck up a conversation with the attentive barmaid. There were few customers and soon the woman was telling me her life history, which included getting pregnant in the tenth grade when she was 16, and now struggling to get herself through school. I shared that I had married at 16, had five kids, and then went back to school.

Sometimes the world seems such a small place. The sandwich was excellent, the conversation stimulating, and I left a generous tip before strolling over to where the tour of the Mark Twain home complex was to begin.

The celebrated home was a narrow two-story structure painted a glistening white with quaint flower boxes beneath the windows. Like with the Molly Brown home, I wondered how closely the restoration resembled the original. Even so I enjoyed Hannibal's efforts to let me step back in time, and into a sliver of Twain's early life.

I particularly enjoyed the Twain quotes hanging on the walls. My favorite was: "I don't know anything that mars good literature so completely as too much truth." It made me smile, particularly as I decided that the town's promoters felt the same way about what they presented to the paying tourists.

Another Twain quote that stuck with me was: "A man's experiences of life are a book. There was never yet an uninteresting life." I already knew this, but if I hadn't, the fascinating people I had met on my travels would have taught me this lexicon.

An exhibit of Norman Rockwell paintings, which illustrated the 1930s' editions of Tom Sawyer and Huckleberry Finn, ended the tour. The artist had visited Hannibal to lend authenticity to his work for Twain's books, and later donated the paintings to the Twain Museum. Copies of the books with Rockwell's drawings were available in the museum gift shop. But since living in an RV does not allow for much collecting, I bought a cheaper set to re-read for nostalgia's sake, which I would later pass on to a young grandson who enjoyed reading.

After leaving the Twain complex, I strolled over to Cardiff Hill, at the base of which stood a Tom Sawyer and Huckleberry Finn statue. At the top of the hill – 253 huffing and puffing steps up – was the Mark Twain Memorial Lighthouse, along with a road that more sensible people took to reach the hill's summit.

There was also a tiny blue-gray gnatcatcher flitting about in a tree next to the lighthouse, a new bird species for my slow-growing trip list. I had expected the list to be longer by now, given that once I had seen 102 birds in a single day. But then I remembered that I had been at a birding hot spot that day, and also had a professional bird guide with me who knew where each bird species liked to hang out. Had I been on my own, I would have been lucky to have seen even half that number.

Thinking on this made me rethink my bird-count expectations and vow to just enjoy any birds I did see. My joy of birds had nothing to do with numbers, although I do enjoy compiling my bird lists. But then I'm one of those people who makes lists of everything, from things to do before I die and writing ideas, to grocery lists and all the towns I was passing through on this trip. Putting numbers out of my mind, I simply watched the gnatcatcher. A tiny, pale bluish and white bird with a tail about as third as long as its body, it was a constant blur of motion. Even when it briefly sat on a branch, its tail continued moving from side to side. But through my binoculars, I was able to see the white circle that outlined the gnatcatcher's tiny dark eye, so perfectly round that it seemed magical.

Only when the bird flew out of sight did I turn my attention to the lighthouse. The glistening white, round structure, which looked out over Hannibal and the Mississippi River, had never been an aid to navigation. It had been lit for the first time in 1935 by President Franklin Roosevelt to mark what would have been Samuel Clemens 100th birthday. It was rebuilt and rededicated to the great author in 1964 by President Kennedy, then refurbished in 1994 and rededicated by President Clinton.

I wondered what the sharp-tongued author would have said about that. For all that I've enjoyed Twain's light-hearted writings, it's his little-known essay, "The War Prayer," in which he explains exactly what praying for victory means, that had left its mark on me. Thinking about the ugliness of war somehow made the hike down Cardiff Hill's 253 steps harder than going up them.

My mood was lighter the next day when I boarded the Mark Twain Riverboat for a jaunt on the Mississippi River. Even though it was still morning, the air felt as thick as my mom's cream gravy – but with a less appealing smell. The fishy, dirty-sock odor, however, dissipated as a slight breeze thinned the air once the riverboat was paddling along in the middle of the stream. A flock of ring-billed gulls followed in our wake, occasionally swooping down to forage from what the boats paddles had churned up From a distance, Hannibal had a child's picture book quality about it. The huge barge being pushed down stream had me thinking of Twain's time spent on this river – and the red engine chugging along the bank with a bunch of coal cars behind reminded me of one of Thomas the Tank Engine's friends.

Sitting on the deck of the boat listening to banjo music playing over a loud speaker. I found myself spelling Mississippi the way I had as a kid. "M, I, crooked letter, crooked letter, I, crooked letter, crooked letter I, humpback, humpback, I." The tune was fresh in my mind from Maudine's rendering of it the day before.

Sitting next to me on deck were a middle-aged couple from Minneapolis who were on their way to Waterloo, Iowa, to visit the John Deere plant. I wondered who would choose a tractor plant as a vacation destination – until they told me they were farmers. I suspect people would find some of my destinations just as odd. For example, after Hannibal, one of my planned stops would be Battle Ground, Indiana, where I was going to howl with wolves.

But before I left Hannibal, I had to make one last stop. I wanted to visit the infamous Mark Twain Cave in which Tom and Becky had gotten lost. My tour group included one young family and a giggling gaggle of Girl Scouts led by an enthusiastic elderly gentleman. I use the gentleman adjective literally, as the kind man loaned the jacket he was wearing to a shivering young girl who hadn't thought to bring a coat along.

As caves go, this one was all narrow passages and ledges with nary a stalactite (holds tight to the ceiling) or stalagmite (might reach the ceiling one day) in sight. The cave, according to our guide, was a place where Jesse James hid out after a big robbery. It was a fascinating bit of trivia, but while I thoroughly enjoyed the hour walk though it – my claustrophobia lets me do caves as long as I keep moving – I doubt this rather plain cave would have the popularity it does today if not for its tall-tale role in Twain's books.

It had none of the awesomeness found in Carlsbad Caverns, or Timpanogas Cave near Provo, Utah, where red lights single out the rock formation said to be the heart of the Indian maiden whose profile can be seen on the mountain top above.

BIRDS ALONG THE WAY:
European starling, northern mockingbird, red-tailed hawk, mourning dove, eastern meadowlark, northern cardinal, American crow, bank swallow, common grackle, belted kingfisher, chipping sparrow, American robin, *blue-gray gnatcatcher, eastern phoebe, rock pigeon, great blue heron, house finch, house sparrow, eastern bluebird, turkey vulture, killdeer, ring-billed gull and red-winged blackbird.
*First sighting of this species on the journey

THE JOURNEY

INJUN JOE CAMPGROUND,
HANNIBAL, MISSOURI TO CHATHAM, ILLINOIS
107 MILES

CHATHAM TO WELDON SPRINGS STATE PARK
65 MILES

WELDON SPRINGS TO KICKAPOO STATE PARK
72 MILES

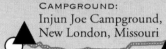

CAMPGROUND:
Weldon Springs
State Park
Clinton, Illlinois

CAMPGROUND:
Kickapoo
State Park
Oakwood, Illinois

CAMPGROUND:
Injun Joe Campground,
New London, Missouri

HANNIBAL
MISSOURI

CAMPGROUND:
Double J Camp-
ground and RV Park
Chatham, Illinois

"We live in a wonderful world that is full of beauty, charm and adventure. There is no end to the adventures we can have if only we seek them with our eyes open."

– Jawaharal Nehru

12

MEANDERING THROUGH ILLINOIS
WHERE KICKAPOOS ONCE ROAMED

Itook Interstate 72 out of Hannibal. It took me across the Mighty Mississippi and into Illinois, where a flock of red-winged blackbirds welcomed me as I crossed the river into the fourth state on this six-month journey. I lingered a bit near a pull-off on the Illinois side of the river to watch the cheerful red wings as they flew among the trees, their scarlet epaulets sparkling every time the sun bounced its rays off them. While I was watching, a golden-throated meadowlark flew down and began taking a bath in a drainage ditch. What a great start for the day. Even Maggie watched the birds from her co-pilot perch. I wondered what she was thinking. As if reading my thoughts, she turned her brown eyes toward me and seemed to smile. I assumed she thought it was going to be a good day, too.

Back on the road, I jogged south to catch Highway 106, and continued heading east. This was a narrower road that roughly paralleled Interstate 72 but left behind more than 90 percent of the traffic, including all of the blow-you-off-the-road semis. I was able to stay on these twisting lesser roads as they passed through tiny villages and small towns all the way to Chatham, Illinois, where I checked into the Double J RV Park for four nights. After non-stop sight-seeing in St. Louis and Hannibal, I felt a need to settle quietly for a while. My gas allowance also needed a reprieve to catch up with my budget.

Chatham is a small village of less than 10,000 people located on the outskirts of Springfield. It was a quiet, pleasant place to relax, and the activities I engaged in for the next three days were short walks with Maggie, reading, writing, sketching, playing computer games and watching TV.

Each of the walks started with a scolding from a mockingbird that kept a reproachful watch in a nearby tree. I suspected the bird had a nest nearby, but never could locate it in the thick summer foliage. American robins, finches, sparrows, bluebirds, mourning doves and killdeer were plentiful around the park, but my best bird find here was a dickcissel, a small sparrow-like bird with a thick beak, yellow eyebrow and chestnut on the side of the wings. The male often wears a large black bib, which at a distance allows it to be mistaken for a meadowlark. I had done just that until a closer look showed me my error. The bird was a new one for the journey, and one I had only seen once before. Part of me was sorry I had been such a late-bloomer when it came to watching birds. Another part of me was glad – because I would be seeing lifers for a long time to come.

All too quickly, or so it seemed, it was time to move on. After four days of solitude and quiet, I was ready for something different. I found it at the nearby Henson Robinson Zoo that was located next to Lake Springfield, a 4,200-acre reservoir owned by the city of Springfield. I arrived just as the animal park was opening for the day, and so had the animal park mostly to myself for the two hours that I strolled through its landscaped paths. As zoos go, there weren't a lot of animals, but among them were a couple of rare species: the black-footed penguin, which is found in the warm waters around southern Africa, and two red wolves thought now to be extinct in the wild.

Red wolves once roamed Smoky Mountain National Park, and in 1991 an effort was made to reintroduce them to the area. But almost all the pups born to the released wolves died, and the adults strayed out of the park. The effort ended in 1998 with the capture of all the surviving wolves. I was glad to hear later that the mated pair I had watched this day at the zoo had given birth to three pups sometime after my visit. The births were a significant increase to the known red wolf population of only about 200.

When I left the zoo, the heat and high humidity were quickly becoming oppressive – a state of the climate that would stick with me until I had I left both Illinois and Indiana behind. I had never suspected that these two states could get as hot as Texas, but they certainly did. And they were just as humid as the Lone Star State's Gulf Coast, where I had lived for 15 years.

On leaving the zoo, I skirted Springfield as I wasn't in the mood for a big-city visit. Springfield, the capital of Illinois, was home for many years to Abraham Lincoln, who lived and practiced law and politics in the small town for a quarter of a century. With a current a population of over 100,000 residents, Springfield has come a long way from its 1818 beginnings, when trappers and traders plied their business along the area's Sangamon River. which I crossed twice during the day's journey.

Once Springfield was behind me, I took the Highway 54 exit off Interstate 55, a choice that took me away from most traffic and through the small communities of Bissell, Spaulding, Barclay, Buffalo Hart, Cornland, Lake Fork and Pulaski, the biggest of the towns even though its population was less than 2,000 people. I wondered about the name and discovered that the town had been named after Casimir Pulaski, a Polish nobleman and military commander who immigrated to America, and joined Washington's Continental Army. He is said to have saved the life of this country's first president. Pulaski has also been called the father of America's cavalry.

I wondered if the Pulaski tool, which has a combination axe and adze head – which I had used a few times when I had volunteered to help build Forest Service trails – had also been named after the Polish hero. Nope. Ed Pulaski got the credit for that after he gained hero status helping save firefighters during a 1910 outbreak of Idaho wildfires.

Finding answers to satisfy my wondering-wandering mind always pleases me.

After Mount Pulaski – which could have more appropriately been called Hill Pulaski since its elevation was less than 2,000 feet – I passed through another round of small communities until I reached Clinton, a town with a population of about 7,000 residents. It was named for an 1800s' New York governor, and is the place where Lincoln is said to have given the speech that includes the quotation: "You can fool all the people some of the time and some of the people all the time, but you cannot fool all the people all of the time."

From Clinton, I took Highway 1 south and followed the signs to Weldon Springs State Park, where, since it had been a short day's drive, I checked in for only one night.

The springs that gave the manicured park its name began life two million years ago as a huge river known as the Teays. This ancient stream was 15 miles across in some places before glaciers moved down from the north and buried the area. When the glaciers receded, the till they left behind obliterated the Teays, but groundwater still flows through the layers of bedrock below, seeping out to form the springs and the lake that are the dominant features of the park.

Before leaving the park the next morning, Maggie and I hiked the two-mile trail that encircled the lake. Along the way, we saw great blue herons, American robins, blue jays, cardinals, ring-billed gulls and a gaggle of geese. The latter were of the domestic variety, and we herded them along the bank ahead of us before they finally returned to the water and swam their get-away. The trail meandered: past landscaped docks and picnic areas, through untamed stands of oak, sycamore, maple, ash, walnut and hackberry, and then onto boardwalks through lush wetlands. Reflections of pink-tinged sunrise clouds, and the many-hued greens of the trees, painted the lake, offering an ever-changing kaleidoscopic view as we traversed around it.

While my eyes scanned the sights, and stored them in memory scrapbooks, Maggie, with her cocker nose to the ground, got drunk on the aromas of the lake and trees. We both arrived back at the RV richer than when we had started our morning hike. I was glad my next stop would be another Illinois state park – one whose name made me smile and think of kicking Maggie's dog poo around, instead of picking it up as good dog owners always do. The park was called Kickapoo.

Just for the record, I am a good dog owner, and my pockets, when walking Maggie, always hold a bag or two to pick up her poop. Far more than once on my journeys, I have wished other dog owners were as considerate.

To get to Kickapoo, I backtracked to Clinton, and then took Highway 10 east, past Clinton Lake. The reservoir was created in the late 1970s as a cooling source for a nearby nuclear power plant that became operational in the late 1980s. Today, the lake is popular with fisherman, as it is home to catfish, crappies and bass.

The day's drive took me past the small communities of Weldon and Bondville before passing through Champaign. Located about 135 miles from Chicago, Champaign has a population of about 82,000 – and its own song. Bob Dylan and Carl Perkins wrote music and lyrics for a little tune named "Champaign, Illinois."

"I got a woman in Morocco, I got a woman in Spain, Woman that's done stole my heart, she lives up in Champaign. I say Champaign, Champaign, Illinois; I certainly do enjoy Champaign, Illinois."

I drove slowly through Champaign, but didn't stop. I still wasn't in the mood for city life. I left Highway 10 in Champaign, and caught Highway 150 east, which would take me the rest of the way to Kickapoo State Park, which was named after the Kickapoo Indians – to whom I probably owed an apology for my earlier poo thoughts. The area was their home between 500 and 1500 A.D. Some suspect that the word *kickapoo* is derived from the Algonguian word *kiwigapawa*, meaning *he who moves about*. Others have their doubts. Regardless, one has to admit it's a funky word that's fun to pronounce. Or is that just my own weird sense of humor?

The resource-rich area had been strip-mined for coal from about 1850 to the late 1930s. Then the state, with the financial support of local residents, bought the property, and with a lot of help from Mother Nature, turned it into a riparian and water playground for hikers, fishermen, canoeists, flower lovers, scuba divers – and of course birders. The park provided yet another nature feast for my eyes, but because it had been yet another short driving day, I planned to stay over only one night.

My plans changed the next morning when I learned there was a severe storm watch for the area. I decided it would be best to stay put until the storm had passed. As it was, Maggie and I barely managed to get in our morning walk before rain drops started falling. They were gentle at first, but soon picked up velocity and density. I fixed myself a second pot of coffee and settled down to watch. The something in me that loves a wild storm was fulfilled. Lightning flashes lit up the dark sky for nearly an hour, while the roaring thunder echoed deep bass replies.

Sitting inside my RV, with Maggie curled up beside me, my whole body felt the vibrations of the lightning and thunder conversations going on outside. I thought about the 19th century artist, Joseph Mallord William Turner, a controversial English watercolorist. I had written a college paper for an art class on Turner, who was best known for the light he captured in his paintings. My research turned up a tall-tale about him tying himself to the mast of a ship so he could experience the drama of a storm at sea. While such an experience was miles from my own dry and comfortable seat on the couch, I still felt adventurous and savored every minute.

Even after the rain had stopped I continued to enjoy the beat of it. I was surrounded on three sides by trees and each slight shift in breeze would send leftover drops of water dripping onto the roof of my RV. Anna Quindlen wrote, in *Thinking out Loud*, that sometimes we should examine our life, and sometimes we should just live it. Today I was living it.

BIRDS ALONG THE WAY:
Red-winged blackbird, eastern meadowlark, great blue heron,
northern cardinal, northern mockingbird, chipping sparrow,
house finch, house sparrow, eastern bluebird, American robin,
turkey vulture, killdeer, mourning dove, American crow,
*dickcissel, common grackle, *ring-billed gull, Canada geese,
mallard, blue jay, eastern phoebe, white breasted nuthatch,
European starling, Carolina chickadee, downy woodpecker,
red-bellied woodpecker, and red-headed woodpecker.
*First sighting of this species on the journey

THE JOURNEY

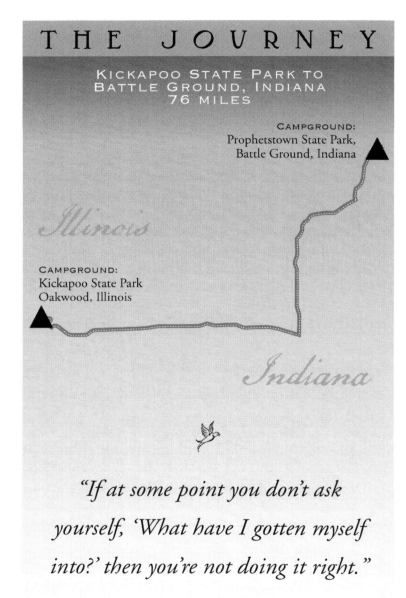

KICKAPOO STATE PARK TO
BATTLE GROUND, INDIANA
76 MILES

CAMPGROUND:
Prophetstown State Park,
Battle Ground, Indiana

Illinois

CAMPGROUND:
Kickapoo State Park
Oakwood, Illinois

Indiana

*"If at some point you don't ask
yourself, 'What have I gotten myself
into?' then you're not doing it right."*

ROLAND GAU

12

THE PROPHET —
AND HOWLING WITH TRISTAN

During my final walk with Maggie at Kickapoo, I stopped to chat with the campground hosts, a congenial older couple with a small barking terrier that Maggie pretended didn't exist. If it had been a drooling Rottweiler, she would have been growling ferociously, displaying her usual serious lack of judgment. Maggie, who wiggles all over with delight and approaches the most disreputable looking human, is either standoffish or alpha-dog growly when it comes to her own species. Well, except for golden retrievers. Oddly, she actually wants to play with them. I suspected this behavior had something to do with her experiences before I rescued her.

While the Kickapoo camp hosts scolded their yapping dog, Maggie quietly sat beside me with a feigned-innocent look. When the yapping wouldn't stop, they put their pet in their RV and closed the door. I swear Maggie grinned. She then tail-wagged her way toward the couple in anticipation of being acknowledged and petted. Charmed, they cooed to her about being such a "beautiful, good dog," and obligingly scratched her cocker ears. The smug glance she slyly gave me was one I had seen hundreds of times.

When human conversation could finally begin again, I told the couple where I was headed, and asked for sightseeing and camping recommendations. It was in this way that I learned about Prophetstown State Park, an Indiana campground so new that it wasn't in any of my camping directories. With directions to it in hand, I said my good-bye to Illinois, and crossed the border into Indiana via Highway 24. My destination was the small town of Battle Ground, where I would find both the recommended campground and Wolf Park. I had read about the park in a travel magazine after beginning my journey, and had immediately replotted my route so I could visit. It was as if I knew that I had wanted to howl with wolves all my life.

My drive this day took me through Danville, and shortly after that out of Illinois and into Indiana. It was one of the few times I've crossed state lines and couldn't feel where one state ended and the next began. The different hum of the wheels on different paving material was almost always a clue, even when just crossing into a different county. Other noticeable differences included the age of buildings, the variety of foliage or sudden litter, or the absence of it. But nothing this morning looked or felt different.

My back-road route took me through farm lands with only two Indiana towns big enough to note: Williamsport, with a population of less than 2,000, was one. Its most striking feature was a 90-foot waterfall on the Wabash River that flowed through the middle of the town.

The second city of note was Attica, once home to the Wabash and Erie Canal that linked the Great Lakes to the Ohio River, and then flowed all the way to the Gulf of Mexico. Stretching for 426 miles, it is the longest canal ever built in America. Even so, Attica's population today is only about 3,500.

Once beyond Attica, I turned north onto Highway 25, also known as the George Rogers Clark Memorial Highway. Clark, in case you don't remember from your history lessons – and I didn't – was a hero of the American Revolutionary War. He was hailed as the Conqueror of the Old Northwest. The parkway with his moniker took me through the outskirts of Lafayette, Indiana, named after the French general, Marquis de Lafayette, who fought on America's side during the Revolutionary War.

I didn't stop in Lafayette this day, but would find myself getting an unexpected better look at the city two days later. During my four-day stay in Battle Ground, my phone died, and Lafayette was the closest place it could be replaced. I also acquired my first computer air card in Lafayette, a fantastic upgrade from using my phone as a modem for internet access. With my better connection to the internet, I thought that sometimes the good old days are here and now.

The journey between Lafayette and Battle Ground reminded me of traveling to grandmother's house. The road went beside the river and through the woods of Tippecanoe Park, and then on Prophets Rock Road to Battle Ground, a sleepy little Indiana town with a large history. It was named for the 1811 Battle of Tippecanoe, in which Gen. William Harrison and his forces defeated the followers of two Shawnee brothers, Tecumseh and Tenskwatawa (The Prophet). The brothers had set up a village in 1808 on the site of the former Trading Post Kethtippercannunk (Tippecanoe), which had been destroyed by white settlers moving into the area in 1791. The brothers' goal was to consolidate the various tribes into one large Indian confederacy and revenge the razing of the Indian trading post. According to the Tippecanoe County Historical Association, the eventual defeat of the Prophet's Indian confederation by Harrison's forces all but ended the Midwest's Indian Wars.

The Prophet was scorned by the Indians after the defeat, while Tucumseh joined with the British Forces and fought in the War of 1812. He was killed in battle. Harrison also fought in the War of 1812, but he survived to return to his Ohio home, and to venture into politics. After several years in Congress, he ran unsuccessfully for president on the Whig platform. On his second try in 1840, he chose John Tyler as his vice-president mate, and used the slogan "Tippecanoe and Tyler, Too." Harrison then held a huge campaign rally in Battle Ground to implant the idea that he was the man who won the war against the Indians. The ploy was successful, and Harrison became this country's ninth president. Thirty-two days later he died of pneumonia and John Tyler became our 10th president.

It is history such as this that brings travelers to Battle Ground, a city of only a square mile of land that is laid out haphazardly. Its population is less than 2,000.

Prophetstown Campground sits on the city's outskirts, near the junction of the Wabash and Tippecanoe rivers, and in the middle of a meadow that at this season of the year was carpeted with wildflowers. The park wasn't crowded, and I was able to get one of the few sites that offered the shade of large trees. Most of the sites, although nicely outfitted and freshly landscaped, contained trees too young to offer much comfort from the overhead sun.

"Historic Prophetstown," a recreated tourist attraction, is located nearby. It consists of the former Gibson Farm, as it looked in the 1920s, and an Indian Village. There was a $5 entrance fee, and the main attraction was the restored 1918's "Hillrose" home. The farm house had originally been ordered from the Sears Roebuck catalog and shipped to the site by rail. The cost of the house was $6,880, which included all plumbing and electrical lighting fixtures. The refurbishment cost "a heck of a lot more" I was told by a staffer.

Other farm buildings on the site were a chicken coop, a blacksmith shop, a Model T garage and a large red barn, in which a small number of sheep and cows were kept. The cows produced five gallons of milk a day, which was churned by volunteers to make butter and ice cream. The Indian Village at the rear of the farm included a medicine lodge, council house, chief's cabin, and granary. A self-guiding map let me explore this recreated past at leisure, but made me thankful I was wearing good walking shoes. Actually they're the only kind of shoes I wear these days.

My unexpected visit to Prophetstown was enjoyable, but it was Wolf Park that provided me with the more memorable moments. My fascination with wolves began at a young age, triggered when I read for the first time, but not the last, Jack London's "Call of the Wild." I discovered the book when I was about eight years old among my late grandfather's book collection.

Down through the years I read many more books that encouraged this love affair, but it was Farley Mowat's, "Never Cry Wolf," which details the summer the author spent observing wild wolves in the Arctic tundra, that created a desire within me to see one of these wild creatures outside of a zoo environment. Given the way we humans had been eradicating these animals for decades, it was a miracle I doubted would ever happen. Then it did, in 2005.

I was traveling in Yellowstone with my youngest son when we unexpectedly came upon a magnificent gray wolf. That moment touched me in a way that brought me closer to nature at its purest than I had ever felt before. My son and I had stopped at an overlook to check out an unkindness of ravens in some trees, beneath which were a dozen or so camera-carrying tourists. We thought the humans were taking pictures of the ravens until we noted that humans and birds alike were focused on something moving on the far side of the small pond below. When I saw it was a wolf, I almost stopped breathing.

The overlook placed the wolf center stage while the morning sun, just capping a ridge to our east, spotlighted it. The wolf ignored our presence until a small dog, left in a vehicle by its owner, began yapping. Only then did the wolf tilt its head in our direction. It clearly knew we pitiful humans were watching. The barking dog, as if feeling the heat from that glance, became silent, and the wolf again continued its ground-covering stride. Through my birding telescope I could almost count the hairs on the wolf's back.

In comparison to seeing a wolf in the wild, which I would rate 20-plus on a 10-point scale, Wolf Park was a mere 10.

I arrived at the park just in time for an afternoon guided tour of the 75-acre grounds. While much more than a zoo, the wolves here were not free and only half wild. Wolf Park is a research facility, created to allow researchers to make closer observations of these animals than would be possible in the wild.

While the wolves are kept in large enclosures that encourage them to form, and live, in packs as they would in the wild, they have been conditioned to human contact to facilitate researchers.

This begins when they are only a couple of weeks old, at which time they are removed from their wolf mothers and given to human mothers to continue the raising of them. At about four months old, the cubs are returned to their packs.

A tour guide explained all this as he walked us around the park. His spiel included a genealogy of the pack affiliations, and stories about the personalities of each of the park's 24 wolves – a number which, give or take a few, is maintained. I was fascinated.

The Main Pack, which occupied the largest enclosure, and would later be the pack I howled with, was led by Tristan. As wolves do in the wild, he had gained his position by asserting his dominance over higher-ranking wolves. This pack in-fighting, unless death of an animal seems imminent, is not interfered with by the park staff, our guide said. Occasionally to avoid serious bloodshed, an animal is moved to another pack or even to its own enclosure. Fights for the alpha female role, our guide said, tended to be more vicious than those of male wolves fighting to become alpha male. The right to breed belongs only to the female alpha.

I returned to the park for the Friday Night Howl, and found myself sitting on bleachers in front of a large fenced enclosure. A couple of staff members entered the compound and were greeted enthusiastically by the wolves, much as my daughter's Great Dane, Tara, greets me. She is extremely loving, but if I'm not careful of my stance, she could easily bowl me over.

With the greeting between humans and animals completed, the staffers talked a bit about the work at the park, and then invited us to start howling to encourage the wolves' response. I found the howling a bit weird at first. I didn't sound at all like a wolf. Tristan seemed to agree – and looked at us humans as if we were missing our brains. But just then, somewhere in the background, one of the wolves from a different pack howled back. Tristan went to a high point in the pen and answered the wild night song. Other members of his pack quickly joined him. The chorus of human and wolf howls went on for a while, but at some point, I stopped howling and simply listened, feeling a freedom in my soul that I find hard to describe. It's a writer's block that actually gives me pleasure.

When I began my human, screechy imitation of a wolf's howls again, Tristan gave me a disdainful stare. Then, never taking his eyes from mine, he decided to take pity on this mere human and howled with me. Shivers of delight rolled up my spine. It was a moment I will never forget.

My bird list, meanwhile, grew by only one new species while I was in Battle Ground, Indiana. I spotted several Henslow sparrows hanging out in the meadow behind my park campground site. I was fortunate in that they hung around close enough and long enough for me to identify them, since they are one of more than a dozen brown sparrows that all look alike. They have large flat heads for their body size and broken stripes on their breast.

My best bird while here, for pure bird-watching enjoyment, was a catbird that spent a lot of time in and beneath a bushy tree next to my RV. It did a lot of hopping from place to place with its tail cocked, giving me a good look at its red under tail feathers. It yapped a lot, but only once did I hear it mew like a cat.

More about Yellowstone wolves: You can find it in *Decade of the Wolf: Returning the Wild* to Yellowstone by Douglas Smith and Gary Ferguson. A great read!

BIRDS ALONG THE WAY:
American crow, brown thrasher, red-winged blackbird, northern mockingbird, mourning dove, American robin, killdeer, black vulture, white-breasted nuthatch, eastern bluebird, house finch, northern cardinal, Carolina chickadee, downy woodpecker, red-bellied woodpecker, red-headed woodpecker, chipping sparrow, dickcissel, house sparrow, *Henslow sparrow, catbird, tree swallow, barn swallow, turkey vulture.

First sighting of this species on the journey.

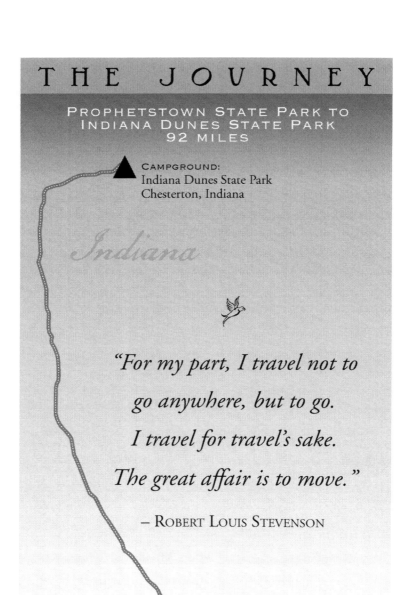

THE JOURNEY

PROPHETSTOWN STATE PARK TO INDIANA DUNES STATE PARK
92 MILES

CAMPGROUND:
Indiana Dunes State Park
Chesterton, Indiana

Indiana

"For my part, I travel not to

go anywhere, but to go.

I travel for travel's sake.

The great affair is to move."

— ROBERT LOUIS STEVENSON

CAMPGROUND:
Prophetstown State Park,
Battle Ground, Indiana

13
HOTTER THAN HELL IN INDIANA

The message on the large wooden bulletin board outside a red brick church read: "Hell is hotter than an Indiana summer day." I felt this was debatable. Although warm temperatures had plagued me for much of my trip, today's heat and humidity topped the charts. It was a true heat wave, making me quite thankful for Gypsy Lee's air conditioning.

Maggie and I were headed toward Indiana Dunes State Park, which sits on the southern edge of Lake Michigan. I had taken Highway 43/421 north from Battle Ground, and had almost reached my destination when I saw the church sign – and questioned its accurateness.

Today's drive took me through Brookston, home of the annual Apple Popcorn Festival begun in 1978 to celebrate the local harvest of apples and popcorn, and through the tiny towns of Chalmers and Reynolds. Monon, just up the road from Reynolds, seemed a little more interesting. It was the former hub for the Monon Railroad, also known as the CIL (Chicago, Indianapolis and Louisville) Railroad, that operated from 1897-1956. The city hosts the Monon Connection Museum, which houses a large collection of railroad memorabilia. It was closed when I passed through the town, or I probably would have stopped.

Francesville, the next town of note, claimed on its welcome sign that it was "A small town with a big heart." As tiny rural towns go, I didn't find Francesville much different than the other farm cities I passed through this day. My journal notes simply summed the day's drive up as "Indiana at its rural best."

I left the farm country behind me at Valparaiso, where I hooked up with Highway 49 that would take me into Chesterton, Indiana, and then on to Indiana Dunes State Park. I had chosen this stopping spot because the park was on a commuter rail line that went into Chicago, where my youngest son lived. He had a few days off from his flight attendant's job, and had agreed to meet me at the park so we could spend some time together. It was a much better plan than me driving Gypsy Lee into the traffic-packed Windy City.

I arrived at the park early on a Wednesday afternoon, and was lucky to be assigned one of the last few camp sites available. Indiana Dunes State Park sits on the shores of Lake Michigan. It is where botanist Henry Cowles, the father of ecology, did his study on sand dune vegetation, which is probably why the park and the nearby Indiana Dunes National Lakeshore are known as the birthplace of ecology.

Along with sand dunes, sun-bathing beaches and designated swimming areas, the park's habitats include a black oak forest, wooded wetlands and a marsh, each with scenic nature trails running through them. Sadly, the heat kept my enjoyment of the hiking opportunities to a minimum.

Mike and I spent a lot of time in my air-conditioned RV playing cards, reading, laughing at fat squirrels as they scampered from tree to tree, and viewing the entire first season of "The Amazing Race," on DVDs. After Mike left early Saturday morning, I took a brief hike on the marsh trail, where dragonflies floated above water lilies and reflections of clouds painted the bare patches of a pond, until the heat chased me back indoors.

A goodly portion of the rest of the day was spent in the park's air-conditioned nature center watching birds through wall-sized windows. It was a colorful show starring ruby-throated hummingbirds, scarlet northern cardinals, white-breasted nuthatches, crisp yellow and black goldfinches, gray titmice, red-crowned chipping sparrows and rosy mourning doves. They had all been lured to the windows by numerous feeding stations kept filled by the park's staff.

The next morning, on my way out of town, I visited the Indiana Dunes National Lakeshore's Dorothy Buell Memorial Visitor Center. Buell founded the Save the Dunes Council in 1952 when she was 65 years old. Her tireless efforts to save the dunes are credited with the creation of both the park and the larger Indiana Dunes National Lakeshore.

After my tour of the quaint visitor's center, I parked myself on a beach in Beverly Shores, a tiny resort community just off Highway 12, where I sat a while watching Lake Michigan's waves surge back and forth onto the sand. The Ojibwa Indians called the lake, Mishigami, meaning great water. Over 300 miles long and 100 miles wide, and with a depth that can reach over 900 feet, the lake is the largest body of fresh water in the United States. The continuous line of curling waves rolling into shore, and the pair of herring gulls sauntering along at the water's edge, made me feel as if I were on an ocean coastline instead of sitting on a sandy shore 800 miles inland.

This was my first visit to Indiana, and it changed my mental picture of the state as merely the home of the Hoosiers and the Indianapolis 500. Like my home state of Texas, which some people think of as only being dusty, cattle-strewn flatlands full of blowing tumbleweeds, Indiana is a complex piece of property with a variety of habitats. The beaches, woods and marshes of the dunes sitting beside Lake Michigan is a microcosm of the whole – and another example of nature reminding us that stereotyping always misses the mark.

BIRDS ALONG THE WAY:
American robin, dickcissel, killdeer, chipping sparrow, house sparrow, gray catbird, red-winged blackbird, American crow, mourning dove, tree swallow, barn swallow, turkey vulture, northern cardinal, white-breasted nuthatch, *ruby-throated hummingbird, American goldfinch, Carolina chickadee, tufted titmouse, common grackle, house finch and *herring gull.
*First sighting of this species on the journey

THE JOURNEY

INDIANA DUNES TO
CADE LAKE COUNTY PARK,
THEN ON TO YPSILANTI
194 MILES

Michigan

CAMPGROUND:
Indiana Dunes State Park
Chesterton, Indiana

CAMPGROUND:
Detroit-Dearborn KOA
Ypsilanti, Michigan

CAMPGROUND:
Cade Lake County Park
Sturgis, Michigan

Indiana

The greatest reward and luxury

of travel is to be able to experience

everyday things as if for the first time,

to be in a position in which almost

nothing is so familiar it is

taken for granted."

– BILL BRYSON

14

HIGHWAY 12, CADE LAKE, THE BRICK DICK AND HENRY FORD

I eventually left the Indiana Dunes behind, and continued toward Michigan on Highway 12. This old road, with its colorful history, would take me all the way to Detroit. Constructed in the 1820s between the Windy City and Detroit, Highway 12 is known as the Chicago Road. Over time, it was extended westward from Detroit to Grays Harbor on Washington's Pacific Coast – a distance of about 2,500 miles.

Thirty or so years ago, I traveled a 200-mile section of Highway 12 between Lewiston, Idaho, and Missoula, Montana, as it made its scenic passage through the Clearwater National Forest alongside the Clearwater River. I was a passenger at the time, and the vehicle's driver was a person who believed a destination more important than a journey. My pleas to stop along the way were ignored. When an opportunity to retrace that drive reappeared a few years later, I eagerly grabbed it, and happily gave the awesome landscape the attention it deserved. The river's gurgling, heard through my car's open window, called to me around every bend in the road; and the intense scents of fir and pine, untainted by human industry, was a calming incense to my soul.

Many years, and many roads later, that section of highway still lingers in my memory. I consider it one of America's best drives – right up there with the Going to the Sun Highway in Glacier National Park and the Blue Ridge Parkway through Virginia and North Carolina.

Much older than the western segments, Michigan's section of Highway 12 bounced me around through some of the state's smaller towns and farming areas. After my early morning stop in Beverly Shores to sit on the beach, I followed the highway, which followed the lake, to Michigan City, home of a huge outlet mall, a riverboat casino and a huge cooling tower. I saw only the tower, which I thought at first was for a nuclear power plant, but later learned was for a large coal-burning unit.

Continuing on 12, I passed several small lake resort communities, including Pottawattamie Park, Michiana Shores, New Buffalo and Lakeview, before Highway 12 turned inland, and began once again passing through small rural communities. These included Three Oaks, an artistic theater town with its own poet laureate; Galien, pronounced *Guh-leen* by the locals; and Edwardsburg, a village that celebrated its 100th birthday in 2012.

I found the passing rural landscape peaceful and pleasant, but not spectacular.

Mid-morning, Maggie and I shared a cinnamon-raisin bagel with cream cheese at the Mottville Bridge Historical Marker that sits beside the St. Joseph River. Only the stone block abutments of the first of the three bridges built at this site exist today. The first bridge across the river was built in 1834 to accommodate settlers heading west. The second bridge is still standing but is used only for foot traffic. It's an eye-catching, three-humped, white camel-back structure built in 1922. The third, built in 1990, is wider and better suited to today's larger vehicles – like Gypsy Lee – but is not as picturesque as bridge No. 2.

After reading the historical marker and walking across the foot bridge – just because it was there – I crossed the river and drove through the small towns of Mottville, White Pigeon and Sturgis. I had started the day with no campground reservations for the night but had noted there was a suitable RV park in Ypsilanti, about 200 miles east of Indiana Dunes State Park. I was hoping, however, to find something closer. My wish was granted shortly after I passed

Sturgis – where I had looked for motorcyclists until I remembered the well-touted motorcycle rally was held each year in Sturgis, South Dakota, not Sturgis, Michigan.

The inviting campground that popped up was Cade Lake County Park. There were about a dozen camp sites right by the small lake and about twice that many on a hill overlooking it. I took the last vacant spot by the water, but by evening I had the lower campground all to myself. It was a Sunday, and I suspected that all the other lakeside occupants were nearby residents who had to go home and get ready for the work-day week.

The 32-acre lake was charming, with a swimming area and beach along one shore and a large patch of water lilies near the water's edge where my RV was parked. A few white flowers floated atop the lily pads, while nearer the shore, clusters of pink smart-weed blooms attracted butterflies.

A clump of orange day lilies encircled a tree near a foot bridge, which crossed a small stream flowing into the lake in a section of the campground that had been groomed. Everywhere I looked was a photograph waiting to happen. I took one picture through the rear window of RV and e-mailed it to my daughter-in-law, along with a lengthy description of my eden-esque stopover. She e-mailed back, expressing the right amount of envy – and the wish that a bee sting me.

A grandfatherly park worker checked in on me once or twice a day to ask if I was OK or needed anything. I think he wasn't used to seeing a lone female traveler, and was actually a bit worried about me. I assured him I was fine, but that I appreciated his kind-ness. It felt as if the entire park were my own personal backyard, which made me reluctant to move on. Since my budget could use a reprieve, I stayed four days, a bonus being that the fourth night of camping was free.

My next overnight stay would be that RV Park in Ypsilanti about 30 miles outside Detroit, the one I had looked up in my campground directory as a last-chance stop on my previous leg of the journey. To get there, I continued on Highway 12 through more of Michigan's small towns, including: Bronson, which is on the Environmental Protection Agency's watch list with three contaminated Superfund sites requiring clean-up action; Coldwater, which supports a scenic park on the Coldwater River; and Quincy, which has a welcome sign proclaiming it as the "Gateway to the Chain of Lakes." The chain is a 75-mile string of 14 charming lakes connected by rivers.

Continuing on Highway 12, which my map was now calling the East Chicago Road, I passed through Jonesville, where almost everyone seemed to be having a garage sale; and Moscow, where Maggie and I stopped at a park featuring the headwaters of the Kalamazoo River. Kalamazoo, my wondering brain discovered, is a Native American word, one with dozens of meanings that has even the language experts confused. The meaning I like best is the Potawatomie word that translates as "otter tail." I wondered if that was because otters once swam, or perhaps still swim, in this 130-mile long river that dumps into Lake Michigan.

I finally gave up on the wondering, and Maggie and I continued our journey – our stomachs full of bologna, mustard and white-bread I had bought when I had filled up Gypsy Lee's gas tank earlier in the day. The lunch fixings were the result of an impulse craving. Neither bologna nor white bread is on my normal menu, probably because they were a daily lunch box offering when I was a kid. But about once every three years I get a craving for them, perhaps to refuel the child within me.

Just up the road from Moscow, the highway passed through two state parks: Cambridge Junction and Walter J. Hayes. Cambridge is a historic park with a restored tavern as a visitor center. The tavern, which was also an inn, was a major stopping place for stagecoach travelers on their way between Chicago and Detroit in the mid-19th century.

The second park, originally called Cedar Hills, was renamed after former Michigan Senator Walter J. Hayes, whose family donated the land to the state. Both parks are located in an area called the Irish Hills, which is named after the Irish immigrants who settled the area in the mid-1850s. The landscape here is polka-dotted with lakes, which made my Michigan drive on Highway 12 almost as scenic as the western section that I had driven years earlier.

Saline, best known for its annual Celtic Festival, was the only other city of note before the day's journey ended at the Detroit-Dearborn KOA in Ypsilanti. The day's 100-mile drive had taken five hours because of my dawdling to check out the sights along the way.

Originally the site of an early 1800's trading post, Ypsilanti is named for Demetrius Ypsilanti, a hero of Greece's successful War for Independence from the Ottoman Empire in the 1820s. Today it is best known as being home of the "World's Most Phallic Structure," a title its 147-foot limestone water tower claimed after winning Cabinet magazine's 2003 contest to find the building most resembling a human phallus.

One look at the tower – built in 1890 by someone either with a macho bent or a sense of humor – and I could see why it must have easily won the contest. Locals call it the "Dick Brick." It's said that if an Eastern Michigan University student graduates while still a virgin the tower will fall down.

Travel is so enlightening.

While in Ypsilanti, I spent a day going back in time at the Henry Ford Museum and the adjoining Greenfield Village in nearby Dearborn. The landscaped village, with both horse-driven and horseless carriages to spin you around the grounds, contains more than 80 original or authentically recreated structures that pay tribute to some of America's greatest minds.

One can wander through Thomas Edison's Menlo Park Laboratory and imagine the excitement exuded when that first light bulb cast its glow. Or marvel at the dreams of fanciful flight that Orville and Wilbur shared while working at their Wright Brothers Bicycle Shop. Greenfield Village is also where you can visit the home in which Noah Webster wrote America's first dictionary, and where you can walk through a replica of the first Ford Motor Home factory.

My favorite structure was less imposing. It was the modest home of Robert Frost that had been relocated to the site. I found myself alone as I wandered the rooms where this great poet once lived and wrote. Enriching the experience was a recording of Frost personally reciting "The Road Less Traveled:"

> *"Two roads diverged in a yellow wood*
> *And sorry I could not travel both ..."*

This poem, which so accurately describes my frequent state of mind while on the road, has always moved me. Like Frost, there's a yearning within me to know what lies down that road not taken. Whenever possible, like Frost's poem suggests, I take the one less traveled.

I sat on the porch steps of Frost's home and listened to the recording three times, letting the words fill me with wonder and inspiration. I was a bit teary-eyed before I finally moved on, but it wouldn't be the last time this day that my eyes needed a tissue.

Among the hundreds of automotive milestones on exhibit in the Henry Ford Museum, I found myself mesmerized by a sleek black Lincoln, the very one that President John F. Kennedy lost his life in on that fateful November day in 1963. The vehicle represented a loss of innocence for my generation, and a very personal blow to me as a Dallas native. How, I wondered many times. Not just how such a thing could happen, but how could it have happened in my own home town?

While I had so eagerly lingered at Frost's home, the memories the Lincoln exhibit brought up made me want to hurry away. So I turned by back, as I tend to do on most unpleasantries in life. Walking away may not be the best way of dealing with pain, but I've finally come to realize it is my way. And it wasn't difficult in the vast automotive museum to find things to distract me.

The many auto exhibits soon had me thinking about the first vehicle I ever drove. It was a 1948 Studebaker convertible that belonged to my boyfriend. The first time I was behind its wheel, I backed it out of the driveway and directly into a bush. I hadn't remembered that in a long time. It's interesting the things that trigger memories stored away in some dark passage of the mind, like in that gigantic warehouse in an Indiana Jones' film where the "Ark" ended up being stashed away.

Meanwhile, the Volkswagen vehicles on exhibit brought to mind the first car I owned that was all mine. It was a 1963 VW that I named "Chigger," a suitable name for a red "Bug." I bought it used in 1967, put 100,000 miles on it as a reporter for a small Texas newspaper the next four years, and then sold it for more than its purchase price. You can safely bet on that never happening again.

I was a working mother at the time, and the hours I spent alone in that vehicle were the only quiet and peaceful ones in my busy life. Perhaps that is why, whenever I get behind the wheel of any vehicle, a sense of peace comes over me. Not even traffic jams unnerve me.

Another vehicle from the past that attracted my attention was the Rosa Park bus exhibit, which so aptly portrays this country's civil rights issues – and speaks of how far we've come since those dreadful days of segregation.

But my absolute favorite vehicle on display in the Henry Ford Museum was Charles Kuralt's "On the Go" RV. He was my traveling hero. How could it not be so?

BIRDS ALONG THE WAY:
Common grackle, mourning dove, northern cardinal,
chipping sparrow, Carolina chickadee, house finch,
house sparrow, barn swallow, American robin, herring gull,
eastern kingbird, Canada goose, and American goldfinch.

THE JOURNEY

YPSILANTI, MICHIGAN
TO AMHERSTBURG, ONTARIO
61 MILES

Michigan

DETROIT, MICHIGAN

CAMPGROUND:
Detroit-Dearborn KOA
Ypsilanti, Michigan

Ontario

CAMPGROUND:
Yogi Bear's Jellystone Park
and Camp Resort
Amherstburg, Ontario

"To awaken quite alone in a
strange town is one of the
pleasantest sensations in the world."

– FREYA STARK

15

CELEBRATING A SUMMER HALLOWEEN

After leaving Ypsilanti, I followed Highway 12 to Detroit, passing through Dearborn, headquarters of Ford Motor Company and the home of its founder Henry Ford, along the way. The city is named after Henry Dearborn, a general during the America Revolution and secretary of war under President Thomas Jefferson.

I didn't linger in the city, but hurried on to Detroit, where I also didn't linger. The largest city in Michigan, Detroit is both known as America's automotive center and the home of Motown, the record company founded by Barry Gordy. The city gets its name from the Detroit River, which was called Riviere du Detroit, or River of the Strait, by the French when they occupied the area. It's actually a good description for the 28-mile-long Detroit River as it links Lake Huron with Lake Erie.

My plan was to cross the river to Ontario, Canada, where I planned to follow Lake Erie's northern shoreline to Buffalo, New York. I had two choices to get across the river: a bridge that spanned the water, or a tunnel that burrowed beneath the river. It wasn't a difficult decision for someone with claustrophobia. I took the exit off Highway 12 that would take me across the Ambassador Bridge, instead of the exit that would take me down through Windsor Tunnel.

The bridge, being 7,500 feet long and rising 152 feet above the water, made the trek across the water memorable.

At the border crossing, I was required to show my passport, which I had handy, and Maggie's current rabies vaccination certificate, a detail I had forgotten. The paper took me a while to locate – even though it was exactly where it was supposed to be. I had overlooked it in the first file folder I had checked. Thankfully, the crossing guard remained patient and pleasant. I wondered if I would have received the same courtesy if I had been traveling in the opposite direction. I would like to believe I would have.

After the border crossing, I took Highway 3 through Windsor, which sits on the opposite river shore from Detroit. The city was named after England's Windsor Castle following a lively debate. Some wanted to call it South Detroit and others wanted to call it Ferry, in honor of the ferries linking the two cities before the bridge was built.

Once past Windsor, I took Highway 20/18 to Amherstburg, where I had reservations at the Yogi Bear Jellystone RV Park for the next three days. I had now been on the road for two months and was deep into enjoying each day. I would later regret all my dallying, but for now I was as happy as a cheery robin after a rain shower brought fat worms wriggling above ground so as not to drown.

"Sweet is the melody, so hard to come by ...
So hard to make every note bend just right."
- Iris DeMent

My life was bending right.

As the Yogi Bear name suggests, Jellystone is a family campground with lots of activities for kids. The day I arrived, a whimsical August Halloween celebration was in progress. After checking in and hooking up, Maggie and I begin an inspection of the large park. About a third of the sites in the campground were decorated with linen ghosts, glowing pumpkins, and human-woven spider webs. Above, a mixed flock of cliff swallows and barn swallows were flitting about. I stopped to watch, which gave Maggie an opportunity to try and chase after a black squirrel that scampered up a tree and began chattering at her.

Cliff swallows lack the forked tail of the barn swallows, and also sport a spot of white on their foreheads that makes them easy to identify when flying toward you. I was once fortunate to observe five different swallows flying together at Utah's Bear River Migratory Bird Refuge. I spent about two hours searching out their differences before I finally could tell them apart as they whipped back and forth over a stream near a bridge. It's gotten easier with time, but as a late-blooming birder, I've often felt like the child who didn't learn language at the appropriate age, and then must work twice as hard to get its intricacies sorted out.

Today's swallows flew off at the same time Maggie decided to ignore the saucy squirrel, and so we continued our stroll — me gawking, and she sniffing, before ending our walk at the camp store, where I bought a bag of candy in anticipation of trick or treaters.

My campground neighbor, Claire, who had a permanent appearing setup and visiting grandkids, told me the park celebrated three Halloweens annually. She was a friendly lady near my own age, but wasn't a traveler like me. Her rooted home was only five minutes away; she said her grandkids usually spent a day or two with her most weeks, and that she spent about six months of each year living in her RV because it meant less housework and her days were more laid-back. She wasn't the first non-traveling RV-er I met who shared that attitude and lifestyle.

The next day found me visiting the former site of the Amherstburg Royal Navy Shipyard, which served the British between 1796 and 1813. The original yard was burned, abandoned, and relocated during the early stages of the War of 1812. Today, it is a neatly landscaped park with a large, well-scrubbed anchor on display, and a polished-up "King's Navy Yard Privy" to pay homage to the past. A red-brick walkway and flower beds full of blooms next to the water encouraged aimless strollers, while tree-shaded benches offered a chance to relax and simply take in the sights. I walked a while and then sat and watched a blue-winged teal swim around in the harbor.

This small duck, well at least the male, is easy to recognize because of the large white crescent moon on its face. The blue on the teal's wing is usually not visible unless the bird stretches its wings, which the lone fellow I saw this day didn't do. The cliff swallows I had seen the day before, and the blue-winged teal seen today, were birds 61 and 62, respectively for my species journey list.

I also watched a flock of house sparrows that were searching for tidbits of something beneath a tree before taking out my journal to capture my thoughts. It was nice to feel I had nowhere to be, or anything I had to do. But then my stomach rumbled, reminding me it was time for lunch. Claire had encouraged me to try the food at Duffy's Tavern located adjacent to the historical park.

It was good advice. The grilled perch I ordered was excellent and the view from my upstairs patio table was entertaining. I could see the channel where the Detroit River flowed into Lake Erie, and I watched as boats floated or raced past to reach the open water. The temperature was pleasantly warm but not hot. Combined with a hair-ruffling breeze it was the most perfect weather of my trip thus far. I slowly sipped a fruity drink of pineapple and cranberry juices spiced with rum for dessert, and lingered to enjoy the moment.

The rest of my stay in Amherstburg passed quickly. I read, wrote, walked Maggie, chatted awhile each day with Claire, and awoke each morning to bird song. All too soon it was time to move on.

BIRDS ALONG THE WAY:
Mourning dove, great egret, American robin, European starling,
barn swallow, bank swallow, *cliff swallow,
brown-headed cowbird, common grackle, killdeer,
house sparrow, ring-billed gull, herring gull,
*blue-winged teal, American crow,
double-crested cormorant.

*First sighting of this species on the journey

THE JOURNEY

AMHERSTBURG TO
WHEATLEY PROVINCIAL PARK, ONTARIO
44 MILES

WHEATLEY TO PORT BURWELL, ONTARIO
144 MILES

Ontario

CAMPGROUND:
Jellystone RV Park
Amherstburg,
Ontario

CAMPGROUND:
Wheatley Provincial Park
Wheatley, Ontario

CAMPGROUND:
Sand Hill RV Park
Port Burwell, Ontario

"The world is a book and those who do not travel it read only one page."

— AUGUSTINE OF HIPPO

16

TRAVELING BESIDE LAKE ERIE

After leaving Amherstburg, I jotted south to catch the little-traveled backroads that would let me stay as close to Lake Erie as possible. The route took me through several small Canadian towns, including Holiday Beach, a tiny spot on the landscape dominated by a large viewing tower that was an ideal prop for the town's annual hawk festival held each fall. Since there was a place to park Gypsy Lee, Maggie and I got out and investigated the tower. But all we saw were a few ring-billed gulls flying overhead. It was too early for the raptors.

Shortly after passing Kingsville, I veered away from the shoreline toward Leamington, home to a large Heinz canning factory. The town claims to be the Tomato Capital of Canada, and I wondered if any of the many cans of Heinz tomatoes that had found their way into my cupboard had come from here. After Leamington, it was just a short distance to Wheatley Provincial Park, where after checking in for the night, I quickly left to explore nearby Point Pelee National Park – Canada's southernmost spot on a map.

The Point is a 10-mile long land spit, shaped like a pizza slice that juts into Lake Erie. While the park is located right next to the water, its landscape has forests and grasslands as well as beaches and wetlands. The site was designated a national park by Canada in 1918, and is probably best known for the thousands of monarch butterflies that briefly gather there in the fall before they fly across Lake Erie and head south toward Mexico. Although as many as 10,000 monarchs land at the point daily during migration, I didn't see a single one this day. It was only mid-August, about two weeks before the migration that peaks in September would begin.

The monarchs' migration between Canada and the high volcanic mountains of central Mexico is a generational journey, with perhaps it being a great-great-great-great offspring that finally completes the round trip of almost 4,000 miles.

The colorful butterflies follow a route that provides them milkweed plants, the only thing monarch caterpillars eat before spinning their chrysalis and transforming into creatures of the air. The monarchs lay their eggs on these plants before joining Mother Nature's otherworld garden. It is estimated only 1 percent of monarch eggs, which are delicacies for birds and other insects, survive, and milkweed habitat loss is threatening even these low odds. Some conservation experts say monarch habitat has declined up to 90 percent in recent years.

Point Pelee National Park also attracts migrating birds in spring and fall – but my timing was off for seeing them as well. I had to satisfy myself with what the park offered in the here and now. First, I climbed a tower overlooking a marsh so as to get an overview of the lush wetlands, then I walked a mile through the wet landscape on a boardwalk designed to keep hikers dry and clean. Thick patches of water lilies hugged the raised wooden walk that provided a path looping though stands of cattails and small ponds where blue-winged teal swam. Here and there great blue herons and great egrets statuesquely posed in the shallow edges of the water, while the dark iridescence feathers of log-sitting cormorants shimmered in the sunlight.

A photograph was waiting every few steps, and I wasn't the only one stopping often to record the scenery and wildlife. After the boardwalk trek, I spent an hour wandering through the park's informative visitor's center, then hiked two short nature trails, one that led to a pond and the other to the shore of Lake Erie, before heading back to Wheatley Provincial Park.

On arriving there, I received an offer to share the campfire of our young, neighbor family, and eagerly accepted. Maggie briefly, accepted the attention of the couple's two young children before scooting beneath my lawn chair. She's good with kids but tires of their attention quickly.

The family and I had actually become acquainted earlier in the day when we exchanged campgrounds. We were both trying, unsuccessfully, to get hooked up in our assigned sites, but my electrical cord was too short to reach the outlet in my large site, and they were struggling to situate their large RV in a too small site. Both our dilemmas were easily solved when we agreed to switch sites. The father of the family, seeing me standing dumbfounded with my RV's electrical cord in hand, had suggested the solution. Five minutes later both our vehicles were hooked up, and camaraderie established.

While I enjoyed the company of fellow travelers this night, along with the crackling fire and the star-filled sky, I retired early. It had been a long day and I planned to get on the road early the following morning.

Keeping to Highway 3 that ran along Lake Erie's northern shoreline, I weaved my way eastward from Wheatley Provincial Park to Rondeau Provincial Park, where Maggie and I stopped briefly. The park sits on a spit of land jutting out into Lake Erie that creates Rondeau Bay on the inland side.

Rondeau Provincial Park is home to the endangered prothonotary warbler, which of course I was hoping to see but didn't. I did, however, get a new bird species for the trip. It was a common yellowthroat, a male whose vivid colors had me gasping in delight.

Its throat and belly were the color of a golden sun, while its black mask topped with a fringe of white made it easy to identify. It was flitting about in a patch of grasses growing in a marshy pond. A dull yellowish-green warbler was nearby, the female yellowthroat that I always find difficult to identify when the male isn't hovering about.

After reluctantly leaving Rondeau, because I wanted to get a few more miles down the road, I continued following Highway 3 before jigging south to Highway 16 so as to continue staying as close to Lake Erie's shoreline as the roads would allow. It was a peaceful back road drive with little traffic and awesome views of the lake. One of the things I noticed was the lack of slickness so commonly seen in the states. This lack of sophistication, felt as much as seen, reminded me that I was in another country.

Weeks later, when reviewing my notes, I saw that the most notable thing I had recorded in my journal about this day's drive after Rondeau, was that Port Stanley looked like a fun place to live, and that I was finally seeing kestrels, North America's smallest and most common falcon. I passed dozens of them sitting on fence posts or wires running next to the road.

I ended my day's driving in Port Burwell in mid-afternoon. The campground for the night was the Sand Hill RV Park, which sat on the inland side of tall sand dunes. After doing laundry, Maggie and I hiked over the dunes, where we came upon the lake and a nice beach. I sat for a while staring out at the water while Maggie walked along the edge of the lake, carefully keeping her toes daintily dry. It reminded me of the first hike we took together. It was one in which the trail crossed back and forth across a small stream. Maggie would stop at each crossing until my hiking companion would give in, and carry her across the water. I smiled thinking of it.

Back at the RV, I quickly took a shower to wash away the sweat of our trek back up the dunes, and then decided Maggie could use a bath as well. Once we were both fresh and clean, I heated up a Stouffer's Cheesy Spaghetti Bake for dinner, and topped it off with some yogurt for dessert. Maggie had the last bit of my spaghetti to go with her dried dog food and one of her doggy treats. While not exactly gourmet, it was a quick and easy meal and left no dishes to wash before I crawled into bed with Jack Kerouac's *On the Road*.

I had started this book twice before, but could never finish it. While it's on all the lists of "The World's Best Travel Books," almost all of which I've read, Kerouac is an author with whom I've had problems connecting. As I made this third attempt to read the book, I found little had changed. Kerouac and I were traveling different roads. Whereas I can envision myself traveling beside such authors as Tim Cahill and Charles Kuralt, I can never see the adventure through Kerouac's eyes. If I ever get to the end of his "road," maybe I'll feel different.

Even so, I recorded Kerouac's thoughts in my journal, the ones on receding people and their good-byes vaulting him "... forward to the next crazy venture beneath the skies." These were words I did connect with, and they triggered my own thoughts about good-byes. While I love my family and my friends, leaving them for a road trip is always an uplifting experience. I get this tremendous feeling of being free that outweighs any hint of sadness, and before I've gone too far down the road, I find myself literally dancing a jig of joy. I fell asleep with these thoughts jangling around in my head, and awoke the next morning to say good-bye to Canada and hello again to the United States, a land where I've found beauty around every corner – even if sometimes it is a bit too slick and orderly. If I had any say about it, "America the Beautiful" would be our national anthem. I've seen its spacious skies, its amber fields, its purple mountains and found the paths that freedom beat. The United States is my country, and in my eyes, there is none more beautiful.

That's not to say I don't enjoy visiting other countries. I loved traveling through Canada, and every other foreign place I've ever visited. But as the saying goes: There's no place like home – even if home is the road.

BIRDS ALONG THE WAY:
Canada goose, red-winged blackbird, American crow,
turkey vulture, northern cardinal, American robin,
dickcissel, mute swan, American goldfinch, ring-billed gull,
common grackle, great egret, European starling, bank swallow,
cliff swallow, killdeer, mourning dove, barn swallow, herring gull,
house sparrow, *common yellowthroat, blue-winged teal,
great blue heron, double-crested cormorant,
*kestrel and brown-headed cowbird.

*First sighting of this species on the journey

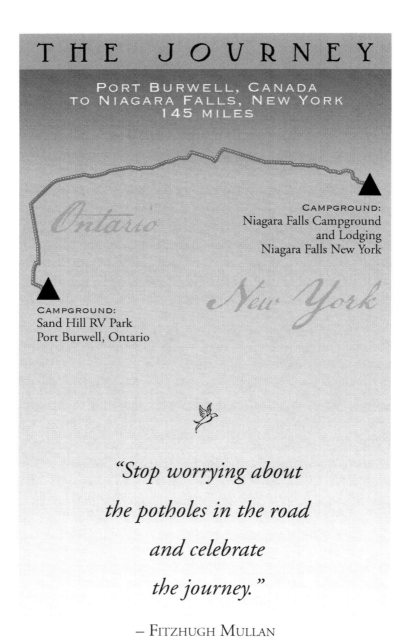

THE JOURNEY

CAMPGROUND:
Niagara Falls Campground
and Lodging
Niagara Falls New York

Ontario

New York

CAMPGROUND:
Sand Hill RV Park
Port Burwell, Ontario

"Stop worrying about

the potholes in the road

and celebrate

the journey."

– FITZHUGH MULLAN

17

NIAGARA FALLS AND NEW IN-LAWS

After leaving Port Burwell, I zigged and zagged my way back to Highway 3l, then followed this little-traveled road past the huge Nanticoke coal-burning power plant and across the Grand River into Dunnville, which was once home to a tribe of Iroquois known as the Cayuga. Continuing on, I passed through Welland, a town of about 50,000 that sits just about half an hour west of Niagara Falls, and then it was on to Port Colborne, home of the Welland Canal Lock that allows ships to pass from Lake Ontario to Lake Erie.

My final stop in Canada was at Fort Erie, which sits on the opposite side of the Niagara River from Buffalo, New York. Here, I took a brief tour of the structure for which the city is named – rather I toured a replica of the original 1764 fort. The original was lost by the British during the American Revolution, and the Americans later burned it when they were losing the battle to defend it during the War of 1812. The fort replica was built as a work project during the Great Depression – in hopes that it would become a tourist attraction. Since I was not alone in visiting the structure, and enjoying its landscaped grounds, I would say the workers' goal came to fruition.

But soon I found myself saying good-bye to Canada and driving across the 5,800-foot-long Peace Bridge over the Niagara River that would take me back into the United States. This border-crossing between Fort Erie and Buffalo is jointly maintained by the two cities – and the view I had from the bridge across the Niagara River, which connects Lake Erie with Lake Huron, was awesome.

The river's short 35-mile path splits to circle around Grand Island north of Buffalo, then joins again before dropping dramatically to create the world wonder known as Niagara Falls.

I had never seen the famed falls, and was eagerly looking forward to the experience. But seeing it wasn't the only reason I had plotted my route to include a stay in New York's Niagara Falls. I had plans to meet up with my middle son's new in-laws, and was looking forward to again being around people whom I could consider family. I had been on the road long enough now that I missed the loved ones I had left behind.

Going through customs to get back into America was an easy breeze – of course this time I had Maggie's papers close at hand. I would never know if my own country's border-crossing guard would have been as patient with me as the Canadian guard had been, but the American guard did have a nice smile about his eyes when he welcomed me back onto American soil.

A traffic roundabout at the bridge's exit easily put me onto Interstate 190, which carried me out of Buffalo. I wondered if the city, which is New York's second largest, had been named after the bison that roamed the area before it became a metropolitan complex. Buffalo, by the way, are found only in Asia or Africa. It is their cousin, the bison, which inhabits North America, but which we usually call buffalo. The difference between bison and buffalo was just one of many eclectic thoughts whizzing through my head as I maneuvered my way away from city traffic in search of more nature and fewer vehicles. I stayed on the busy interstate all the way across Grand Island, twice crossing the Niagara River on bridges, before turning off onto Highway 62, and heading toward the falls and the RV park where I had reservations for the next four days. As so often happens, I zigged instead of zagged at some fork in the road, and was treated to some unexpected sights as the bonus for getting lost. Eventually, of course, I reached my destination.

After hooking Gypsy Lee up, and walking Maggie twice around the modest campground, I called my son, Lewis, and his wife, to let them know I had arrived in Niagara Falls. Sadly, my daughter-in-law informed me her father's brother had died, and that his funeral was the next day. Since it seemed best to not call them until the day after that, I decided to take a commercial tour of Niagara Falls to get my bearings.

A 24-seat Bedore Tours' van picked me, a grumpy man – still complaining that his breakfast eggs had been cold – and his cheerful wife, up at the RV park the next morning. The couple's clothes, I noted, matched their moods. He was wearing black pants and a dark gray Polo shirt, and she was wearing bright pink pants, a pink blouse and a pink hat that put a smile on my face. I love color.

The van was driven by a cheery blonde woman named Sue, who was colorful, too. She wore a bright orange shirt that matched her bubbly personality. The orange shirt would also let us quickly find her in a crowd. As our van driver skipped around town the next half hour, picking up other paying passengers along the way, Sue kept us entertained with her lively fact-filled chatter. All the other tourists came in couples. They ranged in age from a pair of spry young newlyweds in blue jeans, to a more sedate couple in a matching pair of neatly pressed khaki slacks, who announced that they were celebrating their 50th wedding anniversary. The pair told us they had visited the falls on their honeymoon, and decided a return trip to the falls would be a perfect way to celebrate.

Sue, meanwhile, pointed out the hotel where Marilyn Monroe stayed when the movie, "Niagara Falls," was being filmed. I wondered if the young newlyweds sitting across from me had even heard of the 1953 movie. Co-starring Joseph Cotton, the film had a dark plot that I hadn't particularly enjoyed, particularly since back then I was still only seeing the world through rose-colored glasses. These days I've mostly removed the glasses, but I still don't think I would enjoy the movie's dark mood if I were to see it again.

The tour's first stop was Three Sister Islands, which were little more than stepping stones of land with connecting bridges that offered us a mystical backstage view of Horseshoe Falls before it splashed downward. The falls were below the horizon, and couldn't be seen from this viewpoint, but the shimmering rainbows created by the falling water lit up the air. In the background, across the fast tumbling river before its plunge, were a line of tall modern buildings, mostly hotels. Niagara Falls is a two-country event, with Horseshoe Falls on the Canadian side and American Falls and Bridal Veil Falls on the United States' side. The treatment of the scenic attraction by the two countries differs greatly. Americans turned the land surrounding the falls into a state park and have managed to keep development of the area to a minimum. Canada went the glitzy tourist attraction route. Today's tour would give us a taste of both worlds, which was not a bad thing. While nature is best observed without man-made distractions, such commercialism is necessary to meet the needs of hordes of visitors attracted to the falls. The nature lover in me, however, was glad of my country's choice.

Following our exploration of the Three Sisters, we headed to the Cave of the Winds, where we would be taken, in a crowded elevator, down 175 feet to the base of Bridal Veil Falls. I have mentioned that I'm claustrophobic, haven't I? It is times like these that I think of what Georgia O'Keefe once said: "I've been absolutely terrified every moment of my life – and I've never let it keep me from doing a single thing I wanted to do." If she could live her whole life terrified, I certainly should be able to endure a few minutes of having to remember to breathe.

The Cave of the Wind's name is deceiving, as there is no cave these days. It was destroyed by a rock fall in 1954, a fact I'm glad I hadn't known when I was in the elevator. The ride down left us off where we could access the Hurricane Deck, a bright orange wooden platform with a looping series of walkways and steps leading to and from the falls. The deck, I learned, is torn down each year before winter's destructive ice arrives. It is then rebuilt again in late spring.

Unlike the elevator ride, I loved the deck. It sits only 20 feet from the full force of the mighty falls, giving tourists an opportunity to get an authentic taste of nature. The bright yellow ponchos provided for the adventure, sufficient to keep us dry on the approaching walkways, were twisted into uselessness by the force of the pummeling water on the deck. Most of the camera-shooting tourists bypassed the deck, but I tucked my small camera away and weathered the "hurricane."

As I stood on the platform, deafened by the fall's cascading roar, I thought again about J. M. William Turner, the artist who once had himself tied to a mast so he could both experience and observe a storm's fury. While I had only experienced the sight and sound of the storm that I had previously watched from inside my RV at Kickapoo State Park, here I was privileged to feel the falls' savage intensity. It was like completing the "rest of the story," as Paul Harvey loved to say; or, as a Zen saying goes: "If you walk in the mist you get wet."

The pulsing waterfall, however, didn't allow me to linger on the deck. She pushed me along, leaving me both exhilarated and humbled. I arrived back at our van wet to the skin, and glad it was a quite warm day.

Next on the tour was yet another face-to-face experience with the falls – a cruise aboard the Maid of the Mist. Tourists have been taking this boat ride to the base of American and Horseshoe waterfalls for over 160 years, the original Maid having begun operations on the river in 1846. Six vessels bearing the same name followed, with the last four still operating today. Two dock on the Canadian side and two on the American side, the latter being where our group boarded Maid of the Mist VI, and this time handed blue ponchos.

On boarding, I scampered between the mass of people to claim the bow on the main deck of the two-tiered, standing-room only vessel. I wanted to experience the falls as fully as possible, as I'm sure Turner would have if he'd had the opportunity. But as our Maid approached what seemed extremely close to the base of the falls, I suddenly experienced a moment of fear that we would be sucked down to the bottom of the river. The fear lasted only seconds, as I immediately reminded myself that millions of people had safely taken this same ride before me and all had survived –

unlike some of those who got their view of the falls as they tumbled over its edge, usually in a barrel.

I was drenched again as I boarded the tour van, but once again thankful for the experience of the raging falls. As Native American author Hyemeyohsts (Wolf) Storm talks about in his writings, I had experienced becoming "one with life."

Our next stop was Canada's version of the falls. To get there, we had to cross the Niagara River via the 950-foot long Rainbow Bridge that joins the two cities of the same name. Rainbow Bridge is shorter than the Peace Bridge because the river here narrows as it flows into the Niagara Gorge before spilling out into Lake Huron.

The first order of Canadian business was lunch, which was served on the top floor of one of the tall hotels whose glass walls overlook the falls. The view was magnificent, but the food, hurried through because we were behind schedule, was only so-so. Afterwards, we walked through a neatly landscaped park that rimmed the falls and offered stunning vistas. Hundreds of people jostled for places at the best viewing overlooks. I mostly stayed back of the crowds, satisfied with enjoying the park for itself, simply as I would have done if there had been no other attraction. I guess I was still feeling water saturated as blue jeans and cotton T-shirts don't dry quickly. My automatic search for birds only turned up a few ring-billed gulls flying overhead.

After recrossing the bridge into New York, our last stop of the day was the Three Sisters Trading Post, which our guide told us was owned and operated by three sisters. As we had started our day with the Three Sisters, it seemed an appropriate ending.

Back at my RV, where I was enthusiastically greeted by an eager-for-a-walk Maggie, I received a call from my daughter-in-law's parents, Annette and Dave Yash. We made blind-date plans for them to pick me up for breakfast the next morning. Nothing was said of the day ahead, so either side could plead a previously planned activity if things didn't go well. We ate at a local casino, where the food was good and the company enjoyable. The three of us hit it off, and after breakfast they played gracious hosts and showed me around the area, hitting spots that I hadn't seen the day before. It was a very pleasant morning; I even sighted two new birds for my journey's list.

Several dark-eyed juncos, a species I had seen many times, were pecking away at something beneath a large tree. They belonged to the slate-colored subspecies of juncos, which was the one I usually saw in Texas, while the Oregon subspecies was the one I usually saw in Utah. Juncos are easily recognizable for their tendency to feed on the ground, their sparrow-like appearance, and the white on their outer tail feathers that brightly flash as they fly away from you.

The second bird was a little gull, a bird I had never seen before. It was flying above the falls at an overlook. It was much smaller than the ring-billed gulls that were circling overhead that had initially attracted my attention. The little gull – yes, little gull is the bird's name – was a young one, not yet having a black head. Fortunately, I had a long look at it, and finally was able to identify it from the black pattern on its wings.

After our morning tour – and seeing that we were still enjoying one another – the Yashes drove me back to my RV, where we retrieved Maggie, and then went back to their house for the rest of the day. They later told my daughter-in-law that I had been a fun person to be around and a good distraction following the previous day's funeral. I told her she had delightful parents, and I now knew why she had turned out so wonderful.

BIRDS ALONG THE WAY:
European starling, mourning dove, killdeer, double-crested cormorant, turkey vulture, common grackle, American crow, Canada goose, kestrel, black vulture, herring gull, red-tailed hawk, ring-billed gull, red-breasted merganser, American robin, *dark-eyed junco, ** little gull, rough-ringed swallow, mallard, rock pigeon.

First sighting of this species on the journey.
** A lifer

THE JOURNEY

NIAGARA FALLS TO
HAMLIN BEACH STATE PARK
72 MILES

HAMLIN BEACH TO MEXICO, NEW YORK
112 MILES

CAMPGROUND:
J & J Campground
Mexico, New York

CAMPGROUND:
Hamblin Beach State Park
Hamblin, New York

CAMPGROUND:
Niagara Falls Campground
and Lodging
Niagara Falls New York

*"I see my path, but I don't
know where it leads. Not
knowing where I'm going is
what inspires me to travel it."*

— ROSALIA DE CASTRO

18

UPPER NEW YORK'S NOT A BIG APPLE

I took the Robert Moses Parkway out of Niagara Falls, following it north to Lake Ontario. Moses, the parkway's late namesake, played a major role in shaping New York during the mid-20th century, and was both revered and hated. I came across his name several times more as I traveled through the Empire State, noting that a bridge, a park, a dam and a school had also been named in his honor.

This day's drive took me through the small village of Lewiston, which some say is the most historic square mile in America. Formerly called The Landing, because of its location on the Niagara River, it was one of New York's first settlements, a battleground during the War of 1812, home of the earliest recorded U.S. railway, and the final stop on the Underground Railway for escaped slaves.

Lewiston is also home to the Joseph Davis State Park, where the 2005 Amazing Race TV show ended. As a big fan of the reality show – in which the contestant, who crosses the finish line first after a grueling around-the-world adventure, wins a million dollars – I stopped and checked out the park, which sits on the banks of the Niagara River, and has a 27-hole Frisbee disc golf course. It was the park's short nature trail, however, that interested me and Maggie. Although we hadn't been on the road long, it was too good an opportunity to stretch our legs a bit, and converse with Mother Nature, to pass up.

A lone, long-tailed duck – which was called an oldsquaw until we hit the age of politically correctness – was floating in the pond near the park's entrance. It was easily identifiable with its white face markings and slender tail sticking out in antenna fashion. It was only the second of its species I had ever seen, the first sighting being on Great Salt Lake in Utah. This alone made my stop at the park memorable. The status of these ducks, I noted when adding its name to my travel bird list, is "vulnerable," meaning their numbers are declining. Hopefully this would not be the last long-tailed duck I would ever see.

Back on the parkway, I followed the road's parallel path beside the Niagara River all the way to its junction with Lake Ontario and Fort Niagara State Park. The old fort, which played an important role in America's struggles against Britain, has stood at the entrance of the river and the lake since 1726. Now a designated historic landmark within the park, the fort is visited annually by upwards of 100,000 tourists.

I only took a quick drive through the park, stopping just once to take a better look at a flock of gulls that were in a picnic area next to the lake. They were mostly ring-billed gulls, but with a couple of larger herring gulls off to one side, and a couple of smaller Bonaparte's gulls in the middle of the flock. Yea! I thought. Another bird for my trip list. It was the Bonaparte's bright orange legs that made it stand out from the ringed-bills, – and a careful study of my bird field guide that finally let me identify them. Doing so made me feel as if I had just read a mystery thriller and correctly identified who-done-it before the book's author revealed the name of the killer.

On leaving the park, I followed Highway 18, also known as Lake Road, east alongside Lake Ontario. The route took me past several other New York parks. The first of these was Fourmile Creek State Park, followed by Wilson Tuscarora State Park, and then Krull Park. I didn't linger but for a few minutes at any of them because I wanted to put more miles on Gypsy Lee before stopping. Krull would have been a great place to dawdle for a while, and not just because the park's name got me thinking about the time my oldest grandchild, David, lived with me for six months. We played endless games of Krull, a popular board game in the 1980s. The game is now available in a video edition, while the original board game, I noted, was selling for up to $75 on eBay. I wondered where in the world the game board David and I had used had ended up. Later, while trying to find out where the park (which was older than me) had gotten its name (which I didn't discover), I learned that Krull Park had placed second in a Coca Cola contest to find "America's Favorite Park."

The park, however, that was our destination for the day, was Hamblin Beach State Park, which is located beside Lake Ontario. It was perfect for our night's stay, with trees in abundance, landscaped lawns, camp sites that didn't sit on top of one another, launch ramps for boaters, nature trails for hikers, paths for bikers, fish for fishermen, a beach for swimmers, and wetlands and forest areas for the birds and birders. In addition, there was an American Revolution re-enactment, complete with canon volleys, taking place when I arrived.

I wandered over to the staging area to check out the action, but quickly got antsy. Having grown up in the South, I was quite familiar with Civil War re-enactments, and this one of the Revolutionary War didn't seem much different – just a bunch of grown men playing toy soldiers on a large scale.

I decided to go play at bird-watching instead, but it turned out to be a slow game, with a circling osprey, several house sparrows and a couple of mute swans in a small pond being the only sightings. The swan was a new species for the journey, but I wasn't altogether happy spotting it. It's an introduced species, an aggressive one that is threatening native water fowl. It was beautiful, however. As for the few other bird sightings, it could have been that I was at the right place at the wrong time – or that the noisy re-enactment had scared the birds away. I suspected a little bit of both.

When it began to drizzle, I returned to the RV and spent the rest of the afternoon catching up on my journal. Just before dark, Maggie and I strolled through the large park one last time. The booming had stopped, but the only birds to be seen was a pair of mourning doves already snoozing in a tree. Still, it was a pleasant walk. I knew I would be sorry to move on in the morning – but I still had many miles to go to reach Maine and the Atlantic Coast.

An early morning walk with Maggie along the beach added a new bird to the trip list, a ruddy turnstone. Three of these birds, which belong to the Sandpiper family, were strolling along the edge of the water ahead of Maggie and me. Their feathers were duller than the ones I had seen on the Texas Gulf Coast, but I easily recognized them from the pattern of the black bib markings on their chest, and their bright orange legs.

From Hamblin Beach, I continued east on Lake Ontario Parkway, which hugged the lake's south shore. Lake Ontario is the smallest of the five great lakes, and like Erie, whose northern beaches I followed earlier, it separates the United States from Canada. It was a scenic, zig-and-zag route, taking me past several lake communities and across quaint bridges that spanned watery inlets bisecting the road. People who picture the state of New York as being one Big Apple, as I once did, would have been amazed. Upper New York is quite rural.

The drive this day took me through the touristy town of Irondequoit, and then across Irondequoit Bay. Created by melting glaciers, the bay is a half-mile wide, and four miles long. On a 17th century French map, it was called Swamp of the Senecas. The parkway ended at Sodus Bay and the small village of Sodus Point. I turned south here and followed Highway 14 to Highway 104, and followed it east, passing through the small inland towns of Wolcott and South Hannibal before veering back to the lake and Oswego, a port city set on the Oswego River that began life as a British trading post. After crossing the Oswego River, which after Niagara is the largest river flowing into Lake Ontario, I took a break from driving and visited the Fort Ontario State Historical Site. It didn't claim my interest for long, although I did find its many lives – even more than a cat's—fascinating.

The original fort was built in 1755 by the British. A year later, the French came and routed the British from the area and destroyed the garrison. In 1759, after reclaiming the Oswego area, the British rebuilt the fort, this time making it larger and better fortified. But this structure was also destroyed, this time by the

Americans during their war for independence. In 1782, the British returned to Oswego and rebuilt the fort for the third time, and then in 1796 they turned it over to the Americans. It was an ironic generosity because a decade and a half later along came the War of 1812, and once again the British were at war with America. This time the British destroyed the fort.

With such a disastrous background, one might think this would have been the end of it. Not so. The United States began rebuilding the fort in 1839. While it was never destroyed again, it declined because of a lack of maintenance funds, and was abandoned in 1901.

Like that nine-life cat, however, the fort was revived a few years later, and by 1941 its grounds contained over a hundred buildings that were converted into a refugee center for victims of the Nazi Holocaust. After World War II ended, the property was given to the state of New York, which eventually developed it into a historic tourist site.

Whew! And this is merely an abridged version.

After Oswego, Highway 104 began veering inland again, passing a nuclear power plant and the small towns of Scriba, New Haven and finally Mexico, New York, where I would spend the next two uneventful, and evidently unmemorable, days. I wrote little in my journal about my stay here except for watching an early morning robin catching a worm outside my window. I can't recall what I was thinking at the time, and belatedly berated myself for not keeping better notes. I think, perhaps, my brain just needed a break.

BIRDS ALONG THE WAY:

American robin, house sparrow, mallard, rock pigeon, *long-tailed duck, herring gull, ring-billed gull, *Bonaparte's gull, European starling, mourning dove, killdeer, barn swallow, great blue heron, American crow, *mute swan, osprey, *ruddy turnstone, eastern meadowlark, Canada geese, turkey vulture, white-breasted nuthatch, Carolina chickadee, eastern bluebird, raven, chipping sparrow and northern cardinal.

*First sighting of this species on the journey.

THE JOURNEY

CAMPGROUND:
Country Haven Campground
Chestertown, New York

CAMPGROUND:
J & J Campground
Mexico, New York

New York

"It is better to travel well

than to arrive."

– BUDDHA

19

THE ADIRONDACKS

The continuation of our journey through more of rural New York took Maggie and me through a pasture of fake cows – honestly. It seemed like every other house had one standing in their yard. They reminded me of the pink-flamingo lawn ornaments so popular in Florida, the plastic deer Texans scatter about in their front yards, and the carved wooden bears that Idahoans favor as their outdoor accessories. Such lawn decorations have always amused me, and the New York black and white cows were no different. Once I even chuckled out loud, causing Maggie to lift her head and give me a stare that said: You're disturbing my nap.

The chuckle was partly because of the fake cows, and partly because I had suddenly remembered the Canada geese my son, Lewis, and I had once encountered while out bird watching. I had missed seeing them as we passed, but my son had caught a glimpse. He pulled a U-turn to better check them out so we both could add another bird to our day's bird list. We both giggled until we about peed our pants when we realized our birds were fake geese, and super-sized as well. But that's OK. Laughter is good for the soul. The world could use a bit more of it.

With the plaster cows accompanying us, we made our way into Rome, New York, which would be the only city of any size we would encounter on this day. Rome is where Paul Revere had his brass and copper foundry, which is probably why it's called both the Copper City and the City of American History. It sits on an early trade route between the Great Lakes and Canada, and played significant roles in both the French and Indian War and the Revolutionary War. In addition, Rome was also where the 1817 construction of the Erie Canal began. This 363-mile waterway, from the Hudson River to Buffalo, New York, was this country's first transportation system, carrying goods from the Atlantic Ocean to the Great Lakes region.

The first time I ever heard about the canal was in a song I had sung as a kid. I still remember the lyrics.

"I've got a mule, and her name is Sal,
Fifteen miles on the Erie Canal.
She's a good ol' worker and a good ol' pal,
Fifteen miles on the Erie Canal.
We've hauled some barges in our day,
Filled with lumber coal and hay ...
Low bridge, everybody down.
Low bridge, we're coming to a town ..."

I sang to Maggie. And like most beings who have heard my off-key singing voice, she looked pained.

The canal, today, is used primarily by water recreationists, although it still has a bit of commercial transportation business. I paused for a while in Rome so Maggie and I could take a short walk alongside the historic canal. Maggie got into a fit of frenzied sniffing along the path, and I fancifully wondered if she was catching any trace of those ol' mules.

After Rome, I veered northeast a bit to catch Highway 8, which would take us into Adirondack Park, a six million acre tract of land that the state of New York has been protecting out of concern for its vast water and timber resources since 1892. The area contains over 3,000 lakes, thousands of miles of rivers, huge tracts of forest, and a scattered permanent population of over 100,000 people. About half the park is private property, but local land owners are required to abide by state conservation rules regarding development.

Our route took us past several tiny communities nestled into a landscape of ponds, lakes and trees that most often kept the Adirondack Mountains hidden from view. These were gentle mountains, quite different from the jagged peaks of the Rockies that I had lived among for many years. Johnsburg was the only village after Rome that had more than 1,000 residents.

My destination this day was Chestertown, which was a small town located in the southeastern quadrant of the park. I spent a good hour hunting for the RV campground where I had planned to stay. Thankfully I hadn't made advance reservations because I never found it. Instead, I came across the Country Haven Campground, which turned out to be such a pleasant place that I decided to stay a few days, at least long enough to once again let my mail catch up with me.

A large, carved wooden bear with a fish in its mouth, was situated at the entrance to the park. It made me smile – and wonder if the park owners were from Idaho. I described the campground to my daughter-in-law, Cindi, when I called to give her its address so she could forward my mail. She said I had quite a stack, including a lot of birding magazines, and that she would forward it all on. And then, with a tinge of envy in her voice, she hoped I would fall in a creek.

Actually, Cindi, who seldom leaves home because of caring for an autistic child, regularly thanked me for sharing my travels with her. She says I'm her eyes to the world's beautiful places. As for me, I'm grateful to have Cindi in my life. I feel safer knowing that one member of my family always knows where I am – and cares.

Chestertown, located at the junction of Highway 8 and Highway 9, was incorporated in 1799, making it one of the oldest towns in the Adirondacks. Its many recreational opportunities – fishing, canoeing, rafting and hiking in summer, and cross-country skiing and tobogganing in winter – made it popular with tourists, which is why I assumed the campground, located just outside of town near the Schroon River, was almost full. Even so, the campground area offered plenty of space for Maggie and me to take quiet walks, and to recharge our batteries from days of driving.

This part of the journey, however, turned into a slow-motion melancholy film. I suspect it might have been because here I felt strangely out of step with traveling down the road, and was suddenly missing loved ones. I used the lazy days as a time to identify trees and butterflies with nature guides in hand, to stare long at river ripples flowing downstream, and to welcome the morning sun each day with my coffee, and by catching the solar god's last wink before he disappeared at night.

A flock of cedar waxwings, a delightful bird dressed in feathers suitable for a costumed ball, were part of the everyday scenery. Cedar waxwings have a jaunty crest, wear a black mask, sport a yellow-tipped tail and red-tipped wings and travel in flocks. They daily filled a couple of trees full of blossoming berries in sight of my RV – and joined my slow-growing trip bird list.

I was glad it took my mail several days to arrive. And a chat with a fellow Texan during my one foray into downtown Chestertown to mail postcards, which I had bought in Niagara Falls to send to family and friends, cured my brief bout of homesickness. Upon seeing my Texas license plate when I pulled into the post office, a gray-haired female rushed over to greet me. While that might seem strange to New Yorkers or Californians, such behavior is typical of Texans. I know of no other people who are as proud of where they were born as Texans. It's bred into us. I can still hear my grandmother, who died when I was just 10 years old, telling me: "People who weren't born in Texas probably didn't deserve to be." I only partially share that attitude. While it's true my roots are in Texas, I happily chose to live for many years where mountains, which I love, were my backyard instead of in Texas' flatlands.

The Texas woman who approached me this day was spending the summer in the Adirondacks. With an accent dribbled with y'alls, she said she just wanted to talk to someone from home. Our 10-minute conversation cheered both of us, especially after the talk turned to how hot it was in Texas in August. We both decided we would rather be right where we were.

BIRDS ALONG THE WAY:
American robin, herring gull, osprey, house sparrow, mallard, rock pigeon, European starling, mourning dove, ring-billed gull, killdeer, barn swallow, great blue heron, American crow, mute swan, eastern meadowlark, Canada goose, turkey vulture, *cedar waxwing, white-breasted nuthatch, Carolina chickadee, eastern bluebird, raven, chipping sparrow and northern cardinal.

*First sighting of this species on the journey.

THE JOURNEY

CHESTERTON, NEW YORK TO GIFFORD WOODS STATE PARK, VERMONT
83 MILES

CAMPGROUND:
Country Haven Campground
Chestertown, New York

CAMPGROUND:
Gifford Woods State Park
Killington, Vermont

"I think that travel comes from

some deep urge to see the world,

like the urge that brings up

a worm in an Irish bog

to see the moon when it is full."

– LORD DUNANY

20

TICONDEROGA, NORMAN ROCKWELL AND RAINY VERMONT

After spending five days in Chesterton, and getting my mail, which included chocolate treats from my saint of a daughter-in-law, I continued my journey through the Adirondacks on Highway 8. The scenic route took me along the southern shore of Brandt Lake. On spotting some ducks in the water near a place where I could park my RV off the narrow road, Maggie and I got out to stretch our legs. A chatty squirrel scolded us, and Maggie sat down and watched it. I, meanwhile, identified a pair of mallards, and then a pair of common mergansers that were floating not too far from shore. The merganser was a new bird for the trip.

Identification of a flock of ducks off in the distance, however, befuddled me. I finally lugged out my powerful birding scope, and mounted it on its sturdy tripod for a better look. It was worth the trouble, because this distant flock of ducks also included two more species not yet seen on the journey. The first was a common goldeneye, a duck whose golden eyes I had seen often on Great Salt Lake in Utah, where it winters after breeding in Canada. Along with its golden eyes, which both genders have, the male of the species has an almost perfect white circle on its cheek that stands out on a glossy black head. Through my scope, I could see both the yellow eyes and the white cheek marking on one of the ducks. Beside it swam a brown-headed duck – the female of the species.

There were about two dozen ducks in the flock, which except for one pair, all had golden eyes. The exception was a pair of hooded mergansers, beautiful ducks that I had only seen a few times before. The first time I saw one was in 2001 when I had driven the Alaskan Highway. The male of this species also has a white cheek patch on a black head, but is most easily identified by its thin bill and flowing crest that makes its head look elongated. Like the female golden-eyes, the hooded merganser females have brown heads and drab bodies.

What a great start to the day, I thought, as I added the three new birds to my list.

Back in the RV, Maggie quickly fell asleep and I continued following Highway 8 past the small lakeside town of Hague and the northern tip of Lake George, a 32-mile-long narrow, but deep lake that charmed me with its brilliant blue hues. Then I turned north toward Ticonderoga, a name I remembered well from early classroom history lessons.

Sitting on the southern edge of Lake Champlain, with direct water access to Montreal, Ticonderoga and its fort, which was built by the French during the French and Indian Wars, had once been a busy battleground. The town sits in the shadow of Mount Defiance, a steep 853-foot hill, from whose peak one could have watched the battles – or as the British did to the French's surprise, be used as a platform for cannons. During the Revolutionary War, the fort changed hands between the British and Americans several times before it was finally claimed by this country for good.

After the final British defeat, the fort lost its reason for being, and fell into disrepair. It was restored in the early 1900s, and is now merely a tourist attraction.

After Ticonderoga, I turned south on Highway 22, which took me down the eastern edge of Adirondack Park, and through the small communities of Putnam Station, Dresden and Clemons, and then on a bridge across a bay to Whitehall, New York, which sits on the southern edge of Lake Champlain. This small village, once a ship-building port, calls itself the birthplace of the American Navy. Benedict Arnold commanded a fleet of ships built here in 1776 during the Battle of Valcour Island, one of this country's first naval battles, and one of the first battles of the Revolutionary War. Most of America's ships were either captured or destroyed during this battle.

Just after Whitehall, I crossed the border into Vermont, a sparsely populated state of less than a million residents. Only Wyoming has fewer. My drive took me past white churches with tall steeples, covered wooden bridges, green ponds and more cow lawn ornaments – plus a few pastures of the living and breathing creatures. This wasn't surprising, since Vermont's state flag has a cow on it. The gentle lushness of the landscape poured me a glass of serenity. I could feel, as well as see, why Vermont is called the Green Mountain State. Even the state's name of Vermont, given to the area by Samuel de Champlain in 1609, is the French word for *Green*.

In Rutland, which with its population of around 20,000 is Vermont's third largest city, I came across a red, barn-like building that advertised itself as the Norman Rockwell Museum. It was one of those surprise discoveries that keep me eagerly going down the road. Of course, I had to stop.

I grew up reading the Saturday Evening Post with its Norman Rockwell covers that depicted life in times when American values were prioritized by hard work, home, family, freedom, justice and apple pie. It was an era before corporate greed became so prevalent (or before it was so prevalently recognized); it was a time when innocent until found guilty meant something; a time before consumers scrambled to outdo the Joneses with bigger and better until they went bankrupt; and a time before the shenanigans of bratty celebrities dominated world news for days on end. It was the era I grew up in, and although far from perfect, it's still one I'm sad my grandchildren will so completely miss experiencing.

The museum gave me another take on Rockwell. While I was familiar with the artist's magazine covers, I didn't realize the extent of his commercial endeavors. This small museum had hundreds of Rockwell's advertising campaign illustrations. During his career, Rockwell sold everything from socks to bourbon, eye glasses to airlines, and soaps to soda pops. He was a prolific artist, and it took me nearly two hours to meander through the vast collection.

It was raining when I left the museum, as it would be for the rest of my stay in the state. No wonder everything was so green. With raindrops plopping on my windshield, I drove along the southern edge of the Green Mountain National Forest, through the small town of Mendon, and to the forest's southeast corner, where sat Gifford Woods State Park, my day's destination. I was particularly excited about staying here because the Appalachian Trail went through the middle of the heavily wooded park.

I had become fascinated with the idea of hiking the trail as a young reporter who had interviewed a Utah hiker who had done the 2,175 mile adventurous trek over a period of two years. I had immediately wanted to hike the entire trail myself. The opportunity, however, never presented itself.

As age overtook me, I realized covering that much territory, much of it through designated wilderness areas, was way too ambitious. Then I read Bill Bryson's *A Walk in the Woods,* and my goal became more realistic. He only did portions of the trail. This was something I could do. I still never found the time, however, and the years dimmed my expectations even more. Now I finally had the opportunity of hiking at least a few miles on the trail, and I had the entire next day ahead of me to do it, I thought, as I hooked Gypsy Lee up in the rain, and later went to sleep to the beat of raindrops hitting the roof above my over-the-cab bed. It was still raining when I awoke the next morning.

I decided to hike the trail anyway, but I soon let the unending rain turn me into a wimp. Maggie and I hiked little more than a quarter mile down the trail before turning back. Maggie's feet had become heavy with mud, and I realized, as she and I both became as wet as beavers diving to the underwater entrances of their snug burrows, that I wasn't a happy hiker. I hadn't seen a single bird, not even a hermit thrush which is Vermont's state bird.

For the rest of my stay at the campground, I enjoyed Gifford Woods in extremely short walks with Maggie, both of us staying close together beneath my oversized umbrella. One of our short walks was made on an interpretive nature trail near the park's entrance. I learned that Gifford Woods was one of the few remaining old-growth hardwood forests with uncut stands of trees still left in this country.

When not bundled up for rain walks, or staring out the RV window at the birdless lush woods, I read, finishing off Tim Cahill's *Jaguars Ripped My Flesh* that I had picked up at a used book store along the way, and then diving into an anthology of British Lord Peter Wimsey mysteries by Dorothy Sayers. While Cahill tickled my funny bone with his exaggerated travel antics, Sayers stimulated my brain cells with her who-done-it tales, and took me back in time to a place I could only imagine. But Sayer's and Agatha Christie's times would never be my reality, just as my times would never exist for my grandchildren to experience.

I finally stopped caring that the rain wouldn't stop, which was good because it didn't.

BIRDS ALONG THE WAY:
American robin, *common merganser, *hooded merganser,
*common golden-eye, European starling, mourning dove,
eastern bluebird, house sparrow, chipping sparrow, raven,
white-breasted nuthatch, American crow, northern cardinal,
mallard, eastern phoebe and blue jay.

First sighting of this species on the journey.

THE JOURNEY

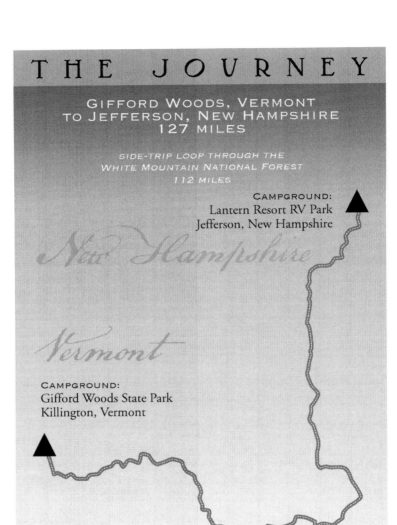

GIFFORD WOODS, VERMONT
TO JEFFERSON, NEW HAMPSHIRE
127 MILES

SIDE-TRIP LOOP THROUGH THE
WHITE MOUNTAIN NATIONAL FOREST
112 MILES

CAMPGROUND:
Lantern Resort RV Park
Jefferson, New Hampshire

New Hampshire

Vermont

CAMPGROUND:
Gifford Woods State Park
Killington, Vermont

"To move, to breath, to fly, to float
To gain all while you give
To roam the road of land remote
To travel is to live."

– HANS CHRISTIAN ANDERSON

21

THE STONE MAN

It was still raining when a couple of Mallards quacked good-bye to Maggie and me as we left Gifford Woods, and continued our journey east on Highway 4. The ducks seemed quite happy with the rain, but by now I wasn't as charmed.

The day's drive began with heavy mist on the windshield, and a road ahead that twisted round and about through scenic land-scapes that would be filled with skiers come the winter snow. Soon after leaving Gifford Woods, we drove through the small town of Killington, the downhill home of Killington Ski Resort and its neighbor, Suicide Six Ski Resort. I wondered about the latter's name, but suspected it wasn't a place I would enjoy skiing. It had taken 15 years for me, who didn't start skiing until I was 40 years old, to get comfortable pointing my skis downhill on Utah's soft powder snow.

My mind continued wondering and asking questions with no answers. Highway 4 followed the Ottauquechee River as it twisted its way through the center of Woodstock, a historic town of about 3,000 people. This small Vermont shire, as county seats are called in this area of the country, claimed to be the only town in America with four Paul Revere bells. Other historic signs told me that Woodstock was also the site of the first ski tow; the birthplace of Hiram Powers (the sculptor of "Greek Slave," for which Elizabeth

Barrett Browning created a sonnet), and that it had been the home
of railroad empire builder Frederick Billings. My favorite roadside
sign, however, was an Aesop-like message that read: "Even on the
right track, you'll get run over if you just sit there."

Or, if you're in Vermont, you'll drown, I thought, and smiled at
my joke.

The rain stopped just before Maggie and I reached the Quec-
hee Gorge Bridge, a steel structure built in 1911 to carry the
Woodstock Railroad across the gorge. At the bottom of the deep
divide, which is sometimes called Vermont's Little Grand Canyon,
flowed my traveling sidekick, the Ottauquechee River.

A large parking lot, along with a souvenir gift shop and an information center, were located on the east side of the bridge, and
I pulled in and parked. A sidewalk across the bridge allowed safe
viewing of the steep gorge and the fast, tumbling river. Even better, there was a hiking trail that led to a waterfall not too far up
the canyon. I felt as if Vermont had given me a parting gift – as if
to say sorry about all that rain and mud on the Appalachian Trail.
Perhaps my stay in Vermont had been too short, but since Maine's
East Coast birds were calling, I bid good-bye to the Green Mountain
state. I had started this journey in May, and today was the last day of
August. The birds I wanted to see might already be heading south.

I crossed into New Hampshire just after passing White River Junction, a small village with a railroad past. During the mid-
1800s, it saw as many as 50 passenger trains pass through daily. I
drove slowly through the town, but didn't stop to explore because
of wanting to get some miles behind me. It turned out to be a good
decision made at the wrong time.

New Hampshire was yet another notch toward my goal of visiting all 50 states. And as usual on crossing state borders, I noted
changes around me. The landscape felt more open than Vermont.
The trees didn't hug the road quite as tightly, and I had occasional views of granite mountains. The state's motto of "Live Free or
Die," which adorned the license plates of passing cars, made me

think of the slogan of my native Lone Star State, and which is shouted on roadside billboards: "Don't Mess with Texas."

I was now following Highway 10 north as it weaved along New Hampshire's border with Vermont, and alongside the Connecticut River. The highway took me through the small towns of Hanover (home of Dartmouth College), Oxford, (which was chartered by King George III in 1761) Piermont, (whose chamber of commerce brags: "It is a great place to spend the summer."), Haverhill (home of the oldest still-standing covered bridge) and Bath (named for the first earl of Bath). While New Hampshire is more populated than Vermont, it's not by much.

At Littleton, where "Pollyanna" author Eleanor Porter grew up, I zigged east on Highway 116 to Jefferson, where I planned to spend two nights at the Lantern Resort, a large Good Sam campground where I could catch up on laundry. Although I was by now in a hurry to push along, my budget was more eager for me to stay put awhile and conserve money.

Unforeseen circumstances threw the battle to the budget. I ended up staying five days at the Jefferson campground, because when I called ahead for reservations for my next stop, which I did because a holiday weekend was approaching, I discovered all the campgrounds a day's drive away were booked up through Sunday night. It was too bad I had left Vermont in such a rush.

OK. It was time to follow the advice of Garth Brooks. "Happiness isn't getting what you want; it's wanting what you got." So, instead of whining, I took an unplanned day trip, a loop through the White Mountain National Forest and a visit to Franconia Notch State Park. But what I didn't have, I soon discovered, was an opportunity to meet "The Old Man" of the mountain. Unbeknownst to me, he had died in 2003 in a rock fall.

The Old Man was New Hampshire's natural and most recognizable wonder, the granite profile of a man's head high atop Cannon Mountain. It and New Hampshire had long been associated – and still is. The image of the Old Man's rugged rock profile adorns

New Hampshire's state quarter, which was issued three years before the avalanche killed him off.

Of this "Great Stone Face," Daniel Webster wrote: "Men hang out their signs indicative of their respective trades; shoe makers hang out a gigantic shoe; jewelers a monster watch, and the dentist hangs out a gold tooth; but up in the Mountains of New Hampshire, God Almighty has hung out a sign to show that there He makes men."

I would have liked to have met the Old Man. Not being able to do so emphasized the disastrous results of procrastination in our lives. Tomorrow simply may be too late. Nothing for me to do now but to content myself with staring at the mountainside where the Old Man once reigned, and continue my journey to Franconia Notch State Park, which my travel guide described as a spectacular mountain pass carved between the Kinsman and Franconia mountain ranges. It was indeed.

After a tour of the park's visitor center, I paid $10 to hike the two-mile Flume Gorge Trail. I more than got my money's worth. It was one of those unexpected travel surprises – and the most spectacular hike of my New England trip. The trail, which begins at the visitor center, led me across the Pemigewasset River on a foot bridge adjacent to a historic 1886's covered bridge. Pemigewasset means swift, or rapid current, in the language of the Abenaki Indians, a name probably given it because of the falls and rumbling cascades that dot its 65-mile journey from Franconia Notch to the Merrimack River.

After crossing the river, the trail jogged across a patch of slick rock where tiny pools of water had formed as water from the flume flowed across the pot-holed granite. The wetness painted the rock into fanciful patterns on its way to join the river. Continuing onward, the trail began its ascent up the flume, a geologic wonder created from molten rock deep below the surface millions of years ago. The lava cooled, fractured and was eventually exposed by the forces of erosion.

A series of bridges and steps anchored to the steep moss-covered walls of the gorge, below which flowed a stream of water, led upward to a ridge. The final section of the trail required squeezing past a torrent of plunging water known as Avalanche Falls, an appropriate name because the falls was created in 1883 after a storm washed away a huge overhanging boulder. Mother Nature has both destructive and creative temperaments, I thought, as I reached out and touched the fall's spray. The water chilled my hand, and sent a cooling tingle through my body.

At the top of the gorge stood a rain shelter with a garish green plastic looking roof and a sign declaring "TOP O' GORGE." I took a picture, not because of its beauty but simply because I wanted to show that I had been at this spot. Hikers reaching this point could now take a shortcut back to the visitor center or continue on to Liberty Gorge, where yet another cascading stream made its way down to the Pemigewasset River.

I continued onward, along with about half of the dozen or so hikers who had made it to the top the same time as me. While they set a fast pace on the trail, I dawdled, taking time to identify the birds and flowers and to photograph the beauty around me. The result was that I soon had the path to myself. Miraculously, it continued that way, except for one fast-trotting hiker who passed by without even a nod. I suspected that because of the lateness of the afternoon no more hikers were being allowed on the trail.

Such peaceful solitude seems harder and harder to find as more and more people discover the soul-healing qualities of getting outdoors. I try not to resent such intrusions, preferring instead to take pleasure in believing such exposure to the calming influence of the non-material world can't help but forward the ideal of world peace. But when I do have the forest or mountain to myself, my heart sings.

I slowed my pace even more, drinking in the tranquility of nature's whimsies right down to my little toes. Hug-able trees, fragrant flowers, a mysterious dark pool, water singing as it splashed playfully about, and scattered glacial rocks, one as large as a cabin with an interpretive sign to denote its importance.

Things got even better. While I only saw four birds during the entire walk, two of these were lifers for me.

The first new bird to join my life list was an ovenbird, a rather plain brown creature whose striped breast and bold white eye-ring often disappear in the shadows. Several other times while birding with friends, this bird had been spotted but never well enough by me to count it. This time was different. Alerted by a slurred call, I slowly crept around a curve and immediately saw the bird standing on the edge of the trail near a large leafy bush.

I froze in place and brought my binoculars up to my eyes. The bird was highlighted by the sun, which made its dull, rusty crown stand out. It stared at me for a full minute before pivoting and disappearing into the brush beside the trail.

The next bird was more distinctive, making it quicker for me to identify. It was a black-throated blue warbler looking just like its name. It sat on a heavily-leafed lower tree limb. Like the ovenbird, it was the warbler's voice that first attracted my attention. The bird only vanished into the greenery when I finally had seen enough and took a step forward.

"Life is good," I told Maggie when I finally returned to my RV. Dogs weren't allowed on the trail. She wagged her tail and asked: So, where's my treat? I gave her two.

BIRDS ALONG THE WAY:
Mallards, white-breasted nuthatch, American crow,
mourning dove, European starling, northern cardinal,
eastern phoebe, blue jay, common merganser, house sparrow,
brown creeper, **ovenbird, dark-eyed junco,
**black-throated blue warbler, black vulture, American robin,
eastern bluebird, chipping sparrow and raven.

First sighting of this species on the journey.
**A lifer*

THE JOURNEY

Maine

CAMPGROUND:
Lantern Resort RV Park
Jefferson, New Hampshire

CAMPGROUND:
Lake Saint George State Park
Liberty, Maine

New Hampshire

*One of the great things
about travel is that you find out
how many good, kind people
there are."*

– EDITH WHARTON

22

GOOD-BYE WHITE MOUNTAINS, HELLO MAINE

I continued east on Highway 2 from Jefferson, following the northern edge of the White Mountain National Forest. It was an uncrowded, pleasant drive with no clue that six million people annually visit the innards of this forest to hike its 1,200 miles of trails, float its numerous rivers, or fish its numerous ponds. The forest has also been designated one of the 500 Most Important Birding Areas in this country. Although not planned, I felt fortunate to have been delayed long enough to hike one of those trails, walk among its life-giving trees, hear the music of its rippling streams, and receive the gift of two new birds for my life list.

The birds this day, however, were doing a great job of hiding. I didn't even get a glimpse of unidentified motion in the shadows of roadside foliage as my morning drive took me through the small New Hampshire towns of Randolph, Gorham and Shelburne. The Appalachian Trail crossed through Gorham, and apple orchards thrived in Shelburne. Soon I crossed into Maine, the forest staying by my side until I had passed the small town of Gilead, which gets its name from the Balm of Gilead trees that dot its downtown area. From Gilead, I had rear-facing views of the White Mountains' Presidential Range. These mountain peaks, which loom large over the landscape and have such notable names as Washington, Adams, Jefferson, Madison and Monroe, attract a multitude of climbers, especially Mount Washington, whose 6,288-foot granite summit is the tallest of the lot.

Because I was only at an elevation of about 600 feet, the peaks looked nearly as imposing as the 9,570-foot Mount Ogden, which was my backyard for 20 years when I lived along the Wasatch Front of the Rocky Mountains. I loved living in its shadow, watching the morning sun pop above the mountain peaks on lazy summer mornings, seeing it frosted with snow as crisp winter days came on, then popping with green hues as winter days gave way to spring. And autumn, when red and golden splashes changed the mountain into a kaleidoscope of color, always bedazzled the eyes. It was on Mount Ogden that I learned to ski, and its benches provided many hours of hiking that kept me sane after a day of chaos and daily newspaper deadlines. As I gazed back at the "Presidents," I realized I was a bit homesick for my Wasatch Mountains.

Born and raised in Texas' flatlands, I was 14 before I saw my first mountain, and still 26 years away from my first tumble down Mount Ogden on skis. It took me a month of lessons before I was brave enough to abandon the bunny hill for something a bit steeper, while my 14-year-old daughter, who learned to ski with me, ventured higher up the mountain at the end of our first day of lessons. But I stuck with it, and because of a leg injury my daughter suffered while jumping moguls on our fourth ski outing (which kept her away from skiing for the next year), I eventually became a better skier than she. I think it may have been the first time in my life that I did something better than my children – and I still treasure the achievement.

Ever since that first sight of a mountain in my early teens, I've been in love with Mother Nature's monoliths. I guess that's why I kept looking in my rear-view mirror until the mountains behind disappeared from view.

Coming back to my flatter surroundings, I found myself driving through Bethel, a Biblical name meaning "House of God." It was aptly named, being home to many high-steeple churches, with a nearby ski resort called Sunday River. I assumed a lot of skiers preferred to go there to worship on their day of rest instead of sitting on a hard pew being lectured about God. I know that such natural settings among Mother Nature's creations always touch my spirit more than sitting in any church on any day of the week.

Letting my mind continue to wander as I drove, I passed several quaint bed and breakfasts nestled among the landscape, and several small Maine towns. As usual I looked for that one thing that would make each town stand out from its neighbors. Dixfield called itself "The Only One," because of being the only town with that name. I doubted the claim but then couldn't find another town with the same moniker when I later looked it up. Not so with the next city I passed through. I found eight states and two Canadian provinces that had towns named Chesterville, making me wonder why Chester was more renowned than Dix.

New Sharon, meanwhile, claimed fame for being home to the world's oldest living man, Fred H. Hale. He was born Dec. 1, 1890, and died Nov. 19, 2004. Fred credited honey and an occasional nip of whiskey as the reason for his longevity.

At New Sharon, I jogged south on Highway 27 to catch Highway 3, which would take me all the way into Bar Harbor, where I planned to spend a week before heading back south. My route now passed by a multitude of shimmering lakes and shaded green ponds that taunted me to stop and stay a while. In answer, I called a halt to my travels for the day at Lake Saint George State Park that sat on the banks of Saint George Lake

Located next to Highway 3, the park had only 38 camping sites. I chose a large spot that backed up to the lake, and angled my RV so that nothing stood between it and me. There were no hookups, but the camping fee was only $10, and the weather was cool enough that I didn't need to turn on my air conditioner. My vehicle's self-contained units met all my other needs: stored water, battery power for lights, and propane for cooking and refrigeration.

After a short hike around the area with Maggie, I got out my lawn chair. After a while, with no birds flitting about to attract my attention, I retrieved a book, *Death in Holy Orders*, by P.D. James, and read until sunset, when I lit a fire in the fire pit with one of the fake logs I haul around to use when wood is not available. I knew I would now have at least two hours to sit by the campfire, time in which I could let my mind wonder through distant planes.

The dark brought a sprinkling of magical fireflies. I had seen these amazing creatures often when I was a kid living on the outskirts of Dallas, but rarely as an adult. Had the fireflies mostly disappeared, or had I stopped looking for them? I savored the present, and thought of past giggling nights when I chased fireflies with a Mason jar and lid in hand. I once wanted to take the closed jar to bed with me so I could see the winged bugs light up during the night, but was persuaded by my grandmother that this would be cruel to the fireflies. I understood, and happily set the fireflies free. I've tried to instill this same respect for all wildlife in my kids and grandkids. We humans aren't the only ones that inhabit this planet.

When Maggie and I finally turned in for the night, I was asleep almost the minute my head touched the pillow. It must have been the lulling sounds of the water peacefully slurping up against the shore that had brought me to such a peaceful state – or else I had worn myself out with all the thoughts racing through my mind.

BIRDS ALONG THE WAY:
American crow, mourning dove, black vulture, eastern phoebe.
I saw fewer birds this day than any other on the trip.

THE JOURNEY

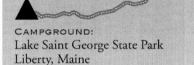

CAMPGROUND:
Lake Saint George State Park
Liberty, Maine

CAMPGROUND:
Bar Harbor Campground
Bar Harbor, Maine

"It is not down in any map;

true places never are."

–HERMAN MELVILLE

23

A WEEK ON DESERT ISLAND

I was on the road early the next morning, eager to reach the most eastern spot of this country that I had ever visited. The landscape along my drive was now waterlogged, and became even more so the closer I got to the coast.

East of Lake Saint George Park, I drove through the small town of Liberty, which claims to be the only city with an octagonal post office, and then edged past Belfast, which sits on the northwest corner of Penobscot Bay. Highways 1 and 3 merge here, and follow the northern edge of the bay to the deep harbor town of Searsport. Although eager to continue on to my destination, I took a bit of time to stop for a bit of historic exploration in Searsport.

Settled in the 1670s, Searsport supported 17 shipyards in the 1800s, and produced 200 ships. While the Penobscot Marine Museum showcases the town's past, the many vintage shops I passed supported the town's present-day claim as the "Antique Capital of Maine." I bypassed all the shops, however, for a visit to the museum that I had read about in *Eyewitness Travel Guide of New England.*

I found the history exhibits fascinating, and the folk art displays charming, particularly the wooden duck decoys. As I observed them, I thought about the rough hands of the carvers, who didn't know at the time they were creating art. Later, I wished I had lingered at the museum longer. It was one of only a few times on the trip that I let my eagerness to reach my destination hurry my journey.

Back in the RV, Maggie and I continued our drive along the edge of the bay, which was dotted with small islands dotted with summer homes. We passed through Stockton Springs and then Ellsworth, which historians say may have been visited by Norsemen in the days before Columbus. Ellsworth was the only city of significant size along the rest of my route, and the passing rural landscape was much as I had pictured Maine in my mind: Quaint bed and breakfasts, verdant wetlands and waterways, sailboats drifting lazily in bays, fishing boats on the water, and also dry-docked in front yards. I crossed many bridges and caught an occasional glimpse of a white-tailed deer among lush foliage.

I left Highway 1 behind at a fork in the road, and followed Highway 3 down through Trenton, which is little more than a general store, and then across one last stretch of water and onto Mount Desert. The island juts out into the Atlantic Ocean, and is home of Acadia National Park and the town of Bar Harbor. French explorer Samuel de Champlain claimed the land for France in 1604 and named it "Isles des Monts Desert," meaning island of the bare mountains. A century and a half later, France lost the island to England, which soon after lost it to the United States. None of the three gave any credence to the original inhabitants of the land, this continent's Native Americans.

For my stay on the island, I checked into the Bar Harbor Campground off Highway 3. It had a waterfront backyard, was the nearest RV Park to Acadia National Park and was only seven miles west of the town of Bar Harbor. The campground clerk told me to choose my own site when I checked in, which I did after two circuits of the large park. All the waterfront spots were taken, but I found a pleasant site surrounded by trees that offered both shade and a bit of privacy. That settled, I placed a lawn chair prominently in the site to claim it, and drove back to the office to pay for a week's stay.

The clerk told me there was a free shuttle that took one all around the area. She gave me a schedule, but since the day was fast dwindling I decided to drive myself around for my eager first look of Acadia National Park. I had been curious about this park ever since I had sailed aboard the Navy's destroyer tender, the USS Acadia. The occasion was a 1990 Tiger Cruise from Seattle to San Diego, a public relations opportunity to show parents and other loved ones how safely their sailors lived, in my case my youngest daughter. The ploy failed because shortly after we sailed out of Seattle, we heard that Iraq had invaded Kuwait. The sailors correctly assumed they would soon be sailing to Mideast Gulf waters, not the kind of thing any mother of a child in the military wanted to hear.

The activities for the guests aboard the *USS Acadia*, however, continued as planned until we reached San Diego. One of these was a Pictograph Tournament, which I and my daughter's team won. My prize was a bright red sweatshirt with the ship's name in gold lettering imprinted across the front. I still wear it on cool days.

These memories, triggered as I drove into the park, also refreshed my unanswered question of why war ships are named after national parks, as in *USS Acadia, USS Yellowstone, USS Grand Canyon, USS Yosemite*. It seems like an oxymoron. Parks are places of peace, and wars are places of hell.

My daughter, who was one of 400 women among the Acadia's 1,200-person crew, was a welder whose job entailed repairing battle ships, which females were not allowed to serve on. That gave me some bit of comfort until she wrote to me about being aboard one of the battleships when it went on full alert. She had been taken aboard the battleship via helicopter to do a bit of welding. She eventually returned home safely, which is the same happy outcome I wanted for my Blackhawk helicopter pilot son who at this time was in Iraq – and thankfully he did.

But what had started out as pleasant memories this day had now dissolved into the tumultuous concern for him that was as much a part of my journey as the passing scenery. I recognized, yet again, that worrying wouldn't change anything, and was not what my son wanted. I forced my attention back to my surroundings and Mother Nature's bounties, and by the time I had reached the park's Hulls Cove Visitor Center, the lushness of the roadside trees, which were just barely beginning to change into their autumn colors, and the cheerfulness of pastel purple asters along the roadside, had put me in a more cheerful frame of mind.

I watched the standard 15-minute film that national park visitor centers usually feature, and which I always view to get an overview of any new park I visit. I learned that Acadia had been designated a national park in 1916 by Woodrow Wilson. It was known then as Lafayette National Park after the Frenchman Marquis de Lafayette, who supported our side during the American Revolution. It was the first park created east of the Mississippi, and today is still New England's only national park.

Its name was changed in 1929 because an English land donor didn't like the French name. That it was named Acadia, however, is kind of ironic. According to a book on the meaning of baby names, *Acadia* is also a French word, although appropriate for the park. The word means *paradise* or *Eden*.

Acadia owes a debt of gratitude for its beginnings to wealthy philanthropist John D. Rockefeller and his family. The roadways that meander through the public land, along with the 17 granite bridges that cross the park's many streams, began as carriage trails built by Rockefeller between 1915 and 1933; and when a deadly 1947 fire devastated 25 percent of the island, the park's restoration was financed by the Rockefeller family.

Over 60 mansions destroyed in that fire were also rebuilt. Many of them are popular tourist stops today, some serving as lodging accommodations for the thousands of visitors to Mount Desert. I viewed some of the cliff-edge mansions from water level the next day during a nature tour of Frenchmen Bay aboard the *Acadian*. Our boat guide, Chuck, pointed them out as we cruised below.

The tour included a close-up of Egg Rock Lighthouse located near the bay's sea entrance. Built in 1875, the lighthouse had a keeper until 1966, when automation took over. The lighthouse, however, was only partially effective as ships continued to slam themselves against offshore rocks through the years. After hearing the tale of an 1899 Christmas Eve incident, I was reminded of more recent ship disasters. The fishing boat *Julia Ann*, which had run aground that long ago winter day, resulted in the drowning of two men. Heber Sawyer, lighthouse keeper at the time, noted in his logbook that the crewmen were "undoubtedly drunk."

Everything was peaceful around the lighthouse this day, with the tiny island being claimed by harbor seals lazing in clumpy packs on the beach and rocks. More energetic were the harbor porpoises that splashed about our boat as our captain dodged the small colorful buoys that bobbed atop the water. Beneath each of these buoys was a lobster trap whose ownership was designated by the colors of the attached buoy. Only lobsters of a middling size are allowed to be kept, and the traps are designed to help with that. Too big lobsters supposedly can't get into the specially designed traps, while those too small can get out. Even so, fishermen have to carefully measure their catches to make sure they meet the size requirement for harvesting. The size regulations and the bay's cold, clean water, are what keep Maine's lobster population viable and prized, our guide bragged. I personally gave the lobsters thumbs up when I gobbled down a boiled lunch of them at one of the bay-side restaurants after the boat tour ended.

Details of the lobster industry were all new and fascinating knowledge for me, and it became even more fascinating after I read Linda Greenlaw's book, *The Lobster Chronicles*. I picked the book up in a Bar Harbor book store on the recommendation of the *Acadian*'s guide. Greenlaw, a rare female lobsterman, was the boat captain who warned Captain Billy Tyne (portrayed by George Clooney in the true-life movie, *The Perfect Storm*) of the danger he was facing by not seeking a safe harbor.

The *Acadian* nature cruise also added four new life birds to my growing list. While satisfying, it was far less than I would have seen if I had made it to Bar Harbor two weeks earlier. I was now paying for all the dawdling I had done at the start of the journey. Familiar with a Texas summer that often lingers well into October, or even December, I now knew a New England autumn comes in August, with winter quickly behind. Many of the birds I wanted to see were already heading south to warmer climes. The ones that were still around included my lifers: common eiders, great cormorants, great black-backed gulls and black guillemots. The guillemots were already wearing their gray and white winter plumage, but because of molting feathers couldn't fly at this time.

The only other lifer I would find on Mount Desert would be a black-billed cuckoo at the RV park. The cuckoo, my 486th life bird, showed itself every time I waited for the shuttle bus, as did a tiny pine warbler, which I had seen many times before. But here at this campground was the first for the trip.

After that first day, I always took the shuttle when I wanted to go someplace on the island. Its environmentally friendly convenience was an amenity that alone should have given Bar Harbor a five-star rating in any travel guide. There was also never a lack of things to see and do while I was on the island, even a bonus for being there so late in the season. I got to watch Maine's fabulous fall, observing each day as more and more of the foliage around me exploded with color.

Acadia National Park was also full of natural wonders to explore. One of these was Cadillac Mountain, the highest summit on the East Coast north of Rio de Janeiro, and the first spot in the mainland states to be hit by the morning sun. I was on its summit one dawn to catch that first ray of rosy light. I laughed, but to myself, when one guy standing nearby spotted a herring gull and got all excited because he thought he had seen a bald eagle. He could have been me a few years earlier. No reason, I thought, to extinguish his excitement; and later in the day I did see a bald eagle soaring over the park. I hoped the guy who misidentified the gull saw it too.

Cadillac, with a road going right up to its summit, is named for French adventurer Antoine Laumet de La Mothe, sieur de Cadillac, founder of Detroit, Michigan, and the governor of Louisiana from 1710-1716. The Cadillac vehicle is also named for him.

Another of my favorite spots in the park was Thunder Hole, into which incoming tides are squeezed and expelled with a boom. Watchers on the cliff eagerly await the show. The boom and whoosh of air and water varies with the size of each wave that forces itself into a small cavern beneath the cliff. I watched six small exhibitions before one large whoosh sprinkled those of us standing on the lower steps of the walkway overlooking the hole. Once again, I was experiencing my travels by getting wet.

For my last day on Mount Desert, I had booked a whale-watching excursion aboard the *Acadian's* sister ship, the *Atlanticat*. Sadly, the trip was canceled because of rough seas. Instead I took a trolley tour of the island. Our guide was full of facts and trivia, such as President William Howard Taft's 27 strokes on the Kebo Valley Golf Club's 17th hole back in 1910, and the fact that scenes for the Dark Shadows TV soap opera had occasionally been filmed on Mount Desert. I had already seen much of what the tour covered, but enjoyed the guide's chatter – and the scenery was well worth a second look.

Back in town at the shuttle stop, I watched two women trimming hedges on the village green. To check out their work, they walked to the other side of the street for an overall look. Their actions struck me as what should be a life axiom. Sometimes we need to stand back a way and look at the whole picture. There were many times in my life that I'm sure I would have made better decisions if I had done just that.

BIRDS ALONG THE WAY:
American crow, mourning dove, turkey vulture, eastern phoebe,
sharp-shinned hawk, ring-billed gull, herring gull,
black-capped chickadee, *pine warbler, cedar waxwing,
brown-headed cowbird, **black-billed cuckoo, rock pigeon,
**great black-backed gull, double crested cormorant,
*bald eagle, **black guillemot, **common eider,
**great cormorant, laughing gull, great blue heron,
American goldfinch, yellow-rumped warbler,
downy woodpecker and blue jay.

*First sighting of this bird on the journey.
**A lifer

THE JOURNEY

CAMPGROUND:
Bar Harbor Campground
Bar Harbor, Maine

Maine

CAMPGROUND:
Paul Bunyan Campground
Bangor, Maine

"The journey itself

is my home."

— BASHO MATSUO

24
STRONG WOMEN AND PAUL BUNYAN

My motor home needed its 3,000-mile oil change, and Bangor, 60 miles up the road from Mount Desert, appeared to be the nearest place I could get it done. I had earlier driven into Ellsworth from Mount Desert to do it, but had failed to find a shop that could accommodate my RV.

What I had found in Ellsworth was a place to do my laundry, a place to buy new tennis shoes and a great lunch at Martha's Cafe. I ordered the crab and cheddar quiche and it melted in my mouth. The friendly waitress also recommended the blueberry-chocolate cheesecake. I couldn't resist, but had it boxed up to take home for later. I also decided to get a haircut while I was in town and asked the waitress for a recommendation.

"Right next door," she said. And so it was.

I got my hair cut by an attractive, chatty woman in her 30s who told me she was recently divorced and now buying a house on her own. To make ends meet she was working a second job as a night bartender.

"I make people look good during the day and make them feel good at night," she quipped.

I laughed at her remark, and thought about how often on this journey I had met strong independent women who had become that way after suffering hardship. An easy life, which is a rare oddity in any case, isn't always the best one. What's important is how we play out our lives when the thunder bolt strikes, be it as an adult who survived an abusive childhood, a cheating boyfriend or a destructive hurricane. I've seen women, and men too, get stuck in a time trap of their worst moments while they let the best of life pass them by. And then there are women like this hairdresser/bartender who makes the best of what life threw at her, and was now moving on to better things. I smiled at her chatter, and at my new haircut in the mirror. Life, for the moment, was perfect.

Today's drive took me once again through Ellsworth, where I jogged north on Highway 1A, which passed by several small lakes and through the nondescript towns of Dedham and Holden. Once in Bangor, I once again let life simply pass by for a few days.

Bangor was once the lumber capital of the world, which is probably why its downtown is home to a 31-foot tall statue of the mythical lumberjack Paul Bunyan. Not quite as tall as Dallas' Big Tex, I noted, but then Big Tex has never been fictionalized by horror novelist Stephen King. The sometimes Bangor resident brought the Bunyan statue to life in "IT," a bit of trivia I learned from RoadsideAmerica.com since horror is the one genre of books and movies I don't read or watch.

I stayed in Bangor's Paul Bunyan Campground for five days. It was an opportunity for my mail to catch up with me, and provided a break after my week of non-stop sight-seeing around Acadia National Park and Bar Harbor. Except for one trip downtown, during which I got my RV serviced and gawked at the Paul Bunyan statue, I never left the rustic campground.

I watched as fall rushed into Maine, waking each morning to an overhead maple tree that was brighter red than the day before, the trill of a chickadee, and the squawky voice of a blue jay checking out recently deserted camp sites for anything the occupants might have left behind. My frequent strolls with Maggie around the park took me past a small pond, dubbed Babe's bathtub in honor of Bunyan's blue ox. The pond was also visible from my RV windows, and through them I daily watched a great blue heron visit the pond's shoreline in the early afternoons. On one of our walks, a knocking sound alerted me to a nearby woodpecker. I found him hanging out in a tall fir tree. It was a hairy woodpecker, looking much like the black and white downy woodpecker that I had seen often on the journey, except this bird was a bit bigger and had a bill as long as his head. The downy's bill is only half as long as its head. I knew this bird was a Mr. Woodpecker by the spot of red on the back of his head, which the female hairy woodpecker lacks.

"It's peaceful here," I wrote in my journal, and not much else.

The one blight on my stay in Bangor was news of the death of Ann Richards, Texas' feisty former governor. She was one of those independent women who served my generation as role models. She was also a woman born with the same git-up-and-go attitude of two other Texas women I admired: the sharp-tongued columnist Molly Ivins and Texas' first Black female senator, Barbara Jordan. I had grieved Jordan's passing in 1996, and did the same now for Richards. As a working journalist, I had heard all three women speak, but I had actually had an informal conversation with Molly.

The year was 1984, and I was regional editor at the Times News in Twin Falls, Idaho. My managing editor had gone to school with Ivins and had invited her to speak at a gathering of area journalists. I don't remember what she said, although I do remember she had me bent over with laughter with her wry clips about life and politicians. What I remember most was sitting in my editor's living room having a drink with her afterwards.

I can still picture that scene vividly in my mind. Molly was wearing a full-circled cowgirl skirt with a wild pattern design that was draped across the cowboy boots on feet, which were propped up on an ottoman. In her hand was a Jack and Coke, which she sipped between deep-throated chuckles as she talked about her life. It's a rich warm memory I treasure. Molly was still alive when I was in Bangor, and would be for another year. It was Richards who dominated my thoughts now. She wasn't perfect and her faults were often aired in public. But unlike some, she never hid from them or from her mistakes either.

"I have very strong feelings about how you lead your life. You look ahead, you never look back," Richards said. The quote, as so many others made by people with something meaningful to say, found its way into my journal. Looking ahead was good advice for someone traveling down the road facing oncoming traffic, or just anyone waking up in the morning to an unknown day.

I don't think the maple tree above my head could have gotten any brighter by the time I decided to hit the road again. I might have lingered longer in the peaceful place, if not that in my search for campgrounds for the journey ahead, I discovered they were all beginning to close down for the winter. Like the birds, it was time for me to head south, where RV parks don't close for the winter.

BIRDS ALONG THE WAY:
American crow, black-capped chickadee, American goldfinch,
yellow-rumped warbler, downy woodpecker, mourning dove,
herring gull, great blue heron, double-crested cormorant,
ring-billed gull, American robin, mallard, Canada goose,
*hairy woodpecker.

*First sighting of this species on the journey.

THE JOURNEY

CAMPGROUND:
Paul Bunyan Campground
Bangor, Maine

Maine

CAMPGROUND:
Wassamki Springs
Campground
Scarborough,
Maine

"If travel is like love,
it is … mostly because it's a
heightened state of awareness,
in which we are mindful,
receptive, undimmed by
familiarity and ready to be
transformed. That is why
the best trips, like the
best love affairs,
never really end."

– PICO IYER
Why We Travel

25
IT'S A LOG ... OR A MOOSE

On leaving Bangor, I continued on Highway 1A, which made a U-turn in Bangor and followed the Penobscot River south to Penobscot Bay at Stockton Springs. This city was originally only called Stockton; the Springs was added when the former lumber and sawmill town had hopes of bottling water and selling it. Sediment in the water, however, dashed those hopes.

From Stockton Springs, I retraced my way back to Belfast, where I took Highway 1 south to Rockport. There seemed to be a sameness to the small towns I was passing, not surprising since the word of the day was port: Winterport, Bucksport, Northport and Rockport. And port was what they all were.

Highway 1 turned appropriately inland at Rockland and made its way over bridges through numerous, sometimes almost non-existent towns, to Brunswick, once the home of *Uncle Tom's Cabin* author, Harriet Beecher Stowe.

The next city of note was Portland, Maine's largest city with a population of about 65,000. Portland's motto is "I will rise again," and the city's seal depicts a phoenix rising from the ashes. It's a theme that fits the city perfectly as it survived four devastating fires during its nearly 400-year history. Portland's founder was English naval Captain Christopher Levett, who was granted 6,000 acres of land in the New World by King Charles I. After building himself a stone house and leaving some of his men behind, Levett returned to England and wrote a book about his adventures. I wondered what the landscape had looked like in Levitt's time, and while I was doing that, I got lost on my way to the Wassamki Springs Campground, which I knew was located somewhere near Portland. I had reservations at the campground for two nights. Eventually I arrived at my destination.

Wassamki was a large park with ongoing activities that included hayrides, horseshoe tournaments and pancake breakfasts to accommodate the many regulars who came each year, and stayed the summer. But two-thirds of the RV-ers had already vacated the place when I arrived. The activities reflected this, having been pared down to Bingo and ice cream socials, which I was invited to attend after being assigned a choice lakeside camp site.

After dinner and the nightly walk with Maggie, I decided to play Bingo. It was a good opportunity to meet some of my RV-ing neighbors. While I never win at Bingo, I usually hit the jackpot on meeting new and interesting people, some of whom are quite lucky at this game of chance. Perhaps there are Bingo gods they pray to, like I've prayed to the river gods before rafting through some hair-raising rapids. I tried never to offend those gods, as did one woman in our annual rafting group. Just before taking a wild white-water ride down the Snake River, she proudly claimed: "I've never come out of a boat." She did that trip – twice.

Evidently at some time in my life I had offended the Bingo gods.

I found the Bingo players a congenial group, with apparent long-standing friendships among them. Usually in such a group there's someone who goes out of their way to make outsiders feel welcome. The kind hospitality came this night from a cheery, long-time married couple. They were quite pleasant company, but sadly it was a one-night stand between us. They were leaving Wassamki Springs for their home in Boston the next morning. I, meanwhile, would linger beyond the two nights I had planned, despite the costly camping fee. Like the just-right size lobsters, Maine's beauty had trapped me.

I blame my decision to stay longer on the moose I saw outside my window when I was having coffee the next morning. At first I thought it was a log floating in the misty lake. But as the object came closer it grew antlers, large ones that spread out across the top of its head. I snapped several pictures quickly through my RV window then went out to watch as the moose swam to a nearby spit of sand about 30 yards from my RV.

By now, there were several other campers watching the animal with me. The moose lumbered through the campground, and then finally back into the forest that fenced the rear of the property. Living each day with the outdoors as my backyard is the best part of being a full-time RV-er, and Wassamki Springs was one of the best backyards I had discovered on my journeys. How could I leave it behind after only two days? It just didn't seem right.

I kept mostly to myself for the rest of the stay, doing little but enjoying the surroundings and admonishing Maggie each time she barked at a fluffy white poodle prancing past my RV with her hand-holding, gray-haired owners. They were the perfect picture of a couple who had been happily married for 50 years. I discovered otherwise at a sundae social the evening before I got back on the road. While devouring butter pecan ice cream topped with chocolate syrup and a generous pillow of whipped cream, I learned that the poodle-walking couple was newlyweds.

Oh how we love to stereotype!

While many of the area's migrant birds had already headed south. I did get one new species for the trip, a semipalmated plover.

About half a dozen of these small shorebirds were pecking around on the sandy spit where the moose had exited the lake. I watched them through my RV window with my binoculars for about 10 minutes before they flew off, spreading their tiny wings and orange legs in unison. It always amazes me how a flock of birds appear to have one brain when they spring into the air at the same instance.

BIRDS ALONG THE WAY:
American crow, black-capped chickadee, American goldfinch,
yellow-rumped warbler, downy woodpecker, mourning dove,
herring gull, great blue heron, double-crested cormorant,
ring-billed gull, American robin, mallard,
*Semipalmated plover and Canada goose.
*First sighting of this species on the journey.

THE JOURNEY

Maine

CAMPGROUND:
Wassamki Springs
Campground
Scarborough,
Maine

*"Twenty years from now you
will be more disappointed by
the things you didn't do than by
the ones you did do. So throw
off the bowlines, sail away from
the safe harbor. Catch the trade
winds in your sails. Explore.
Dream. Discover."*

– MARK TWAIN

Massachusetts

CAMPGROUND:
Black Bear Campground,
which I abandoned,
and Russnik Campground,
Salisbury, Massachusetts.

26

SCARBOROUGH MARSH, BAD VIBES AND BOSTON

The mallards in the lake near my RV had their butts in the air with their heads beneath the water in search of breakfast when I finally forced myself away from Wassamki Springs, and back to heading south on Highway 1. Despite their snub, I told myself I would have to come back one day and visit them for an entire summer.

Maggie, happy as always to once again be driving down the road, gave the mallards a passing glance, then yawned and gave me that wake-me-when-we-get-there look. She was still sleeping a short time later when I pulled into a parking lot at the edge of Scarborough Marsh. The hand-holding newlyweds had told me it was a great place to see birds.

I grabbed my binoculars, jacket and camera and left Maggie sleeping in the co-pilot seat while I went off to explore. A wooden boardwalk took me through the middle of a salt water marsh, past islands of grass surrounded by patches of water, and here and there tall stands of phragmites. Green-turning-gold-turning-red leaves on a few birch trees shimmered in the sunlight, while a splash of white and yellow daisies, entwined with bright red balls of rose hips, formed a playful pattern on the landscape. In the distance a belted kingfisher sat on a lone stump in a golden field of waving grasses. I captured the colorful and lively images with my camera, although I doubted I would need the images to remember this vivid marsh.

A bounteous haven for wildlife, Scarborough Marsh was created thousands of years ago when icebergs advanced and retreated across the land, leaving behind a depression into which the ocean crept. I had only meant to hike about a mile, but the marsh was filled with egrets, gulls, doves, chickadees, sparrows, robins, kingfishers and jays that kept luring me on just a little farther. Repeatedly!

The best bird-sighting of the day was an American bittern, which I almost missed. Although standing two-feet tall, the bird's streaky brown feathers and its reach-to-the sky stance camouflage it quite neatly among its favored habitat of reeds. I wouldn't have seen the bird at all if it hadn't quickly reached down to snatch a tidbit from the waterlogged ground. It was the 82nd bird species for my trip list.

It was with regret that I finally retraced my way back to the RV. Maggie looked up at me as I settled in the driver's seat. I don't think she had stirred while I was gone, but now she appeared to lazily ask: Did I miss anything?

"A grand morning hike," I replied aloud, patting her head before I put the key back in the ignition. She was asleep again almost immediately. I had evidently started the day too early for her liking.

Soon I was following Highway 9 that paralleled the ocean. The route took me past Old Orchard Beach, originally named "Garden by the Sea" by Thomas Rogers, who was one of the original Mayflower settlers. It turned out to be no garden for poor Rogers; he died during that first harsh winter suffered by the Pilgrims. Today the town is a mecca for summer tourists who stay away during its colder months.

At Ferry Beach State Park, named for an old ferry that once took passengers across the Saco River, I had to detour inland a few miles to cross a bridge between Saco, pronounced Sock-oh, and Biddeford, a large tourist town full of strip malls. I then followed the south side of the river back to the beach, where I weaved through several small seaside towns with quaint touristy structures. I said good-bye to Maine in the town of Kittery, and hello to New Hampshire in Portsmouth, pronounced Ports-smith by the locals. These two border cities share historic ship-building pasts and lump themselves together today in advertising their seaside tourist amenities.

New Hampshire's relationship with the Atlantic Ocean is only a small strip of land about 20 miles wide that interjects itself between Maine and Massachusetts. After leaving Portsmouth, it was only about half an hour before I found myself in Massachusetts, my third state for the day. I stopped in the town of Salisbury, which I planned to make my base for exploring Boston. My son, Michael, was going to join me the next day for the adventure, or so I expected. But soon after I got hooked up at my chosen campground, I got a call from him. His work schedule had been changed and he couldn't get into Boston until a few days later.

"No problem," I replied. "I can hang around here until then." But I soon decided I couldn't hang "here." The campground gave me the heebie jeebies, the only time I had them during the entire trip. I had absolutely no concrete reason why, but the feeling was strong enough that when I went exploring the next day, I searched out another Salisbury RV park and checked in, forfeiting the cost of my second night at the creepy campground.

The new park was $8 a night cheaper, so in the long run I recouped my loss. More importantly, it felt like I was where I should be. Almost immediately I was swept into a circle of single women who made the park their summer retreat. Two of the women invited me to go into Portsmouth that night to play Bingo with them. Ready for company again, I accepted the invitation. It was a fun evening – but of course I didn't win.

The next morning while walking Maggie, I bumped into Dick and Kathy, a couple from Chicago who were also walking their dog. It was a black cocker that could have been Maggie's twin sister; she was named Maggie, too. While I'm ambiguous about the thing people call fate, this just seemed one more reason why I had been right to change campgrounds. My Maggie agreed. She allowed the other cocker to actually sniff her butt in normal doggie greeting, an action she rarely allows without an immediate 180-degree turn and a snarly growl that I translate as meaning: *Hey! I'm not that kind of girl.*

When I mentioned to Dick and Kathy that I planned on taking the train into Boston the next day to sightsee, the couple replied they were doing that as well, and they invited me to accompany them. Since they appeared to be responsible pet owners, I deduced they were also people of good character, and readily accepted their offer.

I discovered they were also people with a sense of humor after we missed the train the next day morning – even though we had arrived at the station early. The three of us watched our ride to Boston pull out before we realized that the same train that came from Boston went back to Boston. We had two options: Curse and wait 30 minutes for the next train, or laugh and wait 30 minutes for the next train. We all three laughed. Dick and Kathy were truly my kind of people.

The rest of the day was flawless. We spent it checking out historic sites along the Freedom Trail, a two and a half mile walk that starts at the Boston Commons and travels through town past historic sites and across the Charles River to Bunker Hill. We picked up the footprint-marked path near the train station and the Copps Hill Burying Ground.

With my background in editing, I got a big kick out of the sign near its entrance that explained the Copps family settled on the hill to be protected from "woolves, rattle-snakes and musketos." The cemetery dated back to 1660, with the oldest headstone, that of William Copps, dated 1661. Maybe it stood over William's grave, and maybe not. A second sign explained that some of the gravestones had been moved in 1883 to allow paths to be created, and that many of the stones did not mark their owners' resting places, a detail I thought would provide an interesting plot for an episode of TV's *Ghost Whisperer.*

Among the other highlights along Boston's narrow streets this day were visits to the Old North Church and Paul Revere's home. I had once read that Boston's crooked streets trace their lineage back to ancestral cow paths. That bit of trivia just might be true I decided, as we weaved through the town. To be able to see and touch what I had often read about in books boggled my mind. History truly came to life this day for me.

While I didn't forget to look for birds along the walk, pigeons and sparrows, were all I saw. The only memorable sighting was that of a house sparrow perched in the outstretched hand of a weathered statue of St. Francis, patron saint of animals. It was the place, and not the bird itself, that made the sighting significant.

When stomachs began to grumble, the three of us stopped for lunch at a little Italian place called Mama Maria's. The food was good but our elderly and wrinkled waiter was grumpy. He reminded me of the character Fish played by Abe Vigoda in the old "Barney Miller" police sitcom. I wouldn't have wanted to have been waited on by anyone else.

After lunch, we continued our walk along the trail but stopped short of reaching the Commons. We still wanted to visit the *USS Constitution*, and since time was running out we retraced our steps back to Copps Hill, and then across the Charlestown Bridge to the ship's docking place. We were just in time to catch the last tour for the day. The all-wooden ship, built in 1797 of sturdy oak, is nicknamed "Old Ironsides" because cannonballs once bounced off its sides. The oldest commissioned vessel still afloat, the *Constitution* garnered fame during the War of 1812 after defeating five English war ships.

Our young, blond sailor-guide, one of a crew of 60 active-duty Navy personnel assigned to the ship, was full of facts, figures and tall tales about his subject.

After the tour, the three of us meandered through the ship's museum for a while, then caught the train back to our RV park in Salisbury, where Dick and Kathy pulled out the next morning for their return to Chicago while I stayed on awaiting my son's arrival.

BIRDS ALONG THE WAY:
Mallard, American crow, herring gull, double-crested cormorant,
ring-billed gull, savannah sparrow, belted kingfisher, great egret,
blue jay, *American bittern, mourning dove, American robin,
black-capped chickadee, rock pigeon, chipping sparrow,
great black-backed gull and house sparrow.
*First sighting of this species on the journey.

THE JOURNEY

CAMPGROUND:
Russnik Campground,
Salisbury, Massachusetts

Massachusetts

"Live life fully while you're here.
Experience everything ...
Have fun, be crazy, be weird.
Go out and screw up! You're
going to anyway, so you might as
well enjoy the process ... just be
an example of being human."

— TONY ROBBINS

LOGAN
INTERNATIONAL
AIRPORT

27
HELP! MY RV'S LOST AT THE AIRPORT

When my son Mike called with details of his arrival, he said he would take the train from the airport to Salisbury. I insisted, however, that the rush hour traffic wouldn't bother me, and that I would pick him up at the airport. It would, I said, give us more time together since he only had the next day to spend with me. I was right in that the traffic didn't bother me, but losing my RV in the airport parking lot was something I hadn't planned on, nor was the fiasco that happened even before that.

My drive to Boston's Logan International Airport went way faster than I had suspected, and not wanting to just continue driving around and around until Mike's plane landed, I decided to find a place to park. One option was the airport's enclosed parking spaces, which I would normally have nixed except for a sign at one of its entrances that said "12-foot clearance," a full foot and a half taller than my small RV.

What the sign didn't say was that the 12-foot clearance section was set apart from the rest of the huge underground parking area. I missed that information. Almost immediately on entering the parking structure, I heard a gruff voice yelling "Stop! Stop! Stop!" The shouting actually wasn't necessary as I had already realized I couldn't go forward another foot before doing serious damage to the roof of my vehicle.

The guy, who had shouted, once he knew I wasn't going to continue forward, was actually quite nice. I suspect I wasn't the first dummy he had yelled at. He helped me back up my RV and get it turned around in the right direction to enter the oversized vehicle section of the parking structure.

After parking the RV and telling Maggie to "guard the castle," I walked through a maze of vehicles to Terminal C, where Mike's flight was arriving. Because of the fiasco, I didn't have long to wait before the two of us, after joyful hugs, were headed back to my RV. Somewhere along the way back, reminiscent of my directional skills when driving, I zigged when I should have zagged. The two of us were soon hopelessly lost in the dim cement maze. The train Mike would have taken might have gotten him to Salisbury quicker than it took us to find my vehicle. When we finally did, Maggie greeted Mike enthusiastically, and then gave me one of her easily translated looks: Well it sure took you long enough.

Early the next morning Mike and I caught the commuter train back to Boston, where we started our day of sightseeing at the Boston Commons. Walking through its 50 acres of landscaped gardens and gurgling fountains pushed all thoughts of the previous afternoon's fiasco from my mind. While the statue of George Washington on a horse added dignity to the meandering, those of a strutting mama duck followed by her eight ducklings, and those of the frog statues guarding Frog Pond, kept the mood playful.

Afterwards, we strolled through the nearby Granary Burying Ground with its weathered headstones, which this day were being rained on by gold and red leaves from the autumn-clad trees. The cemetery was the final resting place of three signers of the Declaration of Independence: Samuel Adams, Robert Paine and John Hancock, whose sprawling penmanship has become a byword for anyone's signature. Among the graves were also those of Benjamin Franklin's parents and that of Elizabeth Foster, the woman who is suspected of being America's Mother Goose. She had a penchant for fairy tales and story-telling, and since she married a widower with children named Isaac Goose, she became known as Mother Goose.

For lunch, Mike and I walked across the street to the Beantown Pub, where he ordered the sandwich named for Paul Revere and I the one called Mother Goose. Our stomachs sated with the large sandwiches, we then took the subway to the Boston Museum of Fine Arts. As in St. Louis, it had lots of the Old Masters' paintings on exhibit. This time, encouraged by Mike's enjoyment of them, I tried to look with a more open mind, and actually found things about them I enjoyed, particularly the Dutch masterpieces. A tour guide I overheard should have kept the same open mind.

While comparing two paintings, she haughtily explained why one of them was far superior to the other. Personally, I liked the rejected painting better. Although agitated, and with a desire to lecture the woman about the value of art being in the eyes of the beholder, I properly – this was Boston after all – kept my thoughts to myself.

Still thinking about the incident on the train ride back to Salisbury, I concluded that the art critic's superior attitude was an analogy for what's causing so much turmoil in today's world. Too many people believe their choices in art, politics, religion, or whatever, are the only right ones. The truth is that the choices are usually only different, not right or wrong. What a boring world it would be if we all thought alike.

The next day Mike insisted on taking the train to the airport for his trip back to Chicago. I didn't have to ask why.

BIRDS ALONG THE WAY:
Only rock pigeons and house sparrows, but then perhaps I was too preoccupied otherwise to look much.

THE JOURNEY

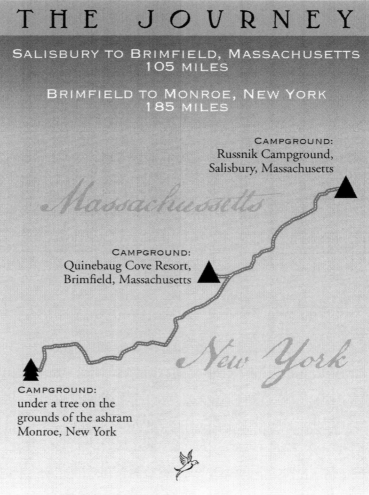

CAMPGROUND:
Russnik Campground,
Salisbury, Massachusetts

CAMPGROUND:
Quinebaug Cove Resort,
Brimfield, Massachusetts

CAMPGROUND:
under a tree on the
grounds of the ashram
Monroe, New York

"Men go abroad to wonder at the heights of mountains, at the huge waves of the sea, at the long courses of the rivers, at the vast compass of the ocean, at the circular motions of the stars, and they pass by themselves without wondering."

— SAINT AUGUSTINE

28

AN EMBARRASSING MOMENT
AND A HUG FROM A GRANDDAUGHTER

From Salisbury, I followed Highway 1 to Interstate 95 that took me on the western outskirts of Boston, and through the tentacles of a mass of suburbs that surrounded Beantown. It was with relief when I hit Highway 20, where I could once again see the personality of the landscape. According to the green dots along the route on my map, I would be following a scenic byway all the way to Brimfield, Massachusetts.

The drive took me through the small town of Weston, with its big homes and large green lawns, and the larger town of Marlborough, where Horatio Alger Jr. graduated from high school in 1847. As a youngster, I was an avid reader of his juvenile rags to riches books, of which he wrote about a hundred. He was also the cause of one of my most embarrassing journalistic moments. It happened in the early 1980s when I was features editor at the Standard-Examiner in Ogden, Utah.

Alger's books were going through a rebirth at the time, and one of them, *Ragged Dick*, was being made into a play. The headline I wrote for the story was "Alger's 'Ragged Dick' comes to life again." The paper came out at noon, and by 3 p.m. I was being kidded unmercifully. I finally shouted: "I can't work and think dirty at the same time." I think there are some bulletin boards around Ogden that still have that newspaper article clipped to it.

Remembering this incident had me giggling to myself and Maggie all the way to the town of Auburn, where Robert Goddard launched the first liquid-fueled rocket from his Aunt Effie's farm in 1926. A city park named after the rocket scientist commemorates the event. Both a model of Goddard's rocket and a Polaris Ballistic Missile are on display there.

On display in the next town, Charlton, is the grave site and tombstone of Grizzly Adams, a California mountain man who toward the end of his 48 years of life performed with his bears for the P.T. Barnum Circus. Barnum is said to have paid for Adams' tombstone, which features the etching of Adams and a pet bear.

The day's drive was pleasant, but with more traffic than I preferred. My own thoughts evidently occupied my time more than sightseeing. The only notes I made of the drive were of the few birds I saw along the way, which included a flock of wild turkeys along a less congested stretch of Highway 20 west of Boston. They were the 83rd bird species for my trip.

Of the Quinebaug Cove Campground in Brimfield, Massachusetts, where I caught up on laundry and spent the night, I simply noted that it had no Internet service and that I had to walk up a hill to use the phone to let my guardian angel daughter-in-law know I was settled for the night and safe.

I think my mind was already occupied with my next stop, which would be Monroe, New York, where I was going to meet up with Shanna, the oldest of my eight granddaughters. Shanna actually lived in New York City, but at the time she was staying at a yoga ashram in Monroe, where she was recuperating from a broken cheek bone that happened when she fell out of a top bunk bed. I remembered her doing the exact same thing when she was a young kid, but without breaking anything. I guess adult bones are more fragile than eight-year-old bones.

The next day, I took a zig-zagging route from Brimfield through Connecticut to New York. It took a lot of determination, but I did manage to escape the heavier traveled highways for most of the day's 185-mile drive. I saw little to distinguish the towns I passed, and for the second day in a row I made few notes in my journal. The one Connecticut town of interest was Hazardville, which was named after Col. Augustus George Hazard. It could, however, have also been named for the adjective hazard as the town began life about 1835 as a village devoted to the manufacture of gunpowder. During the Civil War, its main industry, the Hazard Powder Co., operated in 125 buildings, utilized 25 water wheels and produced up to 12,500 pounds of gun powder daily for the Union Army. Yup! You guessed it. A major explosion in 1913 resulted in the plant finally being shut down.

My travel senses finally came fully awake when I crossed the Connecticut River on Highway 66's Arrigoni Bridge. The bridge is Connecticut's longest, and the river it flows over is New England's largest. When the Arrigoni was opened to traffic in 1938, it won the title of America's most beautiful steel bridge.

Just as impressive was my crossing of the Hudson River in New York, which I did on New York's Bear Mountain Bridge. Once across, I found myself on the Palisades Parkway (Highway 6) driving through Bear Mountain and Harriman state parks. The scenery here was dressed in its best autumn finery. While still eager to get to my destination, Mother Nature demanded my attention. Who was I to ignore her wishes? I stopped for a while in Harriman State Park, which sat on both sides of Highway 6. Maggie and I forgot about traffic and everything else as we let Mother Nature take us to her bosom.

Maggie's reward was that she got to try to irritate a couple of squirrels. Mine was the sighting of two awesome woodpeckers, a red-headed and a pileated. One had a pure red head; the other was a giant of a bird over a foot tall with a red flaring crest. The pileated woodpecker was a new species for the trip, which made me glad I had taken the time to stop. Once again, I was reminded not to miss the journey – even when there's a beloved granddaughter waiting at the destination.

Soon, however, I was back on the road, and soon after that I was at the yoga ashram, where I was welcomed with a big hug from Shanna. I was glad to see that Shanna was recuperating from her fall quite well. Except for a tiny bit of swelling on one cheek, Shanna's face was as beautiful as ever, which I later reported to her worried mother who had asked me for a personal report. Shanna, meanwhile, introduced me to her friends at the ashram, and after sharing a communal dinner with them I felt right at home.

After the meal, a couple of her girlfriends came back with Shanna and me to my RV, where we spent the evening in girl talk that transcended the age gap. The three young women seemed fascinated by my travel adventures while I was awed by their busy lives so lacking the restrictions placed on young girls of my generation.

BIRDS ALONG THE WAY:
Double-crested cormorant, *wild turkeys,
black-capped chickadee, tufted titmouse, rock pigeons,
chipping sparrow, American crow, blue jay, great blue heron,
house sparrow, red-headed woodpecker, *pileated woodpecker,
yellow-rumped warbler and mallard.

*First sighting of this species on the journey.

THE JOURNEY

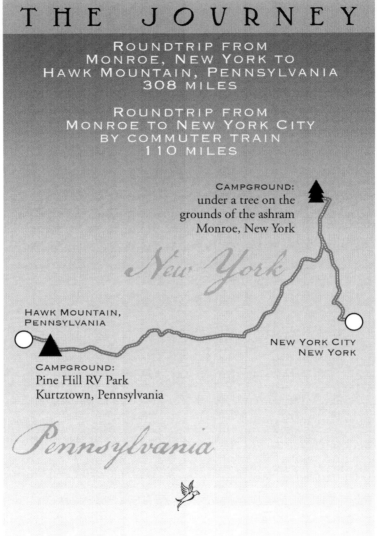

ROUNDTRIP FROM
MONROE, NEW YORK TO
HAWK MOUNTAIN, PENNSYLVANIA
308 MILES

ROUNDTRIP FROM
MONROE TO NEW YORK CITY
BY COMMUTER TRAIN
110 MILES

CAMPGROUND:
under a tree on the
grounds of the ashram
Monroe, New York

New York

HAWK MOUNTAIN,
PENNSYLVANIA

NEW YORK CITY
NEW YORK

CAMPGROUND:
Pine Hill RV Park
Kurtztown, Pennsylvania

Pennsylvania

"To travel hopefully is a better thing

than to arrive."

– ROBERT LOUIS STEVENSON

29
HAWK MOUNTAIN AND THE BIG APPLE

The next morning, with Shanna doing well but still off work for the rest of the week, we set out for nearby Hawk Mountain Sanctuary in Pennsylvania. Maggie was visibly annoyed to lose her co-pilot seat. She insisted on sitting on Shanna's lap at first, but then retreated to the floor between us to nap. Every time Shanna vacated her seat, however, Maggie claimed it back in a blur, and acted pained when she had to vacate it again.

The visit to Hawk Mountain, one of the Blue Mountain ridges in the Appalachian chain, had been on my agenda from the beginning of the journey because of the vast number of migrating hawks that fly over it every autumn. Now, I had the bonus of both visiting it, and time to become reacquainted with a granddaughter I hadn't seen in several years.

So, with Shanna, a non-stop talker, chattering away pleasantly in the co-pilot seat, and with Maggie napping or giving my granddaughter a "you're sitting in my seat" stare, the time it took to drive the 112 miles to Kurtztown, Pennsylvania, passed in a flash. Kurtztown, located in East Penn Valley in the shadow of the Blue Mountains, was just a few miles from the hawk sanctuary, and I had made reservations for us there at the Pine Hill RV Park for two nights.

We loafed around the park for the rest of the day, then hiked to the top of Hawk Mountain the next day. It was a relatively easy walk that led up a rocky trail lined with trees that this day were dressed in erotic reds and royal golds. I stopped often to take pictures of the leaves, mossy green covered rock formations and my granddaughter. When we reached the top of the ridge, we found it crowded with people, all with binoculars pointed toward the sky. Birders are always hopeful a rare bird will fly into view, but today the only birds flying were a few common turkey vultures. The thousands of broad winged hawks, which I had been hoping to add to my life list of birds, plus all the other birds of prey that had been flying overhead earlier, were now well south of Hawk Mountain.

Once again, my dawdling ways came back to haunt me. Even so, the lack of birds didn't mar the day. The panoramic view was well worth the effort it took to get to the top of the ridge. Birding is not always about wings and feathers; sometimes it's simply about being outdoors in good company.

As if to make up for Hawk Mountain's birding lapse, the first part of the drive back to Monroe the next morning turned out to be a good birding day. When Shanna and I made a stop at a scenic spot along the Delaware River near Easton, Pennsylvania, I got a new bird for my life list. Flitting among the branches of a tree at the bubbling stream's edge was a blackpoll warbler, most likely just passing through the area on its way south from Canada. It's bold black cap, white cheek and black striped sides easily gave up the fellow's identity. I'm not sure I would have recognized the duller colored female, which in my trail guide looked the same as several other species of female warblers.

Being able to add the unexpected sighting of the blackpoll to my slowly growing bird list was yet another of those unexpected discoveries that make traveling such a joy. The second half of the day's journey back to Monroe, however, was the kind that made one thankful for simply being in good company. Shanna and I got caught in a traffic jam that stalled us for several hours on the freeway. And that's no exaggeration!

Our plans had been to get back to the ashram in time for dinner, but when that didn't happen, and when we hadn't moved more than a block in an entire hour, and our stomachs started complaining, I put Shanna behind the wheel, just in case the situation changed, and went in the back and made us a quick tuna casserole with noodles and mushroom soup. As so often happens when things go awry, this day spent in the company of my granddaughter will make the list of days I'll never forget. I've discovered that imperfect days leave deeper etched lines in the memory than do the perfect ones. For instance, when the subject of camping is brought up in my family, it's always that "camping trip from hell" that everyone wants to talk about. And just as everyone on that trip survived the late snowfall, the cold temperatures and tent-eating winds, this day Shanna and I eventually escaped the asphalt and hordes of traffic. It was well after dark when we arrived back at the ashram, and so we parked on the grounds and simply chilled out for the rest of the evening.

The next morning, we took the commuter train into New York City. I had visited the Big Apple a half dozen times before so was more interested in learning about my granddaughter's life there than sight-seeing. This was a good thing because she needed to get some things from her apartment, and check in with the yoga center where she worked. What I discovered as I tagged along was Shanna's fascinating, big-city lifestyle.

Her Manhattan apartment was a loft room rudely situated on the third floor of a huge old building in Soho. The floor had been bought by an artist some 30 years earlier, and was filled with his gigantic art work. One corner of the over-sized room held a large modern kitchen while the remainder of it was occupied by the artist's quarters and an open work area for the artist. In addition to Shanna's loft, there were two others that had been created to accommodate renters.

To get into Shanna's living quarters, we had to use a key to open the door of the building, then another key to open the elevator, and then a third key to open the door that led from the elevator onto the third floor. I was charmed by the arrangement, and was sorry when my granddaughter later moved to Africa, denying me an opportunity to revisit her there.

While I'm extremely partial to rural settings, New York City fascinates me. I love walking its busy streets, which we did this day at my insistence instead of taking the taxis Shanna preferred. As we walked, I told her about my best New York City experience, which was seeing one of Pale Male's offspring catch a pigeon in Central Park four years earlier.

Pale Male is the red-tailed hawk that visited the city in 1991 and decided to stay. At this writing, his home is still the ledge of an upscale Fifth Avenue apartment building, where faithful birding fans keep close tabs on his every move. When the building's owners once decided to remove his nest, a huge protest was raised and the hawk was allowed to continue living at the posh address. Bur it actually might be one of Pale Male's offspring. The fellow has been around too long for a redtail's life span, say some ornithologists. I prefer to think he's just long-lived.

While I have enjoyed New York's museums, art galleries, Rockefeller Center, Times Square, and all the other sights, Central Park will always be the best of what the city has to offer in my mind. This patch of green, surrounded and overlooked by skyscrapers, speaks to me of hope in a world gone amok with war, death and greed. But there was no time to visit the park this day. By the time Shanna had finished her business at the yoga center, where she treated me to a healthy vegetarian lunch in the cafeteria, it was time to catch the train back to Monroe. It was a rush in a rush, as we maneuvered our way through workers wending their way home. For some it would be just a couple of blocks walk, during which they would stop at the corner deli for dinner. For others, it would be a train or subway ride to more rural spaces, where stars can still light up the night sky.

I find New York City the one place on earth I'm eager to visit and just as eager to leave, and was glad to know that merely an hour away from the huge metropolis, there were places where cows grazed and people were only five minutes away from their favorite fishing lake. If New York were an astrological sign, it would have to be Gemini, because of its two faces.

BIRDS ALONG THE WAY:
Blue jay, great blue heron, chipping sparrow, house sparrow, rock pigeon, black-capped chickadee, mallard, double-crested cormorant, wild turkey, tufted titmouse, black vulture, turkey vulture, downy woodpecker, *blackpoll warbler, European starling, Canada geese, herring gull, ring-billed gull, American crow, mourning dove and brown-headed cowbird.
*First sighting of this species on the journey, and a lifer.

THE JOURNEY

CAMPGROUND:
under a tree on the
grounds of the ashram
Monroe, New York

New York

"If you board

the wrong train,

it is no use

running along

the corridor

in the

opposite

direction."

New Jersey

CAMPGROUND:
Wal-Mart
parking lot in
North Brunswick

– DIETRICH BONHOEFFER

30

SITTING OUT A STORM
IN A WAL-MART PARKING LOT

After one last heartfelt hug with Shanna the following morning, I headed south, although not straight as the crow flies. I took a mixture of scenic backroads that I had plotted out using the "Microsoft Streets and Trips" program downloaded onto my laptop. The twisting route took me well west of New York City into the state's more rural areas. Along with watching the passing scenery, I kept an eye on my rear-view mirror, which constantly reminded me that rain-laden black clouds were hot on my tail.

While I did manage to avoid the crowded toll ways and interstates so plentiful around this section of the East Coast, I failed to outrun the storm. It caught up with me on a heavily congested city street in North Brunswick, New Jersey. The pelting downpour taunted my windshield wipers, which I had turned to their highest speed, and blurred my vision to only a couple of feet. With nowhere to pull off that I could see, and knowing that to stop might result in a massive pile up of twisted metal, I was reduced to following the shimmering tail lights of the vehicle ahead, and hoping they would not lead me into disaster.

Finally, on the outskirts of North Brunswick, I spotted my white knight stand-in – a Wal-Mart. I knew the huge retailer allowed RVs to park overnight in their lots, and for once I planned to take advantage of the kindness. It was only 2 p.m. But the day was as dark as night already. When the rain finally slowed, I grabbed my umbrella and walked Maggie around the perimeter of the parking lot. She had about a foot's width of grass on which to do her business, and she gave me a pained look that clearly communicated her displeasure.

When we got back to the RV, I toweled her off thoroughly, and then did a bit of grocery shopping. I figured it was the best thanks for the free night's stay I had to offer Wal-Mart, a payback the store's financial wizards had almost certainly taken into consideration when offering their hospitality to RV travelers.

Back in my motor home, I heated up some chicken noodle soup on my propane stove and added a sizable dash of sour cream to make it taste more like gourmet dining. I followed the soup with a bowl of chocolate ice cream. My stomach content, I curled up on my couch beneath a battery-powered light and a fleece blanket, and read the evening away.

A good storm and a good book belong together like Romeo and Juliet. My choice of books for this occasion was Lillian Jackson Braun's *The Cat Who Went Bananas*. Mustachioed former reporter Qwill and his mystery-solving cat Koko were the perfect antidote to lighten the dank darkness outside. I finished the book before I joined Maggie in bed.

BIRDS ALONG THE WAY:
Blue jay, house sparrow, rock pigeon,
black-capped chickadee, black vulture, turkey vulture,
European starling, American crow, brown-headed cowbird
and mourning dove.

THE JOURNEY

CAMPGROUND:
Wal-Mart parking lot in
North Brunswick

New Jersey

Delaware

CAMPING:
Killens Pond State Park
Felton, Delaware

"To get away
from one's working
environment is,
in a sense,
to get away
from one's self;
and this is often the
chief advantage of
travel and change."

– CHARLES HORTON COOLEY

31

LOST AND FOUND IN PHILADELPHIA

The next morning was sunny and cheerful, which was a good thing because I had miles to go to find a campground. The more northerly ones along my route had already closed down for the season. From North Brunswick, I followed Highway 1 to Philadelphia. Because of my flight south to escape the weather, I had no leisure time to explore this historical city that is home to the Liberty Bell; but I thought perhaps I could get a feel for its character by driving through the middle of the city on Highway 13. In reality, I found myself too busy dodging traffic and looking for street markers to do much gawking. Then somewhere in the middle of the city, and not in the best of neighborhoods, I got hopelessly lost.

I finally found a place to park and got out my laptop. After inputting my current location into my map program, I discovered I was actually only two blocks away from where I wanted to be. I decided that perhaps the next time one of my kids offered to get me a GPS device, which I'd shunned, I'd accept the gift.

That was definitely a good idea I decided again, when I accidentally took a ramp onto the turnpike after finally escaping Philadelphia. There was no way to turn around so I had no choice but to pay the toll, although I eagerly took the first exit. No way did I want to drive my RV down the road with a zillion speeding cars and howling semis blowing past me.

Having to pay such strict attention to driving left me little time for thoughts and notes, so this part of my journey filled few lines in my journal. Or perhaps this fact was because the towns I passed through bumped into each other, and gave me little sense of individuality. I was able to relax a bit more once I had weaved my way back to Highway 13, and decided the morning had been an adventure that was probably good for me. I once again felt the strength that comes from overcoming a difficult situation. Still, I hoped the afternoon drive would be less stressful.

It was, although traffic continued to be ever present.

Sticking to Highway 13, my route roughly paralleled the Delaware River as it flowed along the eastern boundary of Pennsylvania. Named after William Penn, a Quaker who championed religious freedom, Pennsylvania was the second state to ratify the U.S. Constitution. Delaware, where I planned to spend the night, was the first.

But before I would cross the border into my third state for the day, I passed through the small town of Marcus Hook. I took note of this port city only because of its odd name. I was curious about it, but the best I could discover from gibberish tales about the place was that Marcus was an early Finnish settler in the area, and Hook refers to the point of land on which the small town sits. What I can say with more certainty is that the city of Marcus Hook takes pride today in its designation as the "The Cornerstone of Pennsylvania." The town sits at the most southeastern spot in the state.

Continuing on Highway 13, I passed through Delaware's capital city of Dover, and then shortly after pulled into Killens Pond State Park in Felton to spend the night. The park was a pleasant place with few campers, and Maggie and I quite enjoyed a walk around the scenic pond for which the park was named. It felt good to get some exercise, even if it was chilly, and I had to bundle up to enjoy it.

With winter still snarling behind us, I got back on the road early the next morning, thinking as I pulled away that Delaware had gotten too little of my attention. Dr. Seuss' rhyme that frequently jingled through my head, "Oh the places we'll go and the things we'll see," was joined by my own, "Too many places to see and too little time."

BIRDS ALONG THE WAY:
Rock pigeon, American crow, blue jay, turkey vulture,
European starling, ring-billed gull,
brown-headed cowbird and Canada geese.

THE JOURNEY

CAMPING:
Killens Pond State Park
Felton, Delaware

Delaware

"Heroes take journeys,

confront dragons, and

discover the treasure of

their true selves."

– CAROL PEARSON

CAMPING:
Tom's Cove
Chincoteague, Virginia

Virginia

32

ALL DRESSED UP FOR PONY WATCHING

I would travel a mere 99 miles this day. But those miles were ones that left the fast approaching winter of the northern East Coast behind me as I traveled from Killens Pond in Northern Delaware through Maryland and into Virginia. Meteorologists consider Delaware the transitional state for climate change, with its southern end having a milder climate and longer growing season than its northern end. I could feel and see the difference. The air felt thicker and moister, and autumn was less pronounced the farther south I traveled.

My drive on Highway 13 took me down the 180-mile long Delmarva Peninsula, which gets its names from the first syllables of the three states that claim it, Delaware, Maryland and Virginia. I skipped through the peninsula's middle section, Maryland, passing along the way through the small hamlets of Princess Anne, founded in 1733 and named after King George's daughter, and Pocomoke, which claims to be the "friendliest town on the eastern shore." My destination was Chincoteague Island in Virginia, which I reached via a weathered swing bridge just after I passed NASA's Wallops Flight Center a few miles off Highway 13.

A pair of brown pelicans sitting on the bridge's railings watched my passage across the bridge, which dumped me onto the skinny island. Bed and breakfast signs advertised it as a tourist resort, while rusty trawlers tied up at docks claimed it has a more traditional fishing village. This late in the season, the locals appeared to outnumber the tourists, I noticed, as I slowly drove to the southern end of the island. I ended the day at Tom's Cove Campground, which would be my home for the next three days.

At the campground, I was assigned a generous tree-shaded RV site that looked out across Chincoteague Bay. In front of the campground waded a long wooden pier with benches where fishermen could sit while waiting for a yank on their hooks, or where a birdwatcher could linger with her binoculars while the lapping sound of the bay lulled her into peacefulness. From this comfortable position, I daily watched birds, spotting among them two new birds for the journey. The first was a boat-tailed grackle, which has a rounder head then common or great-tailed grackles, and also a deeper and rougher voice. Boat-tails are normally only found along the edges of the East Coast or around Gulf of Mexico shorelines, and I hadn't seen many before this. The other bird was a tree swallow, with vibrant emerald feathers that stood out against a white breast. It is a common bird that can be found in both North and South America, and occasionally in Europe. I wondered if it had followed me down from the North, looking for the warm sunshine that we both could now enjoy as winter was still days, or even months, away from our present location.

I had plenty of time to bird watch at Tom's Cove because my goal to drive across the causeway and spend my days on Assateague Island seeing the wild ponies that had roamed there for over 300 years was thwarted. No pets were allowed on the island, and I couldn't find a rental car so I could leave Maggie behind in the RV. The next best option was an afternoon boat tour of the bay that would take me up close enough to Assateague to see the ponies.

While there are several historical tales explaining the ponies' existence on the island, everyone agrees they have been there since the 1600s. Some say the ponies swam ashore from a Spanish galleon, others believe they were the survivors of an English ship that ran aground, and others claim that pirates brought them to the island.

Today, the ponies have been separated by a fence into two herds, one managed by Maryland, which owns the northern half of the island, and the other by Virginia. Both states have taken action to keep their herd's population at about 160 animals. Maryland annually darts some of the females with a contraceptive vaccine, while Virginia rounds up the ponies and drives them across Assateague Channel to Chincoteague Island, where some of the foals are auctioned off each year.

This annual Pony Swim has taken place since 1925, but only became a popular tourist attraction after Marguerite Henry's *Misty of Chincoteague*, a novel about two children who purchased one of the ponies at auction, was published. The annual event takes place in July and attracts around 40,000 tourists. Because the timing of the swim is chosen by the tide and not the clock, the onlookers lining the beach to view the event often wait hours in the hot sun.

While I regretted arriving on the East Coast too late for prime birding opportunities, I decided I was not sorry at all that I had missed the swim. Instead I got my view of the ponies during my tour of the bay aboard a small scow. Instead of being squeezed among thousands for the sighting, my companions this off-season day were only two couples and our tour guide, Captain Mark. He was ruggedly handsome in typical outdoor tour guide fashion, and assuredly maneuvered the scow's rudder while plying us with trivia about the area and the ponies.

While five of us were dressed down for the outing, one of the women wore a stylish white hat over carefully coiffed brunette hair. Lavish Indian jewelry topped an expensive red sweater, which she had tucked neatly into her jeans and kept in place with a wide red belt that matched her lipstick and fashionable boots.

Don't take me wrong. I don't mean to make fun of how the woman was dressed for our outing. I admire a person with the self-security to not blend in, be it one who dresses up when others dress down, or down when everyone else dresses up. If I were brave enough I would always go bra-less and wear cargo pants or shorts with a loose, brightly-hued T-shirt and good tennis shoes. I like to be comfortable, colorful and kind to my feet. But there are times when I dress to meet society's expectations. My reward for doing so is usually scratchy skin and achy feet.

Our chic woman's husband, meanwhile, was an ample-bellied, good-old-boy who agreed with my idea of comfort. He was wearing a University of Kentucky sweatshirt with loose-fitting pants and tennis shoes, making him and his wife fit together like mismatched puzzle pieces. I suspected appearances were deceiving, and was convinced of it by watching their easy camaraderie. Except for their choice of clothing they appeared quite compatible.

The other couple, about my age, was dressed similar to me, only toned down a bit. They could have passed for any of my birding friends, many of whom believe bright color frightens away birds. I believe birds are actually attracted to color, but when birding with those who don't, I opt for muted tones as I lack the security of today's lady in red.

What any of us were wearing, meanwhile, didn't affect the day's outing. We saw quite a few of the ponies, albeit at a distance that made me glad I had my birding binoculars, and thankful for the zoom lens on my camera. I got a striking photograph of a black and white pony, which Captain Mark said was a rare color.

The fascination with these ponies, I decided, was solely related to their survival. There was nothing different about them from any of the other wild horses I had seen in Utah, Wyoming and Montana. But, just as I had been thrilled at seeing free-roaming mustangs out West, I thrilled at seeing the Assateague ponies. It must be this thing we Americans have about freedom.

In addition to watching and photographing the ponies, I was of course keeping an eye on the birds. The most prolific this day were the laughing gulls winging above our heads, and then the double-crested cormorants drying their wings on nearby rocks. But among them I spotted four new birds for my trip list: least tern, Caspian tern, yellow-crowned night heron and a green-winged teal.

The three least terns I saw were flying with a large flock of Forster's terns. It was easy to separate the smaller nine-inch least terns from the 14-inch Forsters, and not just because of size. The least terns had black edging on their wings. I was thrilled to see them because I had only seen one of these birds, previously. That one was a migrant passing through the Bear River Migratory Bird Refuge in Northern Utah. I had been birding at the time with my local Audubon group, and the least tern had been a lifer for half a dozen of us. As you can imagine, well if you know how crazy birders can be when they spot a new species, the sighting was cause for a celebration. While here on the Eastern Coast, least terns are common, seeing one in Northern Utah is a rare occurrence.

Also, easy to identify this day were the Caspian terns. Not only are they the world's largest tern, they sport a deep orange bill that makes them standout from all other North American terns, whose beaks pale in comparison. A whole row of these Caspians were sitting on an abandoned rowboat near the shore of the island. As for the yellow-crowned night heron and green-winged teal, they are fairly common birds everywhere in North America. I was a bit surprised that I hadn't encountered them earlier on the trip.

As we came around a bend of the island, Mark interrupted my bird-watching by pointing out the Assateague Lighthouse. It has been warning ships of the area's shallow waters and rocks since 1833, even though its original 45-foot height and weak lantern lights were not adequate to the task. That problem was addressed in 1867 when the tower's height was increased to 139 feet, and its glass-enclosed top equipped with modern lighting that reached 19 miles out to sea. A lighthouse keeper lived in a small house at the bottom of the tower until technology arrived, and the facility no longer required human overseeing. The keeper's dwelling is now used by volunteers for the Assateague National Wildlife Refuge on whose land the lighthouse sits. It was with laughing delight that I noted the lighthouse was painted bright red and white in candy cane fashion. Self-assuredly, it stood out boldly on the horizon against a cloudless blue sky.

BIRDS ALONG THE WAY:
Blue jay, turkey vulture, great blue heron, great egret,
brown-headed cowbird, belted kingfisher, *boat-tailed grackle,
common grackle, laughing gull, *tree swallow, herring gull,
*Caspian tern, ring-billed gull, Forster's tern, osprey,
double-crested cormorant, brown pelican, rock pigeon,
snowy egret, mourning dove, mallard,
*yellow-crowned night heron, American robin, mallard,
*least tern, black vulture, northern mockingbird,
Brewer's blackbird, green-winged teal,
and Carolina chickadee.

*First sighting of this species on the journey.

THE JOURNEY

CAMPING:
Tom's Cove
Chincoteague, Virginia

Virginia

CAMPING:
Trav-L Park
Virginia Beach,
Virginia

"Remember what Bilbo used to say, 'It's a dangerous business, Frodo, going out the door. You step onto the road, and if you don't keep your feet, there's no knowing where you might be swept off to.'"

– J.R.R. TOLKIEN

33

CROSSING CHESAPEAKE BAY
AND A SICK DOG

I left Chincoteague Island the same way I had come, via the swing bridge with brown pelicans watching my passage. Back on Highway 13, I continued south along a strip of land barely 10 miles across at its widest. On one side of this narrow strip of Virginia was Chesapeake Bay, and on the other side was the vast Atlantic Ocean. The landscape made for a picturesque drive, with egrets, cormorants, terns, boat-tailed grackles and gulls keeping me company along the way.

I stopped awhile to bird at Kiptopeke State Park at the tip of the peninsula. My travel homework had indicated it was an important bird study area because it sits beneath a major flyway for migratory birds. I had reservations for the night in Virginia Beach or I would have stayed longer. Instead I merely satisfied my need to stretch my legs a bit by taking a short hike that took me on a raised boardwalk from the forest area of the park to a beach on Chesapeake Bay – and from Carolina chickadees and robins to floating green-winged teals and cormorants.

On my way back to the RV, I identified my 92nd bird species for the trip. The bird wore a bold, rufus colored cap and had a black spot of color in the center of its chest. I first thought I was looking at a song sparrow, but then noticed its distinctive white wing bars. With the help of my birding field guide, I finally realized I was looking at an American tree sparrow.

Back again in my RV, Maggie gave me a painful look that I translated as: Why did you leave me. I gave her one of her favorite T-bone doggie treats and was immediately forgiven. She was asleep in the co-pilot seat before I had gone a half mile more down the road. While she snoozed, I thought about crossing the water ahead on the "Chesapeake Bay Bridge-Tunnel." At this point I thought it would be one or the other, and knew that I would take the open-to-the-sky option.

Wrong! My homework here came up way short of what is ranked as one of the seven marvels of the engineering world. It had to have been a brilliant mind to come up with a way to cross the 17 miles of water at the mouth of Chesapeake Bay's outlet to the Atlantic Ocean. By the numbers, according to a brochure I picked up describing this passage, this man-made wonder involves 12 miles of trestled roadway, two bridges, two tunnels, four man-made islands and two miles of causeway, plus over five miles of approach roads.

When I started across it, however, all that was on my mind was the passage ahead where the highway disappeared into the water. Suddenly I found myself muttering, "I do not like this Maggie. I do not like this at all." You would think I had just been offered green eggs and ham by *Sam-I-Am*. But down I went beneath the bay, trying to ignore my claustrophobic imagination that made the tunnel walls crack from the water pressure all around them.

I would have made this bay crossing even if I had known what it entailed because I do try to face my fears. But it was all to the good that I didn't have more than a few minutes to worry about it, moments when all I could see in front of me was the magnificent bridge I was crossing disappear beneath the bay. I shivered as I went down into the tunnel's depths and breathed a sigh of relief when I saw natural light around me again. It wasn't any easier the second time.

The two tunnels, the brochure informed me, allowed tall ocean-going ships to enter and exit the bay without any overhead interference, while the bridge's 75-foot height at one end allowed local boat traffic to come and go at ease. Heights do not bother me, and I regretted I had been so preoccupied with what lay below to fully enjoy what was above. I suspected, however, that unlike the character in Dr. Seuss' *Green Eggs and Ham,* who liked the dish once he actually tasted it, I would never come to like enclosed spaces. I did, however, like the feeling of achievement I felt for once again having conquered my claustrophobic nemesis.

Once across the bay, I headed east on Highway 60 and followed it into Virginia Beach. The drive took me past First Landing State Park, formerly Seashore State Park until its name was changed to recognize the site as the "first landing" of the Virginia Company in the New World. Jamestown was established here in 1607. Once again, I was passing through history. Highway 50 continued on, taking me into Virginia Beach via the Atlantic Ocean shoreline. I found a spot to park and a place to sit on the beach, and stared out to sea for a bit. A cool, salty breeze quickly chilled me, however, so I didn't linger long.

The day's drive ended at the large, upscale Holiday Trave-L Park that perfectly fit Virginia Beach's resort image. This late in the season, the park was far from full, which made walking about the landscaped foolishness quite pleasant. I say foolishness because of such things as kooky statues of an ape in a hula skirt and a giraffe decked out in polka dots. There were also comical history sites, like the one containing a wooden cannon and a sign that read "On this spot, Sgt. 'One-Eared' Magda learned to stand behind the cannon."

In contrast to the fun, Maggie developed an ear infection that was serious enough to require the services of a veterinarian. She was cursed with the dreaded cocker ear, and although I carry ear washes and antibiotic drops around with me to keep it in check, about twice a year I lose the battle. The park's handout of traveler information included the number of a nearby vet, who kindly ended Maggie's suffering for the mere cost of $142.

"I hope you know how much I love you," I later told Maggie. And, just in case she suffered complications, I also decided to stick around Virginia Beach a few days before getting back on the road. I really didn't mind. As actress Sophie Okonedo said: "Wherever I am is where I am meant to be."

The extra time in Virginia Beach gave me another chance to walk on the beach and stare out over the ocean, whose vastness my ancestors had crossed to get to America. My mother's side came from England to find a better life, and my father's side from Portugal, all descendants of a sailor who jumped ship in Connecticut, and whose son, moved to Galveston and began the Joseph line in Texas. I also took advantage of my prolonged stay to visit the Virginia Aquarium, a complex that included nature exhibits and a hiking trail through marshlands in addition to the traditional aquarium tanks. It was my kind of place and I spent an entire afternoon enjoying it.

The miracle of modern drugs, meanwhile, worked their magic on Maggie. After four days in Virginia Beach, she and I were both ready to get on the road for our next adventure.

BIRDS ALONG THE WAY:
Blue jay, turkey vulture, great blue heron, great egret,
brown-headed cowbird, belted kingfisher, boat-tailed grackle,
common grackle, laughing gull, *American tree sparrow,
herring gull, Caspian tern, ring-billed gull, Forster's tern, osprey,
double-crested cormorant, brown pelican, rock pigeon,
tree swallow, snowy egret, mourning dove, mallard,
yellow-crowned night heron, American robin, mallard,
least tern, black vulture, northern mockingbird,
Brewer's blackbird, green-winged teal
and Carolina chickadee.

THE JOURNEY

Virginia

CAMPING:
Interstate Motel
Roanoak Rapids,
North Carolina

CAMPING:
Trav-L Park
Virginia Beach, Virginia

CAMPING:
Lake Reidsville Campground
Reidsville, North Carolina

North Carolina

"Our happiest moments as tourists always seem to come when we stumble upon one thing while in pursuit of something else."

— LAWRENCE BLOCK

34
DISMAL SWAMP, ROANOKE RAPIDS AND SIMPLE THINGS

I headed westward from Virginia Beach, zig-zagging on back roads until I reached Highway 17. Now late October, it was a sunny, but cool morning. The brilliant fall I had left behind in Maine was just coming to this part of the country. While it paled in comparison to the northern show of colors, the landscape exuded a gentle beauty as it wandered to the eastern border of the Great Dismal Swamp. Aptly named, this great marsh abounds with waterlogged trees, poisonous snakes and dark waters that hide what lurks below. About 40 percent of it lies in Virginia and the remainder in North Carolina. A huge chunk – 111,000 acres that crosses state lines – is a designated national wildlife refuge.

The place captured both my curiosity and my imagination, and I stopped to explore an edge at a welcome center shortly after crossing into North Carolina. The welcome center provided a pleasant rest stop, a picnic area for both motorists and boaters, as there was a generous parking lot off Highway 17 and a dock at the rear of the building to accommodate boats traveling the Great Dismal Swamp Canal. The creation of the canal was the idea of George Washington and his investor colleagues. They saw it as a means to accommodate trade between Virginia and an isolated region of North Carolina.

Today, the 22-mile long canal provides boaters a shortcut between the Elizabeth River and Chesapeake Bay in Virginia and the Pasquotank River in North Carolina. In Washington's time, it was the only easy passage through the mucky swamp. The arduous labor of digging the canal began in 1793 with slave labor. But the massive project was slow going, and it wasn't until 1805 that a boat could go from one end of the canal to the other. It has been used constantly since, first by commercial vessels carrying cargo and passengers, and now mostly by boats full of recreationists.

This latter use was clearly evident this day. Six large sailboats, quite nifty compared to the small 21-foot sloop I used to sail on the Great Salt Lake, were double-parked at the welcome center's dock. The sight surprised me, until I realized that the boats used their motors to make their way through the narrow, tree-lined passage.

The canal, via a short navigable ditch, also provides access to Lake Drummond for fishermen and other outdoor enthusiasts. The lake may have been gouged out by a large meteoroid based on its round shape, or it may be the result of a huge peat moss burn. Whichever, it is named after North Carolina Gov. William Drummond, who was hanged by Virginia Gov. William Berkeley in the 1670s. Since the lake is located solely in Virginia's portion of the swamp, I guess someone eventually thought an apology was in order.

After ogling the sailboats with an experienced eye, and exploring the visitor center and its manicured grounds, I found a path leading off into the forest. A sign identified it as "The Dismal Swamp Nature Trail," with an added cautionary note to "Beware of Snakes." Actually it was a quite civilized trail, with markers identifying black cherry and mulberry trees, a cheerful squirrel dashing among the foliage, and a tufted titmouse whistling me along its fallen leaf carpet. The narrow path led along the canal for a while, then circled around into a more forested area before dumping me out, far too quickly, near the parking lot.

On the far side of the canal, the landscape was fiercer. There were no paths, only a mass of tangled vines and nature debris hiding and sheltering its wild occupants, like black bears and bobcats – and over 200 species of birds. Its tangled webs of vines, unsure footing and dangerous wildlife keep most people out, which is why it became a refuge for America's former slaves. Some passed through it on their hopeful way to freedom, while others chose to live in the swamp as an alternative to slavery. Harriett Beecher Stow, whose book *Uncle Tom's Cabin* sympathetically described the sad plight of slaves, wrote a second book, *Dred: A Tale of the Great Dismal Swamp*, whose title character was an escaped, angry slave who lived in it.

The swamp is also a designated Underground Railroad Historic Site because of the role it played in hiding slaves on their way to freedom.

Back in my RV, still pondering facts about the swamp I had learned at the welcome center, I continued following Highway 17 south until it intersected with Highway 158, a well-maintained but little traveled road that took me through the middle of the swamp. The 38-mile drive through the quagmire took me from the swamp's eastern edge to its western edge. One of the more vivid images I captured of the swamp with my camera has a grim, fairy-tale feel of evil about it. Its black masts of dead trees rising into the air from a dark sea of muck had my imagination picturing a flotilla of trapped ships that had slowly sank with all aboard.

The swamp, however, was one of those travel surprises that I love so much. While my route to the East Coast had been plotted with detailed research, my return trip some days was simply based on heading in the general direction. While I knew where I wanted to end up – Texas in time to have Thanksgiving with my oldest daughter – what lay ahead was often a mystery. The first method of travel heightened my enjoyment and understanding of what I saw, while the second method had the deliciousness of the unexpected. This day all I had to go on when I started out was that a large area on my map was marked off with blue dashes and weedy looking lines and simply identified as the Great Dismal Swamp. I had decided it would be a fun landscape to explore, and I wasn't disappointed. It's not, I decided, that one method of travel is better than the other. They are only different, as are most of life's choices. I've always found it hard to understand people who believe their way of doing or thinking was the only right one. Sadly I've known far too many such people.

As for me, I often choose friends who think differently from me because my horizon is expanded and I learn new things. On this day, I found the Great Dismal Swamp as magnificent in its own way as the sparkling clean lakes that had thus far dominated my wandering. But life isn't all beautiful surprises, as my stopping place for the night revealed. I found myself camped in a crowded field behind a place called the Interstate Motel in Roanoke Rapids. It was the only place to camp for miles around, a situation that quickly filled all the motel-campground's unappealing sites by early afternoon.

With a population of around 17,000, Roanoke Rapids reminded me of "Small Town Anywhere," USA. It sits beside the river, for which it is named, with the river named for the rapids that hopscotch down its fast-flowing waters. It was too bad the motel wasn't situated by the river, I thought. But then one can't always have everything one wants.

The next morning, I continued westward on Highway 158 through a handful of small towns: Littleton, Macon, Norlina, Middleburg, Henderson, Oxford, Roxboro (formerly known as Moccasin Gap) and Yanceyville. Henderson was the largest, with a population about the same as Roanoke's. Some of the towns I passed had populations that barely topped 100, and while I saw their names on a map, a couple eluded me completely. It was a peaceful drive, but with little variation in the scenery, mostly being a tree lined road that led from one small bit of population to the next, until I pulled into Lake Reidsville Recreation Park.

Here I was assigned a wooded campsite adjacent to a 750-acre lake surrounded by trees dressed in reds and golds. It was the most autumn-colorful camp since I had left the upper East Coast. I stayed two nights, lured both by the pleasant landscape in which to walk Maggie and the cheap camping, $12 nightly. It would have only been $8 if I had been a North Carolina resident.

It rained, a genteel dripping, often while I was there, and I used the time to plot out the next leg of the journey. What surprises are still ahead of us, I asked Maggie? I find that on days when I don't have humans to commune with, I talk aloud more to Maggie. In response, she stared at me, then at the door, stared impatiently at me again, then back at the door. I looked outside and saw the rain had stopped.

Maggie gave me yet another one of her looks, and I comprehended its meaning, just as human companions can often tell what the other is thinking without spoken words. Let's go for a walk and see what flowers we can find to smell. Now! Have I mentioned that Maggie is bossy? My friends tell me I'm the pet and she's the owner. But since both Maggie and I do like to smell the flowers, I put my shoes on and we went for a walk. Since I assumed my interpretation of Maggie's glare was pretty close to perfect, I let the thoughts of one Albert Einstein, about whom I had been reading, flow through my head. "Learn from yesterday, live for today, hope for tomorrow," he said.

It was a great walk. I enjoyed watching a robin take a bath in wet leaves and Maggie sniffed out the path of a squirrel that watched us from a tree. We're both blessed that such simple things can make our hearts sing. But then things got even better. A northern goshawk flew past us and landed in a tree. He was a beautiful bird, and one I was a bit surprised to see here. I assumed he was migrating through.

My last sighting of a goshawk had been several years earlier, when I was writing a story on HawkWatch, an environmental bird-watch organization that was monitoring birds of prey during their migration over the Goshute Mountains in the northeast corner of Nevada. I had hiked to the top of a peak in the mountains to spend a day with the enthusiastic group of volunteers. Once on top, I had put my claustrophobia on hold just long enough to stay huddled in a blind, and watch as a couple of the volunteers used a trapped pigeon as bait to net a bird that came down for what it thought would be an easy meal.

The bird was a goshawk, and I gawked in fascination as the bird was measured and banded. The best part was when the raptor was set free to continue its journey. I then joined the group of hawk watchers sitting on a ridge with their binoculars, and counting the numbers of birds flying overhead. I was much more comfortable out here than in the enclosed bird blind.

One of the watchers, noticing my dinky pair of cheap binoculars, loaned me his binoculars so I could get a better look. This, I should note, was right before I became a passionate birdwatcher. Once this craziness took hold of me, I bought myself a pair of way-too-expensive binoculars, the maker of which suggested they be noted in my will. I was inspired, I'm sure, by looking through that great pair of loaner binoculars, which let me see overhead hawks on that autumn day as I had never seen them before.

But then not everything I saw in the sky that day was a bird. Even now I smile thinking about me calling out to the other hawk watchers when I saw what I thought was a really big bird. Seconds later, I realized I had been looking at a quite distant F-16 flying over Hill Air Force Base's West Desert Bombing Range.

"We call that the silver-winged eagle," joked one of the guys.

BIRDS ALONG THE WAY:
American robin, Carolina chickadee, Brewer's blackbird,
northern mockingbird, rock pigeon, tufted titmouse,
ring-billed gull, laughing gull, mourning dove,
double-crested cormorant, turkey vulture, American crow,
eastern bluebird, Canada geese, black vulture, blue jay,
mallard, pied-billed grebe and *northern goshawk.

*First sighting of this bird on the journey.

THE JOURNEY

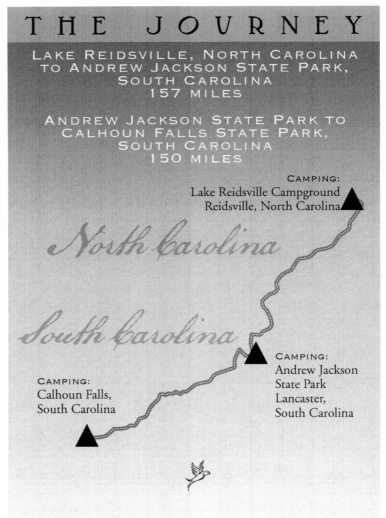

LAKE REIDSVILLE, NORTH CAROLINA
TO ANDREW JACKSON STATE PARK,
SOUTH CAROLINA
157 MILES

ANDREW JACKSON STATE PARK TO
CALHOUN FALLS STATE PARK,
SOUTH CAROLINA
150 MILES

CAMPING:
Lake Reidsville Campground
Reidsville, North Carolina

North Carolina

South Carolina

CAMPING:
Andrew Jackson
State Park
Lancaster,
South Carolina

CAMPING:
Calhoun Falls,
South Carolina

*"Though we travel the world over to
find the beautiful, we must carry it
with us or we find it not."*

– RALPH WALDO EMERSON

35

THE CAROLINAS —
BOOKS, TOBACCO AND ART

Today's travel would take me from North Carolina into South Carolina. As I drove, I thought about the history of these two sister states. I did some online research about them to help pass time during the rain at Lake Reidsville.

Both states stretch west from the Atlantic seaboard inland to the Appalachian Mountains, and both began life in 1663 as a British proprietary colony managed by eight English nobles for profit. As is prone in committee rule, dissension on how this Carolina Colony would be managed became an issue. To resolve the situation, the large colony was divided into north and south colonies in 1712, forming the boundaries for the two states they would eventually become. Dissension continued, however. This time it was between the settlers and the proprietors. The royal crown eventually bought out the nobles, and claimed the Carolina colonies for its own.

Of course, this wasn't the end of the dissension. Americans became fed up with English rule, and eventually became embroiled in a battle to sever their ties with England, and the Revolutionary War followed. After the war was won, South Carolina became this new country's eighth state in 1788, and North Carolina its twelfth in 1789. The battles were over, until the Civil War. Although having fought to gain their own freedom, Carolinians were reluctant to extend that same privilege to their Black slaves. Both states seceded from the Union and joined the Confederacy. While I'm southern to the core, that's one battle I'm glad we lost, just as I'm glad the two Carolinas once again became U.S. states.

I saw no visible remnants of these past lives as I unhurriedly traveled south through a tree-lined, scantly populated section of Highway 158, but just knowing about the history added meaning to the landscape. The history channel in my brain jangled its meandering tune all the way to Winston-Salem, the first sizable city I had encountered since leaving Virginia Beach. The hyphenated name recognizes the merger of the towns of Winston and Salem in 1913, not the cigarettes – although the area plays a major agriculture role in this country's tobacco industry.

Winston, founded in 1849, gets its name from Joseph Winston, a local hero of the Revolutionary War. The older settlement of Salem traces its roots back to 1766, and the Hebrew word for peace, Shalom. A cigarette connection, however, does come with the town's nickname, Camel City, which refers to the city being the home of the R. J. Reynolds Tobacco Co. that produces Camels, the brand my mother smoked until the age of 76 when she quit cold turkey because of the increased cost of the habit.

When tobacco baron R. J. Reynolds died in 1918, his successful tobacco company owned 121 buildings in Winston-Salem. But it wasn't one of these buildings that caused me to call a halt to my drive. It was a large Barnes and Noble Bookstore. While I've never smoked cigarettes, I am a book addict, and a B&N sign usually causes the vehicle I'm driving to forget where it is going and give in to my craving. In fact, Gypsy Lee should have a bumper sticker declaring: "I Brake for Bookstores."

Walking up and down aisles filled with the work of beloved authors, smelling the crispness of new paper and ink, and reading first pages of books with exotic titles, gives me a John Denver high without the Rocky Mountains. My purse was lighter, and my RV a few pounds heavier, by the time I left Winston-Salem behind. The books that I couldn't live without included *The Creative License,* an art instruction book by Danny Greggory that I found on a sale rack; *Living on the Wind,* a book about bird migration by Scott Weidensaul; and a mystery by Sara Peretsky, whose heroine V. I. Warshawski brings Chicago alive to the reader better than most travel writers.

Back in the RV with my treasures, Maggie enthusiastically examined my new purchases in hopes there was something for her. I gave her a doggie biscuit to soothe her visible disappointment after she discovered nothing and cast her disappointed cocker eyes on me.

That settled, and with Maggie snoozing again almost before I left the parking lot, I continued down the road on Highway 52 toward Charlotte, North Carolina's largest town. The city is named after German Princess Charlotte of Mecklenburg, who became queen consort of King George III at about the same time the area was first settled in 1755. The first home in the area was built by Thomas Polk, uncle to our eleventh president, James Knox Polk.

I'm sure this city, named after a German but sounding so like a southern belle, has a lot to offer travelers, but I wasn't in the mood for big city cacophony. I took the 485 Bypass around Charlotte and joined up with Highway 521 on the far side. This quiet highway took me into South Carolina, where I would stop for the night at Andrew Jackson State Park.

It was a weekday, and so the park was uncrowded and peaceful. I had my pick of RV sites, and chose one that looked out onto a small lake – close enough so that the sounds of water lapping against the shore would lull me to sleep this night. After hooking Gypsy Lee up to water and electricity, Maggie and I walked down to the water for a closer look.

A floating squadron of hybrid mallards expecting handouts greeted us enthusiastically, but back-paddled when Maggie approached the shoreline. The ducks were a motley crew of variegated colors and sizes. While most birds are persnickety about mating only with their own species, mallards are unprejudiced. Their pairings with other species produce offspring that can greatly confuse fledgling birders. I finally came to realize that if I saw a duck not listed in my North American bird guide, it was more likely to be a mallard hybrid than a rare species out of its territory.

Leaving the lake and the ducks behind, Maggie and I wandered up to the park's small museum, which supposedly tells all about Andrew Jackson's exploits during the Revolutionary War. I say supposedly because the museum was closed, open only on weekends or by appointment, the sign said. I contented myself with a careful examination of the outdoor statue of a young Andrew Jackson on horseback by American sculptor Anna Hyatt Huntington.

It wasn't the first time I had seen Anna's work. Her statue of El Cid in San Diego's Balboa Park came to mind. When I had first seen that piece, I thought Anna's artistic skill had captured the fiery soul of the Spanish military hero and his warhorse. Now, I thought she had captured the essence of the man who would become our seventh president, not as the hero of the Revolutionary War he would become, but simply as a young South Carolina boy on his farm horse in his formative years.

I'm sure Anna was one of those single-minded people whose lives are totally wrapped up in their work, letting art lovers, like me, enjoy a few minutes of insight into the essence of a thing. People like Anna enrich my life, and I'm thankful for their intense artistic drives.

Returning to my RV, Maggie and I tucked ourselves in for the evening. She went to bed immediately after dinner while I got out my travel maps, computer and brochures, and spent a bit of time planning the next day's adventure. As usual, when I was ready to join her, I found she had managed to spread her small body across the entire bed.

The next morning, after I had put Maggie back in the RV after our walk, I took some stale bread that would have been thrown away down to the lake, and fed the motley squadron of ducks. While feeding wildlife is definitely on my no-no list, I considered these ducks to be non-migrating domestics who had learned to use humans to survive winter without migrating. My reward for coming down to the lake this morning was to spot a pair of Gadwalls. The large ducks swam out from behind some reeds just as I was about to leave. The small white patches near their tails let me easily identify them, especially since they are species I see often in my bird-watching forays. Unlike the Mallard hybrids, they exuded a sense of wildness and kept their distance. That pleased me.

Today's drive took me south and west on highways 521, 9, 121 and 72. It was mostly a wooded route that wound through a section of Sumter National Forest, past a few towns and across Greenwood Lake, which was created in 1940 by a dam across the Saluda River. My destination for the day was Calhoun Falls State Park, which sits on the banks of Lake Richard B. Russell that was created with the completion of a dam on the Savannah River in 1984. The lake straddles the border with Georgia, and both it and the dam are named after a former Georgia governor and senator.

What I vaguely remembered of Russell, who died in 1971 shortly after I had begun my journalism career, was that he was an outspoken opponent of civil rights legislation. While his stance shattered his long-time friendship with President Lyndon Johnson, it must have pleased others because Russell also has a senate building named after him, as well as an airport, a scenic byway, schools and several other projects.

As Maggie and I wandered down a trail that circled through the campground, I wondered what Calhoun the park was named after. I never found out, but I did learn that the falls it had been named after no longer existed. The lake had obliterated it once the dam was built.

A great blue heron flying out of the woods interrupted my thoughts. I was quite pleased with the distraction. While I find names of things fascinating, the sight of a magnificent great blue flying overhead always makes my heart leap. I saw another one, or perhaps even the same one, emerging out of the mist and flying low over the lake the next morning. Gliding through the air in front of a pink and purple sunrise sky, the heron looked magical. Why hadn't someone thought to name this place Misty Sunrise Heron Lake? Or Misty S. Heron Lake, so as to leave someone like me wondering what the S. stood for.

BIRDS ALONG THE WAY:
Mallard, pied-billed grebe, blue jay, Canada geese,
eastern bluebird, ruby crowned kinglet,
northern mockingbird, turkey vulture, mourning dove,
*gadwall, great blue heron, kestrel.

*First sighting of this species on the journey.

THE JOURNEY

CALHOUN FALLS, SOUTH CAROLINA
TO STATESBORO, GEORGIA
175 MILES

STATESBORO TO
LAURA S. WALKER PARK, GEORGIA
117 MILES

WALKER PARK TO
OCHLOCKNEE, GEORGIA
148 MILES

CAMPING:
Calhoun Falls,
South Carolina

*"The everyday kindness of
the back roads more than
makes up for the acts of
greed in the headlines."*

— CHARLES KURALT

CAMPING:
Parkwood RV Park,
Statesboro, Georgia

Georgia

CAMPING:
Laura Walker
State Park,
Waycross, Georgia

CAMPING:
Sugar Mill Plantation
RV Park
Ochlocknee, Georgia

36

GEORGIA ON MY MIND

The name game didn't end the next day, when I followed the example of the migrating birds and headed south on the Savannah River Scenic Highway. The pondering started up again when I passed Strom Thurman Lake about 40 miles downstream. This lake, also created by a dam, was about 30 years older than its upstream, politically named brother. It was originally called Clarks Hill Lake, after the nearby town of Clarks Hill that had been named for Revolutionary War hero Elijah Clark. But South Carolinians pulled some political shenanigans in the late 1980s to get it named Strom Thurmond Lake in honor of their favorite senator. Since half the lake was in Georgia, residents there opposed the change. While they couldn't halt the renaming, they did manage, in the same bill, to name the newly created upstream lake on the Savannah River the Richard B. Russell Lake after their favorite senator.

And that's the rest of the story. Well, except for the fact that Georgians still call it Lake Clarks Hill instead of Strom Thurmond Lake on their maps, which can be a bit confusing to travelers – and why, after being confused, I was prompted to research the issue.

Today's drive, meanwhile, meandered back and forth between river and trees, and beneath a fanciful, cloud-filled sky of dragons and castles. Once again, I was traveling through the Sumter National Forest, this time along its western Savannah River boundary.

In past lives, when the river flowed freely without dam interruptions, the forest was home to Cherokee Indians, served as a battleground for the Revolutionary War, and was a production plant for the timber industry. It still is the latter; logging is one of the multiple uses of forest management.

I left the river and woodlands when I crossed to the west side of the water into Georgia near Augusta. Here was another large city that I decided to ignore. I took the bypass and continued on Highway 25 down to Statesboro, where I checked into the Parkwood RV Park. It was a large Good Sam campground with laundry facilities and other amenities that made it an ideal place to give my stash of mail a chance to catch up with me. I called my daughter-in-law as soon as I had hooked up, and told her to send my mail to Statesboro.

Gen. William Sherman passed through this area on his infamous Civil War March, but there wasn't much for him to destroy in the town. About the only damage Sherman left behind was a destroyed log barn that doubled as a courthouse, according to historians. The town's boom era came after the incestuous war, with cotton being the catalyst for growth until boll weevils conducted their own march through the area in the 1930s. Down but not out, farmers switched to tobacco crops, and life for them went back to normal, which being a farmer's life still wasn't easy.

Agriculture continues to play a major role in the area's economy, but Georgia Southern University, whose green landscaped lawns and pink brick buildings call Statesboro home, is its largest employer. The campus had a cheerfully modern appearance, in contrast to the outdated downtown atmosphere. I suspected the city's center suffered from mall madness, a disease that leaves Main Street businesses lonely and forlorn.

As I explored the city, I kept an eye out for a place to get a haircut, and found it downtown. The cut I got was perfect, exactly matching my instructions to leave the bangs long enough to touch my eyebrows, a simple request not always followed. But once the hair was cut, the stylist blew it dry and puffed it up so much that I looked like I had stepped back in time to the 1970s. I didn't wear big hair even when it was popular, but the beautician looked so pleased at her efforts that I smiled and lied that I thought it looked great.

This was the South after all, a place where politeness and hospitality rule. Southern manners had been ingrained in me by my grandmother, a hot-tempered lady who once told me the secret to staying a lady and saying her favorite cuss word – shit!—was to always pronounce it with three syllables. Sh-ee-it! I had the accent perfected, as it was my favorite (actually only) cuss word. But I refrained from saying it this day. I knew my daily shampoo would have me back to my normal unfashionable self the next morning. I even tipped as usual, although I did avoid looking into reflective windows on my stroll back to my RV. Maggie lifted a sleepy eyelid, but shut it almost immediately, which I translated as "No comment."

A few days later, with mail in hand and my hair back to normal, I took off down Highway 25 again. The first town I passed through was Claxton, where a water tower proclaimed it as the "Fruitcake Capital of the World." I'm assuming they meant the cakes and not the flakes. After Claxton, I jogged onto Highway 301 and followed it for a while before turning west onto Highway 82 at Nahunta. It was a quiet drive with little variation in the rural scenery that ended at Laura S. Walker State Park.

Finally, something named after a woman, I thought – although I had no idea who Laura was. A park brochure answered the question. Born in 1861, this Georgia native was a teacher, writer, civic leader and naturalist with a passionate drive to conserve and protect trees. According to the one-page typed history, Laura, who died in 1955 at the age of 94, was the only living woman for whom a state park had been named, an honor that was bestowed on her by President Franklin D. Roosevelt.

The park had its own golf course and lake, but its nearness to the Okefenokee Swamp, made famous by the antics of Walt Kelly's political comic strip "Pogo," and my desire to explore the place, was the reason I chose the campground. I still remembered when I thought Pogo's Okefenokee Swamp home was only a funky, made-up name.

The Okefenokee had a livelier atmosphere than the Great Dismal Swamp. Wild flowers grew in the greener Okefenokee, with few dead or dying trees. Even the moss looked charming, instead of simply drooping lifelessly above black muck. But then words are powerful things. Was I was letting the names influence me?

Okefenokee means trampoline earth (so named because of the area's spongy moss base) and sounds playful. Dismal sounds drab and dreadful, lacking hope. Slaves fought and died in The Great Dismal Swamp; Pogo lived in the imagination of readers in the Okefenokee. How could I not be influenced, especially since I got my best look of the Okefenokee in a place designed to attract tourists and then to educate them about a swamp's benefits. While not a Disney World, the Okefenokee Swamp Park featured animal plant sculptures, scenic walkways and an open-air train pulled by a black, red and gold painted engine dubbed the Lady Swannee. And the alligators, so boldly on display, were fenced off from the human habitat.

The train tracks meandered through stands of saw palmetto, around a moonshine still, past a *chickee* (a raised wooden platform with a thatch roof used as a shelter by Indians), and through Song-bird Village, an acre-size town whose dwellings were all birdhous-es. If the area had not been in the middle of a drought, I would have also gotten to take a boat ride on a waterway that meandered through the park.

A 30-page picture booklet about the swamp by Dot Rees Gib-son that I picked up at the visitor center confirmed my suspicion that the Okefenokee was not at all like Dismal Swamp. Not only was it much larger, more than 600 square miles containing a dozen islands and 60 lakes, it is more of a giant wetlands watershed than swampy. Both the St. Mary and Suwannee rivers begin life in the Okefenokee. The 266-mile long Suwannee of Stephen Foster fame flows into the Gulf of Mexico, while the 90-mile long St. Mary's flows into the Atlantic.

Swamp Park, the tiny section of the swamp that I visited, is located at the northern edge of the Okefenokee on Cowhouse Island near the headwaters of the Suwannee River. The Okefenokee landscape lay beneath the ocean until a sandbar formed a million or so years ago. The sandbar, now known as Trail Ridge, eventually cut the basin off from the sea, and time and the elements turned it into freshwater wetlands that extended Georgia's eastern coastline by about 75 miles.

I learned a lot more about the Okefenokee during a lecture given by a weathered local, who said he lived in the swamp alone in the winter.

"Bill collectors can't find me, and I feel honored when I hear a panther scream," he told his audience. "The swamp's dark waters are the result of tannic acid leached from plants, and it is good to drink despite its color. We call it gator-ade." At this aside, he brought out several small alligators to give his audience a chance to see details of this ancient reptile survivor up close and personal. I touched the smallest of them, once again thrilled to be part of the experience, and more than a mere spectator.

Before leaving the park, I met a California RV-ing couple who were my neighbors at the campground. We struck up a conversation that continued through lunch at the Swamp Park's snack bar, and before we parted company, they invited me over for a glass of wine around the campfire later that night. Of course, I accepted.

That evening, as we watched the sun set over the lake, I found the congenial couple as eager as I was to talk about the places they had visited. They had been on the road much longer than me, and had a lot more to tell. We exchanged Christmas Cards a couple of months later, and they told me their motor home, which had over 200,000 miles on it when we had met, barely got them back to California. Sadly, they said their RV-ing days were over. Thankfully, my RV still had about 140,000 miles to go to reach their traveling milestone.

The next morning, while watching a purple and pink sunrise while drinking coffee, I read that TV 's star newswoman, Diane Sawyer, was worried about bags under her eyes. I admired Diane because she had gotten to the top of her profession at a time when few women made it there, but I couldn't help but wish she would have been more worried about the dumbed-down news being fed to us these days than her appearance. I mean we're getting too much news about celebrities and too little about issues, too much effort trying to give readers and viewers what they want, and not what they need, too much fascination with youth and good looks, and not enough appreciation for experience and wisdom. I felt my blood pressure rising.

"Maggie!" My voice woke her from a sound sleep but she gladly joined me for a two-mile walk on a nearby trail. About halfway along the trail I came across a sign that cautioned hikers to be on the lookout for bears. I hiked a bit faster at that bit of news, and kept up a running conversation with Maggie so as to warn any bears we were out and about.

By the time I got back to my RV for a second cup of coffee, and had stopped worrying about bears, I had calmed down from my journalistic rant. It was one I felt justified in having because of my 37 years as a journalist. It wasn't a new rant, but one that had grown stronger with the passing years.

My last stop in Georgia was Thomasville, a town of about 25,000 residents that calls itself the City of Roses. I reached it by traveling west on Highway 84 through the middle of Valdosta, also known as the Azalea City after the flower that blooms there so abundantly.

I lingered in Thomasville, a charming, genteel town of old southern mansions, long enough to find what I considered its main attraction, a 350-year-old live oak that I had learned about from a brochure picked up at my last stop. I was appropriately awed. With twisting limbs that stretched out for 160 feet, the live oak made me feel the size of a Barbie Doll as I sheltered beneath her. I had an urge to hug the trunk, but since I wasn't alone I suppressed it. Besides, its massive trunk made hugging impossible. I satisfied myself by letting Seuss once again sing in my mind: "Oh the places we'll go and the things we'll see."

I then drove 10 miles up the road to Ochlocknee and checked into the Sugar Mill Plantation RV Park. It was a pleasant place with three ponds full of catfish and bass, and geese floating atop them. I lazily lingered for three nights.

It felt as if time slowed the closer I neared the end of my journey. Perhaps it was a subconscious desire that my traveling, even for just a few months, never cease. Once in Texas, I would spend the winter there, parking my RV in the driveways of my scattered family members long enough for a good visit, but hopefully not long enough to wear out my welcome. I would visit my daughter and grandchildren in the Dallas area first, and then head south to visit family members along the Gulf Coast, where it would be like wintering in Florida. When the weather was good, I would also take short trips to Austin, San Antonio or back to Camden, Arkansas, where other family members lived. Everyone had a parking spot where I could hook up Gypsy Lee, and had made me feel welcome the previous two winters. Actually, it would be good to once again be among loved ones, even though just thinking about the down time from traveling was already making my feet itchy for the road.

On the last evening at the Sugar Mill Plantation, when Maggie and I were taking yet another walk around the pond, I finally spotted one more new bird species for the trip, a yellow-bellied sapsucker. Its name sounds to me like something you would call somebody you wanted to curse. Don't you agree?

A member of the woodpecker family, this sapsucker was a female. It had a bright red cap, but wasn't wearing a red neckerchief around its neck, as the male does. I discovered this little Miss Woodpecker after hearing a stuttering kind of knocking somewhere above me. The bird was doing what it does best – drilling a hole in a live oak tree. The tree would then send sap to the surface to heal the injury, which is of course what the sapsucker wanted. That's why they are called sapsuckers. If it finds any bugs beneath the bark, well they would be great appetizers.

BIRDS ALONG THE WAY:
Great blue heron, American crow, northern mockingbird,
turkey vulture, mourning dove, eastern phoebe,
*yellow-bellied sapsucker, blue jay, European starling,
American goldfinch, chipping sparrow, black vulture, osprey,
sharp-shinned hawk, northern cardinal, eastern bluebird,
Canada goose and red-winged blackbird.

*First sighting of this species on the journey.

THE JOURNEY

OCHLOCKNEE, GEORGIA TO
FRANK JACKSON STATE PARK, ALABAMA
111 MILES

FRANK JACKSON TO
ISAAC CREEK CAMPGROUND, ALABAMA
91 MILES

Georgia

CAMPING:
Isaac Creek
Campground
Franklin, Alabama

CAMPING:
Frank Jackson
State Park
Opp, Alabama

CAMPING:
Sugar Mill Plantation
RV Park
Ochlocknee, Georgia

Alabama

"You know more of a road by having traveled it than by all the conjectures and descriptions in the world."

— WILLIAM HAZLIT

37

ALABAMA: HOME OF THE BIBLE BELT AND A BOLL WEEVIL MONUMENT

Like Willie's song, this morning found me "On the Road Again." I rejoined Highway 84 after being lost for a while on back roads because of my directional handicap. The first city I passed through was Cairo, also known as Syrup City. Its high school football team is called the Syrupmakers, making me wonder if that made them tough like in the Johnny Cash hit, "A Boy Named Sue."

The city and the football players were tagged with the sweet monikers in recognition of the area's cane syrup production. Another of the city's claims to fame is that it is the birthplace of Jackie Robinson, the first major league Black baseball player.

Cairo slipped past, as did roadside pecan trees, playful squirrels and more small towns. At some point, my drive intersected with the route Hernando de Soto took in the 1540s. The Spanish conquistador was the first European to explore Georgia.

Bainbridge, named after The War of 1812 hero Commodore William Bainbridge, was the only Georgia city of any size I passed through before crossing into Alabama. To keep things in perspective, I should tell you that Bainbridge's population was less than 12,000. This section of Georgia has a pace matching the locals' slow southern drawl, a facade southern politicians have long used to hide their wily schemes. Knowing this made me wonder what lay beneath the surface of the scenery I was passing through.

It was going to be one of those wondering-wandering days, I decided, as my mind once again played hopscotch with my little grey cells.

Soon, however, I was in familiar territory. Highway 84 took me through Dothan, where my Army helicopter-pilot son lived for several years while undergoing flight training at nearby Fort Rucker. If there were great changes since I had visited the area some 25 years ago, I missed them. Dothan looked pretty much as I remembered, a bit on the run-down side with a downtown past its prime and churches on just about every corner. While the denominations were mixed, the majority were Baptist. Dothan is smack dab in the middle of the Bible Belt. The city was even named after a place mentioned in Genesis: "For I heard them say, let us go to Dothan."

The town had changed, however. It was more crowded. When I had last visited Dothan, the population had been about 49,000. Today it's about 65,000. Thirty miles west on Highway 84 is Enterprise, a smaller town than Dothan, but where my daughter-in-law sometimes liked to shop. Enterprise has more character and color than Dothan. Perhaps it is because of the town square's unique Boll Weevil Monument.

It seemed odd to honor a destructive bug that had destroyed the area's cotton crops, but then the monument itself is odd. The sculpture depicts a Grecian female in flowing robes, holding a boll weevil above her head, while standing on a lighted pedestal with a fountain flowing at the base. Area residents put up the monument to honor the boll weevil in 1919 – after they had discovered the new crops they planted were a heck of a lot more profitable than the cotton crops that boll weevils destroyed. This was especially true of the peanut crop, thanks to George Washington Carver's discoveries of numerous uses for this versatile nut during the same time period.

The monument only cost about $3,000 to erect, and locals are still cashing in on their investment by selling boll weevil souvenirs.

I ended my day's drive about 30 miles up the road from Enterprise at Frank Jackson State Park. Wow! While southern state parks top my list of the best places to stay, this one outdid itself. I had a tree-shaded site with full hookups that backed up to the 1,000-acre W. F. Jackson Lake – and a cable TV outlet, a first for me at a public park.

I was in no hurry to move on, and the one night I had planned to stay turned into three, during which I took daily hikes across a wooden walkway to an island in the middle of the lake. One day I even hiked it twice, once to catch the reflecting pink and soft orange glow over the lake as a sunrise welcomed the day, and a second to see bolder orange and red rays of the sunset that ended it. A photograph I snapped at the perfect moment, after the sun had set and the glow had faded, captured a couple of fisherman silhouetted in a small boat floating on a lavender lake beneath a darkening sky. It felt as if I had captured a whole life time of living and reduced it to a single memory.

Maggie missed this perfect moment, however. A squirrel, one of many fat ones that called the park home, distracted her. Actually, it taunted her, letting her get close before dashing up a tree as she lunged at it. She gave me a frustrated look before we walked back to the RV in the peaceful, fading twilight.

Besides frequent walks with Maggie, I spent the rest of the time at the campground catching up on my journal and reading Ami Tan's *The Bonesetters Daughter*. The book reminded me of my own early and uneasy relationship with my mother. I'm thankful that before my mother died, I came to accept her failings and appreciate her strengths – and to recognize that I've inherited both. The failings make me human and the strengths accompany me on my solo journeys.

I eventually tore myself away from Frank Jackson (never did find out who he was), and continued west, past the small towns of River Falls, Evergreen and Andalusia, with its historic Devereux Hill named after an early postmaster, according to a Highway 84 roadside marker. As I drove on, swaying logging trucks, and road-kill raccoons and armadillos, accompanied me – but also scattered pockets of brilliantly colored fall leaves that made the day seem cheerier in spite of the trucks and dead animals.

My destination was Isaac Creek Campground on Lake Claiborne near Monroeville. I had a hard time finding it, following only the instructions I had received from my next-door neighbors at the last campground. The two senior-citizen fishing enthusiasts from Louisiana had praised it for its fine facilities, and for being a part of the national park system that offered half-price camping to Golden Age Passport holders.

When I finally came upon the campground, off County Road 17, I found it just as my new friends had described: an awesome setting with cement pads for RV-ers, full hookups (although no cable TV), a manicured lawn leading down to the lake, trees galore, and plenty of places to hike. I splurged and asked for a spot by the lake, which meant I paid $8 a night instead of only $6 for a wooded site.

Why was this place not listed in my campground directory? I asked the campground hosts.

"We're a Corps of Engineers project, and are forbidden by law from advertising, so as not to compete with commercial campgrounds," was the answer.

"So how can I find other Corps campgrounds?" was my second question. They gave me the address of Cottage Publications (PO Box 2832, Elkhart, Indiana, 46515) that publishes a book called "Camping with the Corps of Engineers." As soon as I found a post office, I sent off for the book, which I now frequently check to see if a Corps campground coincides with my travel plans.

The Corps project for this huge campground was the Claiborne Dam on the Alabama River. The winding road accessing all the camping sites was nearly a mile long, judging from the time it took Maggie and I to walk it. We took the peaceful trek, which offered access to Isaac Creek, twice a day. While I used my eyes to take in the sights, Maggie used her nose to smell them. Saucy squirrels were everywhere, but Maggie finally accepted that she wasn't going to catch one. Her solution was to go into her "just ig-nore them" mode, the same rule she had for small barking terriers.

While the species of birds here weren't numerous, each one I saw seemed to have something special about it. One day I heard a cackling rumble, which I backtracked to a red-bellied woodpecker. Another day it was blue jays, which were everywhere and playfully swooping back and forth above the lake. One actually rippled the water while playing this game, sending sunlit droplets splashing into the air.

Early mornings brought a hazy mist over the lake. When the fog lifted, it revealed a blue canvas, on which was painted an echo of the fall-dressed trees on the opposite shore. "Winter is an etch-ing, spring a watercolor, summer an oil painting, and autumn a mosaic of them all," I wrote in my journal. It felt delicious to linger in a place where the days were warm and pleasant, and the nights cool enough to warrant snuggling up in a quilt.

Also, written in my journal while I was here was some trivia I had discovered —about pine cones. "Female pine cones are fatter than their male counterparts and have harder scales." Perhaps, I thought, that's why we ladies have wider hips than men – and an inner toughness that has nothing to do with brawn.

On the morning of my third day at Lake Claiborne, I received a phone call from my granddaughter, Heidi, who wanted me to meet her in Shreveport, Louisiana, for her 24th birthday that was less than a week away. I enthusiastically accepted the invitation, replotted my route and got back on the road.

BIRDS ALONG THE WAY:
Mourning dove, turkey vulture, American crow,
northern mockingbird, great egret, house sparrow, blue jay,
eastern bluebird, eastern phoebe, belted kingfisher, osprey,
double-crested cormorants and red-bellied woodpecker.

THE JOURNEY

ISAAC CREEK CAMPGROUND, ALABAMA
TO LAUREL, MISSISSIPPI
153 MILES

LAUREL TO
NATCHEZ STATE PARK, MISSISSIPPI
157 MILES

CAMPING:
Sleepy Hollow RV Park
Laurel, Mississippi

CAMPING:
Natchez State Park
Natchez, Mississippi

CAMPING:
Isaac Creek
Campground
Franklin, Alabama

"A good traveler has no

fixed plans, and is not

intent on arriving."

– LAO TZU

38

MISSISSIPPI BIRD ENCOUNTERS
AND GOOD LUCK

My new route began with rejoining Highway 84 just before it crossed the Alabama River, and then following it into Mississippi. The elevation of the day's journey was only about 300 feet, and the landscape was mostly rural wetlands. The few towns I passed through before crossing into Mississippi were tiny, either a tic of blight on the landscape because of boarded up buildings and trash-filled yards, or a dimple of southern charm because of their courtly old buildings and flower-filled lawns. It was much the same as I would have found in any metropolitan area, except here there were less people and traffic, and more nature goodies to ogle.

My drive took me past green ponds, moss-laden live oak trees, and scattered patches of yellow roadside flowers, mostly the not-so-easily-identified-kind that wildflower advocate Lady Bird Johnson would have lumped together as DYCs – those "darn yellow composites." My only complaint about the drive was the logging trucks that frequently whizzed past me, even though I had my cruise control set a couple of miles above the posted speed limit.

One of these weaving, log-laden road hogs scattered a flock of turkey vultures feasting on road kill beside the highway. One of the birds, in its panic to avoid the semi, glanced off my side-view mirror. It continued flying, however, and when I stopped and checked for damage to my vehicle I found none.

A little farther down the road, I had a second near mishap with a large bird, this time with no logging truck in sight. I startled a great blue heron looking for tasty critters in a water-filled roadside ditch. The bird, instead of doing the logical thing and flying away from the road, flew across it. I enjoy seeing birds up close and personal but not inches from my windshield when I'm moving at 57 mph. Fortunately, I knew better than to suddenly jerk the wheel and cause myself to have an accident, and miraculously the stupid heron survived untouched.

With the encouragement of a rumbling stomach, and to celebrate my two near bird mishaps, I decided to treat myself to lunch out for a change. My search for restaurants, however, turned up only churches. When my stomach finally demanded "feed me now," I found a quiet place off the road and fixed myself a salmon, celery and apple-filled wheat-bread sandwich. It was cheaper and healthier than what I would have eaten at a restaurant, so I guess I should have been thankful I hadn't found a restaurant. But I wasn't.

Maggie sat patiently through the meal, but with her eyes glued to the sandwich in anticipation of that last bite I always give her. I tried not to look into those soulful brown orbs of hers until I was actually down to that last bite, knowing if I did she would get more of my sandwich than she needed to maintain her girlish figure. I figured one of us should maintain one, and I knew it was never again going to be me.

As I ate my sandwich, I watched a belted kingfisher out my RV window, which made me a bit more thankful. It was sitting on a wire by a small pond with its feathers all puffed up to keep warm as the chill of the night had lingered into day. After the kingfisher flew away, and Maggie got her bite, I got back behind the wheel and drove on to Laurel, Mississippi. A lumber town founded in 1882. Laurel promotes itself as one of this country's most beautiful and livable cities. I didn't investigate the claim, simply stopped for the night at the city's Sleepy Hollow RV Park near Highway 84's junction with Highway 11.

It was a large park with a free fishing pond for guests. Few sites, however, were occupied. Perhaps it was because the days had turned from cool to cold, and the park managers had turned off the campground's water, fearing an overnight freeze. I kept to my warm and cozy RV, except for a couple of short bundled up walks with Maggie around the campground. We both went to bed when the sun did.

Up early the next morning, I again headed west on Highway 84. I had no end-of-the-day destination in mind, gambling on luck to find us an inviting campground around mid-afternoon. About 10 miles down the road from Laurel, I realized I hadn't filled up with gas before I left town. That might have been a big mistake. There were no gas stations in sight, and my fuel indicator needle was sinking fast. It was 30 more miles of nervous driving, the last 10 while watching a blinking red warning light, before I found a place to refuel and could relax.

The rest of the day's drive took me through small polka dots of scattered populations, mostly unincorporated places sandwiched between woods, wetlands and farm lands. The South's paler version of New England's flamboyant autumn foliage edged the roadside as I made my way through the Homochitto National Forest. It was a pleasant drive, but one in which the passing scenery barely scratched my memory cells.

More deeply etched in my mind was the remembrance of the luck that found me a gas station in the nick of time, and that was again with me when I began thinking of stopping for the day. Just a few miles past the tiny town of Leesdale, I came across roadside signs pointing the way to Natchez State Park.

The campground was yet another of those southern gems that had been enriching my travels. It sat next to Natchez Lake, in which the biggest largemouth bass (18.15 pounds) in Mississippi's history was caught in 1992. It also offered great access to a hiking trail. My assigned back-in RV site was sheltered on three sides by trees and connected to a path that went down to the lake. Twice, while walking down the trail, I stumbled upon a doe and her fawn. Both times they unhurriedly melted back into the trees. I also frequently saw a hermit thrush, which first attracted my attention with its flute-like voice. This bird is one of my favorites, perhaps because it became one of those darn brown look-alike birds that I finally realized I could easily identify. Its upper chest is speckled with brown dots, and it has a tail with a very distinguishable red tint.

I stayed at the park for two nights, one of which I lay awake at 3 a.m., listening to rain pitter-patter loudly on the roof above. Walking Maggie the next morning, I was treated to the smell of nature freshly laundered, a scent sweeter by far than any man-made perfume. I would have stayed at the park a third night except that I was running low on the propane that kept my RV warm and cozy, and propane was one thing this nature-friendly park didn't have.

BIRDS ALONG THE WAY:
Blue jay, American crow, double-crested cormorant,
eastern phoebe, turkey vulture, belted kingfisher, *hermit thrush,
Carolina chickadee, great blue heron, red-tailed hawk, kestrel.
red-bellied woodpecker, house sparrow.
*First sighting of this bird on the journey.

NATCHEZ TO VICKSBURG, MISSISSIPPI
63 MILES

CAMPING:
Ameristar Hotel Casino RV Park
Vicksburg, Mississippi

Mississippi

CAMPING:
Natchez State Park
Natchez, Mississippi

I'd rather wake up in the middle of nowhere than in any city on earth."

— STEVE MCQUEEN

39
THE NATCHEZ TRACE

Early the next morning, I left behind the neatly landscaped campground, which had been named for the city of Natchez that sat 10 miles west on Highway 84. A town of about 20,000 residents, it sits on the banks of the Mississippi River at the western terminus of the Natchez Trace, a 440-mile long ridgeline trail created by prehistoric animals traveling between bottom grasslands along the Mississippi River and salt licks near what is now Nashville, Tennessee. The animal foot path was discovered and used by Native Americans, and then by early European explorers and settlers.

The city was named for the Natchez Indians, a tribe that lived in the area until conflicts with French settlers in the 1700s decimated their numbers – and those of the French colonists as well, although these kept being replaced. Prior to the Civil War, Natchez was considered the wealthiest city in the country, and today its promoters boast that it has more southern mansions still standing from that era than anywhere else in the country. I opted to bypass the city, however. Instead of getting back on Highway 84 that would have taken me through Natchez, I headed north on the park road for about five miles to where it intersected with the Trace Parkway. While I'm sure I would have enjoyed strolling down the streets of Natchez while visualizing its southern past, I was more eager to see what remained of the historic old footpath itself.

While I couldn't recall anything I may have read about the old trail in history books, author Nevada Barr's descriptions of it were etched vividly in my mind. She used the Natchez Trace Parkway, where she had actually worked as a park ranger for two years, as the setting for her murder mystery, *Deep South*.

It was a pleasant drive, with almost no other traffic, through a landscape where human development had been banned. Nature, except for roadside lawn care to control weeds, was allowed room to breathe here. A lone deer watched me from the edge of the trees as I drove by, maintaining its position even when I stopped long enough to photograph it. I've seen this same behavior many times in parks where animals seem to instinctively know they are protected and need have no fear of man.

A wild turkey, startled by my passage, ran alongside my RV, thinking I suppose to leave me behind. I captured its image with my digital camera before it and I parted company. When I came across a place where the original trace was still visible, I stopped for a closer look. The National Park Service marker here informed me that "... The Natchez Trace was politically, economically, socially, and militarily important for the United States in its early development. Among those that traveled the road were American Indians, traders, soldiers, 'Kaintucks,' postriders, settlers, slaves, circuit-riding preachers, outlaws, and adventurers."

I felt like one of the latter when Maggie and I set foot on the remnants of that old footpath. It was as if we were strolling back in time. This section of the trail we walked was closely hemmed in by trees whose limbs formed a roof above our heads. It was like walking through a tunnel, and the dim light that penetrated the ground brought to mind all those fairy tales that warned young girls not to be caught alone in the forest at night.

While my map showed that the Natchez Trace went all the way north to Nashville, I left it after only 28 miles. Perhaps someday I'll come back and drive it all the way to the country western music capital in Tennessee, I thought, as I reluctantly took the fork in the road that would take me to Vicksburg, Mississippi, and back to the harried civilization that I had mostly escaped for the past six months of travel.**

I made my exit from the Trace at its intersection with Highway 61. While not as famous as the Chicago to Los Angeles' Route 66, this New Orleans to Minnesota highway had its own heyday before the characterless interstates came along, and put the mom and pop roadside businesses out of business.

Bob Dylan's "Highway 61 Revisited" album gave the north to south Highway 61 route some fame, but only a distant second to what Bobby Troup lyrics "Get Your Kicks on Route 66" and a television show did for the east to west highway. While I've often driven remnants of Route 66, including a short, well-marked historic section this trip in Oklahoma, I don't recall ever before being on Highway 61. But while tracing its path northward on my map - which wasn't easy to do because it kept getting eaten up by interstates - I noted that it ran just north of St. Louis in Missouri where it joined with Interstate 55, meaning that I probably crossed its original path somewhere in Illinois.

This day, I traveled on it for only about 35 miles, and saw little of its colorful past before I hit Vicksburg and Interstate 20, one of those damn freeways I had carefully avoided for nearly six months and over 6,000 miles. The sad part is that this freeway would now be with me for the remainder of my journey. Interstate 20 runs for over 1,500 miles between South Carolina and Texas, and I would be traveling on it to Shreveport to meet up with by granddaughter, and then all the way to Dallas in time for Thanksgiving at my oldest daughter's home.

BIRDS ALONG THE WAY:

Wild turkey, American crow, northern mockingbird, eastern phoebe, turkey vulture, belted kingfisher, Carolina chickadee, great blue heron, red-tailed hawk, kestrel. house sparrow, house finch.

* I actually did drive the entire Trace a few years later, but I entered it in Nashville, and exited it in Natchez, where I did take time to stroll past some of the city's old mansions.

THE JOURNEY

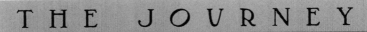

Mississippi

CAMPING:
Shreveport KOA
Shreveport, Louisiana

CAMPING:
Ameristar Hotel Casino RV
Park, Vicksburg, Mississippi

Louisiana

*"Every dreamer knows that it is
entirely possible to be homesick for
a place you've never been to,
perhaps more homesick than
for familiar ground."*

– JUDITH THURMAN

40

KNOW WHEN TO HOLD 'EM
AND KNOW WHEN TO FOLD 'EM

Vicksburg, which is where I ended my day of driving, was once a southern stronghold on the Mississippi River. It held Union forces off until near the end of the Civil War. Its defeat, when it finally came, dealt the Confederates a blow from which they could never recover. But after a shady racial past, Vicksburg finally did regain some ground; today it's a colorful city of about 30,000 where the past is over but not forgotten.

The city's Civil War past can be recalled at the Vicksburg Battlefield Museum and the Vicksburg National Military Park. Tourists can also visit the Biedenham Coca Cola Museum and learn how the very first Coke was bottled in Vicksburg in 1894, back when steamboat traffic was still in vogue; or they can explore Catfish Row Art Park on Levee Street and be reminded of the role the Mississippi River played in this country's history.

I indulged in a stroll through the art park, but passed on the museums. Ready for a change of pace, I took advantage of the fool's opportunity to gamble at one of the colorful casinos that line the river in this Heart of Dixie city. I don't play the slots, but I do enjoy sitting down to a live game of poker or blackjack once or twice a year.

While I couldn't find a poker table, I did find a $3 blackjack table, where I plunked down $50, thirty dollars of which I saved on my RV campground fee – I was hooked up on the Avenue of Aces – by simply walking into the casino. The additional $20 was an amount that I figured my budget could live without, and an amount I was willing to spend for entertainment, much as I would have for a trolley tour through the town.

Being a player more than a gambler, I wisely locked the rest of my cash and credit cards away for the duration of my stay in Vicksburg. I was quite pleased – and surprised – when I left town the next morning richer by $212, my winnings after meals and tips. I decided the unexpected windfall would be the stake for yet another day of gambling in Shreveport with my granddaughter, which is what she told me she wanted to do for her birthday, hence her invitation to meet in the Louisiana town where gambling is legal. Now that she was old enough, she wanted to give it a try.

But before that could happen, I had 237 boring miles to go down busy Interstate 20. Drat it! It was time to dig out one of the recorded books I usually have on hand for just such an occasion. My choice was an Agatha Christie mystery, *A Murder is Announced*, which I put on after I crossed over the Mississippi River into Louisiana. The border between the two states is located in the middle of the river. By the time I arrived in Shreveport, I had successfully solved the mystery's convoluted clues before the final reveal, and was quite proud of myself.

Too bad I wasn't as good at solving the mystery of how to get to where I wanted to go. Patting yourself on the back, I've learned, is a good way to get your bubble busted quickly. This time it was the directional gods who held the prickly pin, as once in Shreveport, it took me a full hour and a half of wandering around on narrow streets in my RV to locate the campground where I had a reservation. Seems I had the right street and right numbers, just the wrong side of town. Oh well! The silver lining was that I got to see more of Shreveport than the average tourist.

When I finally found the campground, got hooked up, walked Maggie, microwaved and then ate a Stouffer's "Cheesy Spaghetti" TV dinner, it was dark outside. I crawled into bed early, and lay there listening to Maggie snore at my feet while pondering the end of my journey so near at hand. I was now only 85 miles from where my journey had started at my youngest daughter's home in Camden, Arkansas, and just 186 miles away from my oldest daughter's home in Rowlett on the outskirts of Dallas where it would end.

Between the beginning and the end were 23 states and almost 7,000 miles of eye candy, new friends, adrenaline experiences and a better understanding of myself. The latter is better than earning reward points from using your credit cards or earning airplane miles.

My granddaughter, Heidi, who was earning her master's degree at the University of Texas at Tyler just a couple of hours from Shreveport, arrived early the next morning. She, like me and almost everyone else in the family, loves to play cards, and was looking forward to a day of gambling. I was hoping to teach her a few tricks and to impress on her that in the end the casinos always win.

"So, let's go play Nana," she said. And we did. I told her about my Vicksburg winnings, and said we could use that for our stake, and that our goal was to see how long we could make it last. We chose Diamond Jack's as our place of operation, and sought out a low stakes blackjack table. It was full, unlike the higher stakes' tables, but we stood guard over it until first one, and then the other of us, was seated.

For the next six hours, sitting side-by-side, we laughed together, met new people and watched our stake go up and down. Finally, the casino busted us. It went exactly as I expected it would. The last thing I wanted was a grandchild of mine thinking they were going to get rich by gambling.

Afterwards I used my original stake in Vicksburg, which I had tucked away in a pocket, to buy us a nice dinner before Heidi had to drive back to Tyler the next morning. I stayed over an extra day, using the time to catch up on laundry and clean my RV inside and out.

I also used the time to do some bird watching around the pleasantly wooded park, and was rewarded with three final birds for the journey, two kinglets and a nuthatch. The first kinglet was a snap for me to identify, even before it flashed me with its red-crowned head. I had seen this bird many times. The golden-crowned kinglet, which I had seen only once before, and which was flitting about even more rapidly than its red-crowned cousin, was a bit more difficult. But finally I saw its golden head feathers outlined by black and made the identification. Kinglets are tiny birds, only 4 inches in size, and they never stop moving.

The red-breasted nuthatch was scampering up and down a tree, as nuthatches tend to do. I felt as if it was a parting gift to my bird-watching trip list, taking the numbers of birds seen on the trip to 101. There were times I thought it wouldn't reach 100.

BIRDS ALONG THE WAY:
Turkey vulture, red-tailed hawk, kestrel, wild turkey,
red-bellied woodpecker, American crow, northern mockingbird,
yellow-rumped warbler, house sparrow, *ruby-crowned kinglet,
great egret, black vulture, osprey, *golden crowned kinglet, robin,
white-winged dove, Carolina chickadee, European starling,
common grackle, eastern phoebe, *red-breasted nuthatch
and great-tailed grackle.
*First sighting of this bird on the journey.

SHREVEPORT, LOUISIANA
TO DALLAS, TEXAS
186 MILES

DALLAS, TEXAS

Louisiana

CAMPING:
Shreveport KOA Campground
Shreveport, Louisiana

Texas

New London Museum
New London, Texas

"I can't change the direction of the wind,

but I can adjust my sails to

always reach my destination."

— JIMMY DEAN

41

MEMORIES OF A DEAR FRIEND

My plan the next morning, when I left Shreveport, was to drive all the way to Dallas, but to time it so that I was in the small town of New London just off Interstate 20 at lunch time. Before Heidi had left Shreveport, we had arranged a lunch date at the small cafe across from the high school where she was setting up an athletic trainer program as part of her master's degree curriculum.

What was amazing to me was that my granddaughter was teaching at the New London High School, whose history was better known to me than to her. A gas leak explosion in 1937 killed 300 of its students and teachers. I knew all the details because a dear friend of mine, Lorine Bright, had written a book, *New London: One Woman's Memories of Orange and Green*, about the tragic event. Her children had been at the school that day, but fortunately had survived.

Lorine, many years my senior and now deceased, was the first person I ever told I wanted to be a writer. She had encouraged and mentored me at a time when I had little confidence in my ability to achieve that goal. She will always have a special place in my heart. I was looking forward to sharing my dear friend's connection to the place where Heidi was now teaching, and did so after lunch in the small cafe across from the high school. The café's large back room was home to the New London Museum that commemorates the explosion. One of the exhibits was a video presentation that included clips of my friend talking about the tragic event. As I watched it, I found myself needing a tissue for leaking eyes. One was supplied by the kindly museum volunteer.

When I commented that I had an autographed copy of Lorine's book, the volunteer said it was now out of print, but that she had recently seen one at a local antique store - with a $150 price tag on it. Wow! I thought. If Lorine, somewhere up there in that great unknown, knew that, she'd be thrilled, as would my oldest daughter, whom I had given my autographed copy of Lorine's book when disposing of my possessions in preparation for my on-the-road life.

Sometimes the world seems an awfully small place, I thought as I left Heidi behind and continued on down Interstate 20 toward Dallas. Reminders that I was back in my native homeland of Texas accompanied me. One of those was that I was being passed by other vehicles constantly even though I was driving above the speed limit. I also saw many Lone Star state flags, right next to American flags, waving at me as I drove past businesses and residences; and when I needed a break from driving, a pleasant rest stop would appear not too far up the road. Texas has some of the best road-side parks in America.

It felt good to be back in familiar territory again, and I was excited about seeing loved ones. Three of my five children had moved back to Texas to live, and all but five of my 15 grandchildren live in Texas. It was going to be especially nice having Thanksgiving at my oldest daughter's home.

But even before I arrived, I was already thinking about where the road would take me next.

Oh the places we'll go, and the things we'll see were words still running through my head – and I sang them in my off-key voice to Maggie, who had suddenly woke up, recognizing that we were in familiar territory.

BIRDS ALONG THE WAY:
Turkey vulture, red-tailed hawk, kestrel, American crow, northern mockingbird, house sparrow, black vulture, white-winged dove, Carolina chickadee, European starling, common grackle, and great-tailed grackle.

EPILOGUE

My travels in Gypsy Lee continued for seven more years after my New England journey ended. I established a pattern of wintering in Texas in the driveways of my large scattered family, taking off the first of March for some new adventure, and then returning to Texas in time for Thanksgiving dinner.

The last four years, I limited my traveling to spring and fall, spending summers volunteering at state parks, where my campground site and utilities were free in exchange for 20 hours of work. The tasks mostly involved simply keeping visitors happy. I especially loved the summers when I was campground host at the small Lake Walcott State Park in southeastern Idaho. It was a win-win situation. I got to become fully acquainted with a scenic area, and the free camp site made my continued travels possible in the reality of rising fuel, food and camping costs.

I continued looking for birds, but I learned that I was more successful in finding them if I planned my travels around birding festivals. One winter, I skipped Texas to winter in Florida, timing my arrival so I could participate in the Space Coast Birding Festival held near Cape Canaveral. Afterwards I spent a month on Pine Island, located just a short bridge across the water from Cape Coral, Florida. I used the island as a base for exploring the western Everglades, then met up with Heidi's younger sister Keri, who lived in Florida, and spent a week exploring the eastern side of the Everglades, with her. This journey included a drive down the chain of islands to Key West and then a boat ride to the Dry Tortugas.

Another year, I timed my summer travels on the West Coast so I could attend the Charleston Shorebird Festival in Charleston, Oregon. In this way, I watched my life bird list grow to over 700.

My faithful canine companion, Maggie, died in 2012 at the age of 15. I still grieve for her, and always will. But I rejoice in her replacement, a bundle of pure energy and joy who chose me at a rescue shelter full of dogs. I was looking for a two to three-year-old cocker-mix replacement when this four-month-old Scottie-mix jumped up into my lap, and with chocolate-caramel eyes that would melt a glacier, she looked into my blue eyes and communicated that she was going home with me.

It was love at first sight, and by the time we reached home we had bonded. Pepper took to the traveling life quickly, but in 2013, I gave up the road for a small, third-floor walkup apartment in Tucson's Catalina Mountains' foothills.

The area is a bird-lover's paradise, but Pepper and I take to the road when my feet get that itch again. And they itch often.

ABOUT THE AUTHOR

PAT BEAN was born with wanderlust in her soul. After 37 years as an award-winning journalist, the author sold her home in Ogden, Utah, and bought a small RV. For the next nine years, she and a mischievous cocker spaniel named Maggie traveled this country from coast-to-coast and border-to-border in the 21-foot motor home Bean named Gypsy Lee. Her goal was to experience all the beauty America had to offer, along with having adventures, meeting new people, and finding and identifying birds. At the time, Bean was a fledgling birdwatcher who had taken up the activity when her body demanded a less strenuous hobby than white-water rafting, her passion for 25 years. Today, Bean lives in Tucson with Pepper, a joyful Scottie-mix canine who helped her heart heal after the loss of Maggie. Her newest work in progress is a book about birds and her late-blooming birding adventures.

You can contact Pat Bean at
patbean@msn.com

And read her blog at
http://patbean.wordpress.com

*"The world is round and
the place which may seem
like the end may also be
the beginning."*

– Ivy Baker Priest

ACKNOWLEDGEMENTS

My journey in writing this book has involved many people, including friends and family members who supported my decisions to live on the road, and the people I met along the way who provided inspiration for my writing. Support for the day-to-day writing and editing of this book came from Story Circle Network, whose efforts to support women's writing is, and I say this without hesitation, the best in all the world. But there is one person who stands out above all the rest in making this book possible. And that is Sherry Wachter, who both created the cover illustration that I feel captures the soul of this book, and then formatted the book and created the maps to make it magically all come together. From the bottom of my heart, I thank you Sherry Wachter.

83039919R00167

Made in the USA
Columbia, SC
08 December 2017